11 1/08 12/14

D0459841

Better Sex for You

Helen Pensanti, M.D.

SILOAM PRESS
Living in Health—Body, Mind and Spirit

iii JUN 1 3 2002   SAN DIEGO PUBLIC LIBRARY
WITHDRAWN LA JOLLA BRANCH

BETTER SEX FOR YOU by Helen Pensanti, M.D.
Published by Siloam Press
A part of Strang Communications Company
600 Rinehart Road
Lake Mary, Florida 32746
www.siloampress.com

This book or parts thereof may not be reproduced in any form, stored in a retrieval system or transmitted in any form by any means—electronic, mechanical, photocopy, recording or otherwise—without prior written permission of the publisher, except as provided by United States of America copyright law.

Unless otherwise noted, all Scripture quotations are from the Holy Bible, New Living Translation, copyright © 1996. Used by permission of Tyndale House Publishers, Inc., Wheaton, IL 60189. All rights reserved.

Scripture quotations marked KJV are from the King James Version of the Bible.

Scripture quotations marked NKJV are from the New King James Version of the Bible. Copyright © 1979, 1980, 1982 by Thomas Nelson, Inc., publishers. Used by permission.

AUTHOR'S NOTE: All of the stories in this book come from my clinical and personal experience with people. Names, places and any identifying details have been changed and altered to protect the privacy and anonymity of the individuals to whom they refer. People referenced are actually composites of a number of people who share similar issues and are equally protected with name and information changes to remain confidential. Any similarity between the names and stories of individuals described in this book and individuals known to readers is purely coincidental and not intentional.

Copyright © 2001 by Helen Pensanti, M.D.
All rights reserved

Library of Congress Catalog Card Number: 2001086221
International Standard Book Number: 0-88419-687-9

This book is not intended to provide medical advice or to take the place of medical advice and treatment from your personal physician. Readers are advised to consult their own doctors or other qualified health professionals regarding the treatment of their medical problems. Neither the publisher nor the author takes any responsibility for any possible consequences from any treatment, action or application of medicine, supplement, herb or preparation to any person reading or following the information in this book. If readers are taking prescription medications, they should consult with their physicians and not take themselves off of medicines to start supplementation without the proper supervision of a physician.

01 02 03 04 05 9 8 7 6 5 4 3 2 1
Printed in the United States of America

ACKNOWLEDGMENTS

First, I want to express my deep appreciation and gratitude to Barbara Biski Hoffman, who for the past fifteen years has been my friend and encourager and who also produces my TV show *Doctor to Doctor*. Her support, input and enthusiasm consistently help my visions become reality. Thank you, Barbara, for always giving so generously of your time, dating back to those early days in my medical office. Your diligence and the endless hours you spent compiling info, statistics, studies and expertly organizing my thoughts have resulted in the "birth" of this book. Thank you for your faithful heart and for always encouraging me to press on toward what God has planned for me.

I wish to acknowledge my pastors, Clifford G. Self and his beautiful wife, Darlene, for all the years they have prayed for me and spoken God's prophetic word into my life.

I want to give a heartfelt "thank you" to Paul and Jan Crouch for allowing me the privilege of serving them as they serve the Lord through the Trinity Broadcasting Network. They have truly been God's hands extended on earth for me. I am deeply grateful for the opportunity they have given me to host *Doctor to Doctor* for the past ten years.

I also want to thank and acknowledge Barbara Dycus at Siloam Press, my wonderful editor, who helped me tremendously in this adventure. I am sure she had a few faint moments as she dealt with my openness in talking about sex, but she took it all in stride as we guided this book to print. I will always remember how she handled this outspoken doctor with such great grace and humor.

Let me express my appreciation to Charlotte Hale, a precious woman of God who humbly works "as unto the Lord" and asks for no acclaim. Meeting her was a highlight of this process. I especially thank her for all her prayers for the success of this book and the support that she gave to help me along the way.

Most importantly, I thank God, the Eternal Creator and Father of Lights. Any gifts I have He gave me, especially my salvation through His Son Jesus Christ. He guides my path daily through His precious Holy Spirit. His providential care and the many tokens of His love for me constantly over-whelm me with His awesome faithfulness.

CONTENTS

Introduction   *xii*

Medical Doctor, Counselor and Friend *xiii*

1   *The Number One Question*   *1*

A Myth 2

Important Benefits 3

Why Sex Is Important 5

My Mission 5

2   *In the Mood*   6

Mood Makers for Women 7

Pure Pleasure 8

You Are Uniquely and Wonderfully Made:
    There Is Only One You! 10

Responding to Him 11

Give Yourself Some Time Out 11

Rediscovering Your Allure 12

In the Mood Again 13

3   *Sexual Arousal*   16

For Men—Arousal in Women 19

Lubrication 20

Vaginal changes 20

Changes in the uterus 21

What Husbands Should Know 21

For Women—the Male Arousal Process 24

What Wives Should Know 25

Initiating Sexual Activity 26

4   *Healing Nonarousal*   29

Nonmedical Conditions That Hinder Arousal 31

Emotional distance 31

Low self-esteem 33

Depression 35

Some major symptoms of depression 36

Drugs That Cause Libido Loss 37

V

Sexual Abuse 38

Other Libido Inhibitors 40

The Ability to Become Aroused 41

5   *Pleasure Areas: Men and Women*   42

What Men Like 43

Your Love Message to Him 44

For Her—Nonsexual "Foreplay" 44

Some Tips 45

For Her—Gentle Touches 45

Obstacles to Pleasure 46

Telephone calls 46

Worries about appearance 46

Resentments 46

Fear and worry 47

Frequency of Intercourse 47

Unexpected Pleasure 48

Kisses 49

Opposites Attract 50

Foot Massage 51

Foot pressure points 52

Using Your Senses 53

6   *From Sexual Arousal to Orgasm*   56

What Men and Women Need to Know
About the Female Orgasm 57

Self-sabotage 59

Why participation matters 61

What Men and Women Need to Know
About the Male Orgasm 64

What has happened 65

The Postcoital Phase: Different for Each Gender 65

7   *Women at Midlife*   68

Hormone Power 69

Hormonal Makeup 70

Hormones and Sex Drive 70

Hormonal Imbalance and Loss of Libido in Women 73

The role of estrogen 75

Side Effects of Premarin 77

CONTENTS

What Happens to Estrogen Levels at Menopause? 78

What Is Natural Estrogen? Who Needs It? 80

How Do I Find Natural Estrogen? 81

How to Use Natural Hormone Cream 82

Weaning Instructions 82

Perimenopausal (or Premenopausal)
  Hormonal Imbalance 83

What Is Progesterone and
  Why Is It So Important? 84

What Should You Do If You Have
  Estrogen Dominance? 85

Symptoms of Low Progesterone 86

What Is Natural Progesterone? 86

Progesterone and Sex Drive 87

How to Supplement With Natural Progesterone 89

General Guidelines 89

Specific Instructions 90

  *Perimenopausal women who are still menstruating,
    either regularly or irregularly* 90

  Women with PMS 90

  *Women who menstruate and suffer from menstrual
    migraine headaches* 91

  Menopausal women 91

  Important advice for all women 92

  My advice to husbands 92

Natural Hormones—a Guide 93

All Hormone Creams Are Not Created Equal 93

What About Those Hot Flashes?
  What Can Be Done? 94

Night Sweats 98

Vaginal Dryness 99

  What causes vaginal dryness as a woman ages? 100

  Other remedies for vaginal dryness 102

Dry Vulva 103

Painful Intercourse 104

  General observations 105

Cystitis/Urinary Tract Infections 105

"Not Tonight, Dear, I Have a Headache" 106

VII

8   *Life After Hysterectomy*   *108*

Your Expectations Affect the Outcome 110

Intercourse Immediately After Hysterectomy 110

Sexual Desire and Fulfillment 112

Some Thoughts on Midlife Medical Issues 113

9   *Men at Midlife*   *114*

Men's Problems 116

Impotency Problems or Erectile Dysfunction 116

What Causes E.D.? 117

Your Doctor and Your E.D. 119

Options for Treating E.D. 120

What About Viagra? 121

Determining the Cause: It May Be Subtle or Complex 122

Premature Ejaculation 123

   Squeeze technique 123

Prostate Problems 125

   BPH 125

   Prostate cancer 127

Midlife Renewal 128

10   *Enjoy Sex Forever*   *129*

Young at Heart 130

Mature Women 132

   Better sex for mature women 133

Begin Again 133

Rekindle the Romance 134

Overcoming Obstacles 136

Recapture Your Intensity 137

What You Say Is What You Get 139

11   *Don't Let Stress Destroy Your Sex Life!*   *141*

Why Is Stress Today Different Than in the Past? 142

What Does Stress Do to the Body? 142

How Do I Know If I'm Getting Too Stressed? 143

How Can I Combat Stress and Restore Adrenal Health? 144

   Tips to restore adrenal health 144

How Does Stress Affect My Sleep? 148

   For women: natural progesterone cream 149

   Calcium 149

CONTENTS

Magnesium 149

B vitamins 149

Herbs 150

5-HTP 150

Melatonin 151

How Does Stress Affect the Libido? 152

Insomnia and libido 152

Doctor's suggestions for prolonged insomnia 153

12   *Sex Despite Medical Problems*   154

Issues Confronting Men 154

Heart Disease 155

Other notes for heart patients 158

Arthritis and Lower Back Pain 158

Urinary Stress Incontinence 160

Kegel exercises 161

Thyroid Disorders 161

Thyroid and natural progesterone 164

Self-test for thyroid 164

Yeast Infections 165

Anemia 165

Allergies/Asthma 166

You Can Find an Answer 167

13   *Is the Answer in Hormone Supplementation?*   168

Testosterone and Women 168

Testosterone and Men at Midlife 173

Testosterone Supplementation 174

Progesterone and Men 177

Some Natural Sex Boosters 178

Tribulus terrestris 178

Avena sativa 180

DHEA 182

L-arginine 184

Androstenedione 185

Human growth hormone 187

Yohimbe 189

Stinging nettle (urtica dioca) 190

Ginkgo biloba 191

Ginseng 192

L-tyrosine 193

Muira pauma extract 193

Saw palmetto 194

Zinc 194

VIP Gel for men 195

Aphrodisiacs 196

Some Tips for Sexual Nutrition 197

Exercise 197

14   *Tips for a Better Love Life*   *199*

General Tips 199

   A note from Dr. Pensanti 200

Tips for Men 200

Tips for Women 201

15   *Common Questions About Natural Hormones* 204

1. What is USP Progesterone? 204

2. How do I know if I should use natural progesterone? 205

3. Does natural progesterone help vaginal dryness? 205

4. I am postmenopausal. Will I start menstruating again or have breakthrough bleeding if I use natural hormones? 205

5. How do I know whether I need natural progesterone alone or natural progesterone with natural estrogen? 206

6. I think I have estrogen dominance, but I felt worse after I started natural progesterone. Why? 206

7. Can I mix synthetic estrogen with natural progesterone? 207

8. Why is transdermal application so good? 207

9. How long before I notice changes in my libido? 207

10. How safe is natural progesterone? 207

11. What happens if I use too much natural progesterone? 207

12. I have had a hysterectomy, but still have my ovaries. Do I need natural hormones? 208

13. What if I don't have a uterus and am taking estrogen? My doctor says I do not need progesterone. 208

14. I have been told that I have very low estrogen levels, yet I fit into the symptoms of estrogen dominance. How can this be? 208

15. What if I have hot flashes and vaginal dryness that are

affecting my libido, but I have had breast cancer—what can I do to get relief? 209

16. How do I use natural progesterone for treatment of PMS? 209

17. I have facial hair, especially above my upper lip, which makes me feel very unfeminine. Sometimes I even have to shave. Can you help me? 210

18. Can natural progesterone help with hot flashes? 211

19. I have had breast cancer. Why is natural progesterone safe for me? I live in fear that my cancer will come back. It is affecting everything I do, including my sex life with my husband. 211

20. Can natural progesterone help me with my "fuzzy thinking"? Sometimes I feel as if I am losing my mind or my memory. 213

21. Will natural hormones affect my thyroid medication? 213

22. How old is too old for natural hormones? 213

23. Why doesn't my doctor know more about natural hormone therapy? 214

24. Why is it important to stay on natural hormones even after my libido is restored? 215

25. What do I say to my physician who thinks this is silly? 215

26. Are there any other benefits of natural progesterone use? 215

27. How long should I stay on natural hormones? 216

Conclusion	*218*
Product Source Guide	*221*
Notes	*222*

INTRODUCTION

Dear Reader:

What was your first response to seeing this book on the shelves? Was it, "Did Dr. Pensanti really write a book about sex?" I'm sure a few of you might be shocked that a nice Christian woman would want to discuss such things. Obviously, there are much "safer" topics I could have chosen. However, this is the book God encouraged me to write. Indeed, perhaps the reason you have opened this book is that this is also the book God is encouraging you to read.

Even though you and I have never met in person, you may already feel as though you know me. For the past ten years, I have been the host of *Doctor to Doctor,* a weekly television program seen on the Trinity Broadcasting Network. I have interviewed experts in every field of medicine and have talked frankly about my personal and spiritual life.

God has given me an ability in my life to go boldly into areas where others may hesitate to tread. My medical credentials provide an umbrella under which I joyfully spread the wonderful knowledge I have gathered through my research studies, clinical experience and through my interviews and teaching on *Doctor to Doctor* and other radio and television shows over the years. Much of that material is assimilated for you within these pages.

Both my mother and father taught me to be fearless and bold. I think that is why God chose me to write this book for you. He knows I will not hesitate to bring you every bit of information at my disposal—medical, psychological and even mechanical—that will help you have better sex naturally—to show you that yes, there is hope for your sex life (contrary to what many of you may feel).

I feel as though I know you also. I have laughed with, cried with and prayed with men and women just like you. I know you from reading your letters, returning your phone calls and receiving your faxes and e-mails.

You have revealed to me your most intimate thoughts and innermost feelings. I am honored at the trust you have placed in me.

In both my medical practice and through the letters I receive from people just like you who watch *Doctor to Doctor* on TBN, I am surprised to find that the number one question I am asked is, "Dr. Pensanti, what has happened to my sex drive? Can you help me?" I have heard heartbreaking comments like, "I feel dead from the waist down." "I love my spouse, but I just hate the thought of sex."

I finally realized I could not delay any longer. I had to write this book—like it or not! I asked the Lord, "Why do I have to be the one? Why do I have to talk about sex?"

He answered, "Because you are a doctor, Helen. My lambs need the information. Who else should do it?" The Lord, of course, knows that I am not too shy to talk about the human body and its functions. And that is precisely what is needed in some of your cases.

When I read a recent study that revealed that books—not health professionals—are the number one source of sex information reported by people forty-five and older, I realized that this book could be an important answer and blessing to many people, and I could not put it off.

MEDICAL DOCTOR, COUNSELOR AND FRIEND

Please keep in mind that I am writing to you as a medical doctor first and also as a counselor and a friend. These pages will not be filled with stuffy jargon or oblique references to body parts. In many sections I need to be blunt and to the point in order to provide information that is practical and useful. With this book I seek to give you a solid base of information about your body and your spouse's body, and how God designed each for your sexual pleasure and psychological fulfillment.

I bring you good news—sex is God's idea. God has much to say about sex in the Bible. We have His permission to enjoy sex in marriage. Knowing what God says about sex helps strengthen and restore relationships in marriage.

Scripture further suggests that just as we can know God, so we can know our spouse in intimacy through the physical act. The Bible uses the same term for *knowing* God as it uses for *knowing* our spouse. The term is used to designate the intimate union of husband and wife. (See Ephesians 5:31–32.)

Anything that is thwarting this God-ordained physical union should be addressed without shame. This book will answer a lot of the questions people just like you (and maybe you) have sent to me. I have tried to do so honestly and fully. If areas of information included in this book are even slightly offensive to you, please skip over them! Not everyone has the same questions. My intent is not to offend anyone. However, I would be remiss if I excluded the discussion of any area of sexuality that is vitally important to another precious individual's success in restoring marital relations with his or her spouse.

If sexual desire is waning at this point in your life, or if sexual relations are disappointing to you or your spouse, read on. Most of all, if you believe that you have lost your sex drive, I want to show you how to get it back. I have been treating loss of libido very successfully for almost ten years with natural hormones and supplements.

I have written this book through the guidance of God's Holy Spirit. May you receive this in love, joy, peace, patience, kindness, faithfulness and long-suffering.

In His love,
—HELEN PENSANTI, M.D.

CHAPTER 1

The Number One Question

C an you help me with my sex drive? I don't have one." This is the number one question I receive from thousands of people of every age, race, class and occupation worldwide. Perhaps this doesn't surprise you—because you are one of these people.

The topic of sexual dysfunction is becoming more and more prevalent in the print and television media. It seems to be reaching epidemic proportions. During the ten years that I have hosted the weekly national television program *Doctor to Doctor,* which reaches millions of viewers in this country and far beyond, I have received countless thousands of individual questions about sexual dysfunction and libido loss. Men as well as women seek understanding and answers. A report in a 1999 issue of the *Journal of the American Medical Association* presented findings showing that 43 percent of women and 31 percent of men have problems with diminished or absent sexual desire.[1]

Libido loss is real and usually physical, not just a "mental" problem. A significant truth related to decreased sex drive is this: Whatever affects one partner also affects the other. Woman or man, it is never just "my" problem, but "ours." If you and your spouse stop having sex, whatever the initial reason, as a couple you will become physically estranged, which often leads to an emotionally aloof state.

When that happens, a rift develops between you and your spouse that can feel like the Great Divide. Soon it feels insurmountable and irreparable. It is because so many individuals have told me that they feel there is no hope for their marital relations that I felt compelled to write this book. God's Word says, "Hope deferred makes the heart sick…" (Prov. 13:12).

But the good news is found in the rest of that verse, for it goes on to say, "…but when dreams come true, there is life and joy." Your dream for a healthy, fulfilling sexual relationship with your spouse can come true. There's plenty that can be done to improve lagging or even lost libido.

This book will help you understand some reasons for this increasingly commonplace medical and marital issue. We'll delineate medical causes and conditions that lead to sexual dysfunction and offer up-to-date, common-sense, practical approaches to restoring normal, satisfying sexual relations. I want you to know: THERE IS HOPE FOR YOUR SEX LIFE!

A MYTH

I believe it's a myth that men and women are psychologically different when it comes to sex. I think we all have the same yearnings and desires, and that God designed our bodies perfectly to satisfy one another sexually. Because I want you to succeed in this area, I'm going to tell you something I have learned in my twenty-plus years "in the trenches" as a physician. The ability to have good sex is not some great secret other couples have figured out but that you and your spouse have failed to discover! No! No! No!

Good sex is not a huge mystery. Your sexual experiences can be as great and fulfilling and satisfying as the next couple's. You just need to understand how your body works and how your spouse's body works. Not every sexual encounter results in ground-shaking orgasms for husband or wife. Sometimes a climax can be just a bleep on the radar screen— or there may be no climax at all. But even with that, each encounter can be totally fulfilling and mutually delightful. This is my goal for you.

IMPORTANT BENEFITS

Why do you think God wants us to have a wonderful experience when we come together sexually with our spouse? There are several important health and emotional benefits.

1. *Good sex builds a firm marriage.* We've all seen those couples, married for years, who still coo over each other. No one can dispute the enormous value of a long, strong, excellent marriage where the husband and wife are content, happy and satisfied. An ongoing, satisfying sex life will help cement your marriage. Good sex, after all, is the physical demonstration of the deep emotional and mental bonds between two people—you and your beloved—who desire and cherish one another.

2. *Sex creates a joyful attitude.* The enjoyment of your sexuality and enjoyment of your partner enhance your enjoyment of life.

3. *Regular sexual intercourse improves health.* There is nothing better for the body than a vigorous sexual interlude. As I have seen in my practice, post-menopausal women who have regular sexual intercourse have much healthier vaginal tissue and urinary tracts than women who no longer engage in sexual activity. In addition, the releasing of endorphins during sex has physiological benefits. A loving sexual encounter can be an incredible mood enhancer. It can have a relaxation effect that is more powerful than prescription muscle relaxants.

4. *Sex also helps lengthen life.* It is common knowledge that married men live longer than single men do. Sex has been identified as a prime factor in longevity.

3

There are many men who think their wives are "just not interested" or "just don't care" about their sexual relationships any longer. But this thinking is just plain wrong! I see many women in my office regularly who are agonizing over their loss of libido. I wish you could read some of my mail. Almost every day, I receive letters from women lamenting their lack or loss of sex drive. They long to feel the desire for their husbands that they know is God's plan for their marriages. They feel desperate about not being able to give their spouses what they want and deserve.

Most of the women with whom I consult thank God for their precious husbands. They desire to honor their mates with their bodies—but somehow "things are just not working." As one dear caller told me, weeping, "I feel like God has set a wonderful feast before me, and I'm just not hungry." Thousands and thousands of women have expressed these same thoughts to me. Gentlemen, your wives are very likely having some of these same thoughts. Be patient! Help is here!

And what about the men? Although it is highly unusual for a man age forty or fifty to experience the almost total loss of libido that many women confront, men still can have problems. For instance, men in their fifties and sixties also begin to notice reduction in their libido and stamina. Yes, men have the same concerns. They too experience doubts and anxiety related to decreased libido or decreased interest in sexual activity.

What is the cause? My research and clinical experience show many causes, and we will explore them. We will examine libido and problems with desire very carefully, as well as problems of stress, painful intercourse, erectile dysfunction, prostate disease and the effects of aging on sexual activity.

Sometimes a couple will experience midlife hormonal changes simultaneously. At the same time that women encounter and deal with significant hormonal changes that affect their libido, men often encounter problems with "performance," both with sex and in their everyday work life. As men pass the age of fifty, many of my women patients say they are confused by some of their husbands' changing behaviors. The midlife years can be a challenging time of emotional and physical turmoil for both men and women.

WHY SEX IS IMPORTANT

God wants you to rejoice in and delight your life partner physically, as in all other ways. God wants you to be a giver of love. If your sexual response is changing, that does not mean that your sexual relationship with your spouse needs to change. You can enhance and strengthen your relationship year by year—just as God designed it to happen. Your human sexuality, as more and more medical studies are showing, can remain intact throughout your life. You just need the knowledge on how to address these confusing physical changes that may be occurring.

MY MISSION

Many Christian "sex" books talk about the wonder of sex and the need to create greater intimacy. They do not address the "mechanics" of the body, failing libido and lack of desire. Ladies especially may know the feeling, "I want to want to, but I just don't want to!" Well, we need to start with some basics. We will start with creating the mood for sex—something that seems to have become a problem for many "old married folks." After all, the *process* as well as the *destination* should be enjoyable. From mood we will move on to the loss of libido and mechanical problems. And we will tell you what can be done so that you can have better sex—naturally.

5

CHAPTER 2

In the Mood

What do I mean by "in the mood"? Do you remember the excitement of the sexual encounters you and your mate shared in earlier days? Does that same excitement now seem always to be just out of reach? It has been lost somewhere in your busy and sometimes stressful life—the life I know most of you are leading. You just fall into bed at night exhausted. Yes, sex remains somewhere on your list, but right now you need your spouse to understand just how overworked, overstressed and resentful you often feel.

This doctor knows all about that. Same song, two thousandth verse, sung by men and women in every city, village and hamlet. Sex? "We're never in the mood anymore. And don't talk to us about getting in the mood, because I just don't feel like it. I seem to have completely lost my sex drive."

That's exactly what this chapter will discuss. Later we'll examine the numbers of medical reasons why sex may not be happening—and why you may honestly no longer care. For now, though, we'll delineate some familiar ways good sex begins—and ideally, keeps on happening. Hopefully you'll recall the intense pleasure and fulfillment of sex and feel the stirrings of your own earlier marital excitement.

MOOD MAKERS FOR WOMEN

In this chapter we will explore ways for a woman to create a mood for sexual arousal and intimacy. We will address some of the same issues for men in a later chapter. But don't stop reading if you are a man—knowing the infinite value and attention that your wife places on "mood making" can be vitally important to you. You can help to create the mood for intimacy that your wife needs.

Men, if you do not want to deal with this aspect, please move ahead to chapter three.

If you are as stressed, fatigued and uninterested in sex as many women today, your closet may reflect it. An overflow of jeans, sweatshirts and ten-year-old clothes are dead give-aways. (We sure didn't wear that stuff when we were trying to captivate our man.)

"But Dr. Pensanti," you say, "you're sounding like those women's magazine articles. Remember, I work. Slinky satins and delicate lacy things don't fit my lifestyle." I believe you, but don't knock those articles. Savvy magazine editors are very aware that lost libido has become a hot issue for their readers.

So here's a quick and easy wardrobe assessment that offers clues to your present state of mind and level of desire. (You won't get this advice from male doctors.)

How long since you bought yourself something red? Or pure white? How about high-heeled or otherwise frivolous shoes? Sexy bedroom slippers? Something silk? Is your hairstyle up-to-date? Your makeup alluring—or blah? Or are you at the other end of the spectrum—polished, up-to-date and too perfect to touch?

Answering such questions provides clues to how happy or unhappy you may feel. Really happy, sparkly, energetic women choose clothes that match their upbeat selves. They look like they want to be alluring, but also accessible to their husbands. There is nothing wrong with black, brown, gray and beige, but if you aren't enjoying some glorious colors in your life, their absence may be giving you an important clue about yourself.

"But I dress for myself, not for a man," you may protest.

That's fine, if you do actually dress for yourself at times, not always for the job or for housework. Wear the clothes, colors and fabrics you truly love, and I guarantee your husband will notice. Learn who you are and what you like, and wear what gives you maximum pleasure. When you do, you'll exhibit the self-confidence that radiates from a woman who is truly secure in herself—and that self-confidence is sexy.

I know of a man whose wife gave him an expensive suede sport coat for Christmas one year. He loved wearing it, because when he did, his wife, daughters and sisters stroked his coat (and him) because the fabric was so touchable.

Many women wear silk for the same reason. It's irresistible to the touch. Silk, suede, even fleece are cuddly fabrics. They invite caresses. Feminine colors—violet, pale green, sky blue, bright red, garnet or baby pink—are flattering and inviting. An elderly woman "doing lunch" with her husband after church remarked, "Richard always asks me to wear this dress, so I wear it all the time." The blue linen dress made her eyes look as blue as sapphires. A beautiful Black woman friend looks yummy in her soft white pantsuit with a lime green blouse, and so invitingly touchable.

Even though this advice may sound decidedly "*un*-doctor-like" to you, the fact is, a wardrobe addition or new hairstyle often works wonders in revving up your *joie de vivre,* or joy of life.

Let's tell the truth. When we know we look knockout, drop-dead gorgeous, don't we also feel sexy? If you don't agree, please stay with me. We are going to get into the medical aspects of the flagging libido, but first I want to cover all of the extracurricular bases, so to speak.

PURE PLEASURE

As a physician, I believe too many women have forgotten all they ever knew about pleasure. Since sex offers pleasure—and somehow pleasure became a nonreality for them—sex, therefore, becomes easy to postpone, sometimes indefinitely.

In chapter three we will discuss the arousal process and the fascinating physiological events that lead to sexual intercourse, providing pleasure, delight and even ecstasy for both partners. But for many, life has become so crowded, harried and tiring that it consists merely of daily struggles to meet everyone else's needs. There seems to be nothing left over for one's own needs. Pleasure, delight and ecstasy seem hopelessly out of the question.

In our chaotic American way of life, one truth must be understood by women who want to bring fresh passion and life to their sexual encounters with their mates: In order to be able to give pleasure to their men, they must restore the capacity for everyday pleasure in themselves. The women to whom I talk about this truth touchingly express their desire to do so!

Sex is meant to be mutually pleasurable to a husband and wife. God designed sex as the means by which a husband and a wife, transported by the bliss of their expressed physical love for one another, literally become one flesh. The miracle of oneness, encompassing not only a physical but also an indescribably spiritual joining, may represent the pinnacle of human pleasure. Such glorious physical pleasure celebrates the uniting of two people. It is the cornerstone of a good marriage.

9

We all desire such tenderness and bliss. But a woman who allows herself to become so self-sacrificing that she offers every ounce of her caring, serving and providing self to the nurturing of others, leaving nothing for herself, soon spins away from the idea of personal pleasure. She no longer perceives her need for pleasure, and at last, she may lose any desire for personal pleasure.

That describes too many women. Does it describe you? Do you regularly fail to take a day off for yourself? Do you habitually postpone friendship opportunities? Was the last movie you saw *Snow White and the Seven Dwarfs* (the black-and-white version!)? If so, then it's not just your libido that's missing—it's your real life.

This modern-day phenomenon of women denying themselves pleasure and self-nurturing is a dangerous habit that is robbing too many women in our society of their femininity, their sex drive and their joy. If you recognize yourself among this number, you should begin now to make regaining your libido a priority.

YOU ARE UNIQUELY AND WONDERFULLY MADE: THERE IS ONLY ONE YOU!

In reality, you probably already know about the potential of all kinds of beauty treatments and makeovers. You may have dieted and exercised for years. When people tell you, "You look good," you are already glancing in the mirror to confirm their opinion.

But what about your opinion? Undeniably, certain childhood messages come back to haunt us. You may never be totally satisfied with what you see in the mirror. No matter what, you are not quite perfect—ever. You may be your own worst critic. Perhaps you are like some women, so self-conscious about your "faults" that you actually cannot believe anyone could desire you; therefore, you actually block your own feelings of desire.

As adult women, we can learn to accept ourselves exactly as we are. We can affirm our beauty. God affirmed it—"God looked over all he had made, and he saw that it was excellent in every way" (Gen. 1:31). That includes all our lovable imperfections—including freckles, big feet or chubby thighs.

You and I are fine. We really need to stop obsessing about "faults" we can't change so we can release the powers of our full-blown womanhood. Long-held anxieties need to be canceled. They are no longer valid. We are grown women now, fully capable of learning to celebrate and enhance our sexual selves. If your physical attractiveness is at question, you will be very gratified at the results of a recent survey. Among men ages forty-five through fifty-nine, approximately 59 percent gave their partners the highest possible rating for physical attractiveness (on a scale of one to ten), and for those men seventy-five and older, the figure was 63 percent![1] So be heartened. Older lovers hold up a different looking glass to each other and see beauty that is ripe and full.

RESPONDING TO HIM

Not only does perpetual fatigue create near total disinterest in sex, but it also can eventually lead to disinterest in your husband. Moving about in a fog of fatigue, we choose to ignore the little hugs, pats and compliments that indicate he's in the mood for intimacy.

Genuinely busy and stressed, we tune him out. (That's simple self-defense, we argue.) We choose to ignore his signals. But the fact is, each time we make that choice we stuff down our own libido. Get busy enough, tired enough, stressed enough, dying for sleep enough…and we have a sure formula for putting out our personal fire of passion.

Sleep experts, whose medical studies show that most Americans are dangerously sleep-deprived, have a lot to say about realistic sleep habits. But sleep is not the only culprit. Make an honest tally of the number of times you have shrugged him off or, at the least, dismissed his affection. The number may surprise you.

No matter how good the reason, these "strike-outs" diminish your health and energy, not to mention the rejection your husband feels. This represents self-defeating behavior at its worst and joyless living at the very least. Welcome love's embrace—it helps to recharge you and gives your spouse the pleasure he seeks.

11

GIVE YOURSELF SOME TIME OUT

When it comes to lagging libido, insecurities flood in. "I feel like a failure as a woman," I often hear. Or, "I've lost touch with my real self, and I've lost touch with my husband. Now I'm too embarrassed to initiate any romantic encounters." Your first priority, obviously, is to restore yourself, no matter what it takes. There's an old country saying that applies here: "You can't keep pouring from an empty bucket." Millions of would-be superwomen, conscientious about their desires for and duties toward husbands, children, parents, bosses, jobs and households, are trying to do just that.

If you notice, men usually seem too smart to make this

mistake. Even on strenuous business trips, they find time for a game of golf. Despite weekend chores, they keep up with their fishing buddies or manage to attend ball games. And sometimes it seems that they can just "turn it on" and have sex at the drop of a hat. Ladies, it is up to smart women to equalize the equation. It's time to realize that you may be guilty of gross self-neglect, which leads to neglect of your husband. We need to find ways to stop it.

Listing things that make you happy is a good starting place. Deciding to take time to listen to music, exercise, sleep, plant a garden or just read a book with a cup of tea in hand is a "worthy" project. You may just need a little time to daydream, but feel too guilty about such a selfish act. Philosopher and author Bertrand Russell, however, once said, "The time you enjoy wasting is not wasted time." AHA! I think that quotation might be important for some of you who are harried, stressed and exhausted from your daily overload of too many fruitless duties.

12

A pastor once commented that most of the marital problems of couples whom he encountered could probably be cured with a good night's sleep and a little cuddling. "And most of their unhappiness, too," he added. Do you know why he may be absolutely right? Because the combination of fatigue and sexual frustration is a deadly one—deadly to the spirit and to the body.

Try his recommendation, and see how it works for you. Make yourself as happy as possible, and realize you owe that to the other people in your world. One way to start the happiness cycle is to dish it out to others via hugs, kisses and sincere words of appreciation and praise. Give yourself time for those important extras, and your happiness quotient will rise.

REDISCOVERING YOUR ALLURE

Remember those teen years when you experimented with Mom's array of cosmetics and "tested" all her perfumes? In those days of long ago, you had plenty of time to experiment with strange new items like eyelash curlers. We tried every shade of lipstick and applied Mom's cosmetics with a generous hand, or we went to the drug store and bought our own.

Part of that experience was plain old childhood curiosity and experimentation. But lying just under the surface were our budding expectations about our soon-to-appear adult beauty, glamour and allure.

Where did all those sweet expectations go? There are different answers for different women, I'm sure. But if you never feel glamorous or alluring these days, or if you never believe you are beautiful, it may be time to return to those long-ago days of experimentation. (Don't get discouraged—we will be getting to the medical aspects soon enough!)

But for now, try some of those little tricks you learned long ago, this time using the fashionable newer shades of makeup. If you're feeling really adventurous, did you know you can even use lip color to give the illusion of fuller, sexier lips? Try dabbing a new perfume on those "gotcha" spots. He may not love the fragrance, but he will notice there is something different about his spouse. Find something, anything, that makes you feel like a different, more desirable woman.

Femininity, that elusive something that makes you know you are a woman, comes from the inside. Despite what Hollywood movies may portray, it doesn't take a man to make a woman sure she is a woman. It happens by continually asserting her inborn feminine self in numerous subtle and largely unconscious ways, all of which reinforce the fact that she's a woman.

But when a woman lets her feminine side get overwhelmed, misplaced or neglected, it soon follows that her sex drive dwindles. Obviously it takes more than clothing, cosmetics and perfume to make a woman, but such things color her self-perceptions, thus steering her libido and sex appeal in the right direction.

IN THE MOOD AGAIN

It's easy enough to allow our womanpower to leak away over the years. Sometimes, though, it's not all that difficult to restore. This chapter, while not strictly medical, nevertheless is rooted in scientific fact and principles. There are numerous medical causes for loss of libido, and as a medical doctor, I

13

am very anxious to address them. However, I recognize that there are many women out there who need to begin at a more basic level with their appreciation of self and their God-given desirability before we move into more succinct and perhaps graphic areas. Here are a few simple tips to get you started.

Let's check your sexual strengths against the following list:

1. *Self-image*—You don't feel sexy because you consider yourself unlovable, unworthy, ugly or fat. I want you to remember, you are uniquely and wonderfully made.

2. *Dowdiness*—Look into some women's closets, and you'd never guess they see themselves as females. One good shopping trip can make a world of difference. If they take "Honey" along and tell him they want to have a "sexier" look, chances are they'll come home with more than they would have bought for themselves. Many men like to be generous, and that makes their women feel loved.

3. *Big sleep debts*—Get an hour more sleep each day by retiring thirty minutes earlier and rising thirty minutes later. Yes, one hour! In just a week you should see a big difference in your moods and energy level. Your usual sunny self will begin to emerge, and your alluring womanhood will return. Begin tonight.

4. *Daily pleasure*—A quiet cup of tea or coffee before the hectic day begins, a new music tape for your car, minutes of undisturbed leisure while you "put on your face" can make a big difference in the way your day shapes up. As queen of your household, you can order in some pleasure just for yourself. Make this a daily treat each day for the rest of your life, and it will transform your outlook about your womanly value.

5. *Accept yourself*—Don't put yourself down. Good women can criticize themselves nearly to extinction, all in the name of virtue and conscience. This is sin, and injurious to one's health. After all, if God and

your husband accept you exactly as you are, why can't you?

6. *Femininity focus*—Try wearing perfume, silky blouses, pearls at your throat. Always wear things you like. Choose yummy colors and flattering designs. These make you happy, self-confident and alluring. I know I love to wear black because I think it makes me look thinner. However, every time I deviate and wear blue, purple or red, I get many, many compliments, teaching me that I don't always know best!

7. *Believe in yourself*—Believe, because God believes in you. As a medical doctor, I can assure you that most sexual problems can be cured, and all sexual relationships can be wonderfully enhanced.

Give yourself permission now to recapture the good feelings, warmth and deep love you felt toward your husband, by first generously loving you. Not only are you worthy and deserving, you also are the daughter of the One who gives all good gifts. Because He loves you lavishly, with absolutely no limits, you have been created, chosen and programmed to love that same way.

This book will explore ways to make that happen. You may find yourself learning, perhaps for the first time, that you are endlessly lovable, delightful and beautiful. You have much to give, and can soon desire to give to yourself, then beyond yourself, from your abundant storehouse of unique gifts. Those gifts, of course, spring from and include your sexual gifts, an inborn and essential element that makes you so uniquely you.

This chapter has concentrated on helping you create a mood, an ambiance, an environment that nurtures intimacy between you and your spouse. In the next chapter, I want to move on to the medical aspects of your lost libido. Together, we will find it.

There is hope for your sex life!

15

CHAPTER 3

Sexual Arousal

What kindles sexual passion? Exactly what makes arousal happen, and why does it occur?

A clear understanding of our sexual anatomy and drives, along with knowing it is God's desire for us to enjoy our spouses physically, paves the way to a wonderful and fruitful sex life. Together, as husband and wife, in privacy, you learn the meaning of God's standard of "two becoming one flesh."

Arousal is perhaps the most fascinating phase of the sexual cycle. In my opinion, most people pay far too little attention to their wonderful, God-given ability to become suddenly, amazingly sexually excited by their mate. In fact, my medical practice has taught me that embarrassment often accompanies the mere acknowledgment that one's body has this great capacity to respond sexually.

Most of us remember the first time we fell in love—"puppy love." Our hearts beat furiously with the pitter-patter of first love. The mere sight of that special person tugged at our heartstrings. Our thoughts turned continually to our love interest, causing our hearts to swell as the endorphins began circulating. That voice on the phone, a certain smile, look or whiff of cologne made us go "weak in the knees."

Wow!...what a wonderful feeling!

You need only to read the Song of Solomon to glimpse the heights of arousal God wants us to enjoy. When the Shulamite maiden opened the door to her beloved, she describes becoming so aroused that "my hands dripped with perfume, my fingers with lovely myrrh" on the handles of the lock (Song of Sol. 5:5). The enamored Shulamite maiden, "sick with love," described "flashes of fire, the brightest kind of flame" (8:6). When you watch a romantic film classic like *Casablanca* or *It Happened One Night*, can't you intuitively understand and identify with the young Shulamite maiden's ardent arousal and sexual longing? Ah, sweet love!

Let me offer my description of sexual arousal. It will not be phrased in the Bible's poetic language, or even in the romantic promises of the silver screen. I offer it in the language I know best: Physiology. If medical terminology offends you, please skip over this part. I think it is important to understand your body's sexual function. Far from being a subject of embarrassment or shame, knowledge of how we are designed to function frees us from incorrect assumptions, fears and all the side effects of human ignorance.

"Know thyself." Socrates' ancient advice still rings true today. Know and understand your own body and how it works, and you will be able to allow someone to "play you like a fine violin."

In some ways, the arousal process is the same for men and women. In other ways, it differs. Let me give you a quick overview of our sexual "wiring."

In the womb, identical embryonic cells become either a penis in the male or a clitoris in the female. The nervous system is "wired" the same in both the male scrotum and the female vaginal lips.

Males and females are created to enjoy the same sensations via their respective organs. Many men do not understand that the many overwhelmingly pleasurable sensations available to men are correspondingly available to women. The sensations that engender pleasure in the male penis and scrotum are the same as in the female vaginal lips and clitoris.

This knowledge alone can immeasurably enhance most couples' sexual enjoyment!

Husband and wife, endowed with differing sex organs, nevertheless have been given identical and equal opportunities for pleasure via the same type of neural pathways, or "sexual wiring."

> FACT: The sensations that engender pleasure in the male penis and scrotum are the same as in the female vaginal lips and clitoris.

Stop now and think about this. If you are a woman, think about how the clitoris feels when properly touched, caressed and adored. Now translate that from receiving to giving to your husband's penis. Remember to touch it gently, caressing and adoring this part of his body. This is God's gift to you, and remember, your husband has a lot to give back to you—later on in the sex act.

If you are a man, you have the capacity to give your wife the same overwhelmingly pleasurable sensations that you are feeling simply by focusing on the areas that have the same neurological pathways as your penis. Whatever feels good on your penis and scrotum, you can simply mirror back on your wife's clitoris and vaginal lips, especially the inner lips, called the *labia minora*. I guarantee you, this tip alone can bring you light-years along in pleasuring your wife! But remember, slow and gentle, please.

As arousal takes place, the pathways to sexual pleasure are again similar. Blood flows to the male pelvis and erection begins. Blood flows to the female pelvis, and the vaginal lips begin to enlarge and engorge.

There is a perfect synchronization of feeling and response between male and female—with one important difference to be considered: A woman's excitement phase is lengthier than a man's. It often seems to women, therefore, that men are too quick to desire penetration. However, as a man ages, the length and pace of arousal seem to become more compatible with that of his mate.

Let's open one of my clinical files:

"Gary makes me feel like something he uses just to satisfy himself," Sue told me. "It seems like thirty seconds after he reaches for me when we go to bed, he's ready, and I feel like he doesn't even care about my feelings. What can I do? It turns me right off."

Gary and Sue had failed to understand the great difference between a man's arousal response time and that of a woman. Sue needed more time. She needed to be able to enjoy her own feelings of arousal without feeling that Gary was only considering his own needs.

I recommended to Sue that she and her husband, Gary, discuss some of the same things that I will be recommending to you in the following pages if she felt comfortable doing so. If she is too intimidated by the thought of an actual discussion, or if she thinks as many women do that you must be very careful with the male ego, she could simply whisper in his ear, "Oh, honey (or other pet name), let's not hurry—it feels too good." Gary can learn or be motivated to slow down his responses and to give Sue time to respond to his lovemaking. She, in turn, will want to give him more pleasure now than she did before.

FOR MEN–AROUSAL IN WOMEN

Sexual arousal is much more than mere emotional response. Our bodies were created to respond physiologically to each other. During the arousal phase the woman's body, in a series of well-orchestrated steps, prepares itself for orgasm. The arousal phase is a very important part of the total act of intercourse and should not be short-changed or overlooked.

As a woman moves through the arousal phase, her vaginal walls begin to produce lubrication, and the muscle surrounding the vaginal opening (the pubococcygeal muscle) tightens. The vagina swells, and the uterus expands and elevates in preparation for penetration.

Let's consider each of these finely tuned actions in sequence.

19

LUBRICATION

While lubrication is one of the first signs of arousal, its appearance does not necessarily mean a woman is fully aroused and ready for intercourse.

During the excitatory phase of lovemaking, blood travels to the outer and inner lips of the vagina, increasing fluid pressures there and causing some fluid to seep into the vaginal tract. Beads of fluid form on the vaginal walls and rapidly spread to form a smooth, moist covering.

> FACT: Vaginal moisture does not always indicate true sexual arousal.

Younger women may find vaginal lubrication occurring within thirty seconds of stimulation. Older women, who may be experiencing decreased hormone fluctuation, sometimes find it difficult to produce natural lubrication.

Anxiety, stress and the use of some medications can affect a woman's natural ability to lubricate. Birth control pills, which can create changes in female sex hormones, may interfere with the production of vaginal lubrication.

VAGINAL CHANGES

As blood moves to the genital area, the inner lips (*labia minora*) become engorged and begin to extend outward. The outer lips (*labia majora*) spread flat, and the clitoris becomes erect and firm, almost like a tiny penis. Breasts may swell, and nipples become firm and erect. After age forty, breasts may lose some elasticity and may not swell as much, but nipples still become hard, erect and sensitive. The *areolas* (the dark pigmented area surrounding the nipples) may also darken and engorge. At this point, the outer *third* of the vagina begins to tighten or narrow.

Many of my patients express worry that childbirth has stretched the vagina so that they cannot satisfy their husband as well as before. Don't worry! God has it all under control. You were wonderfully designed to bear children *and* to please your husband!

NOTE: If you are one of those rare women whose vagina

actually did stretch too much as a result of childbearing, you can consider a surgical procedure called A&P repair.

CHANGES IN THE UTERUS

Once these changes have taken place in the vagina, the uterus pulls up and away from the vagina, pulling the cervix out of the way. (If the uterus is tipped, this does not happen.) Should the husband's penis be inserted deep into the vagina before his wife is fully aroused, he may hit the cervix before it tips forward out of the way. This can cause a sharp, stabbing pain.

WHAT HUSBANDS SHOULD KNOW

It has been said that men are *genitally aroused*, while women are *generally aroused*. Even when genital stimulation has caused vaginal lubrication, a woman still may not feel aroused. The husband should woo his wife into romance. This demonstrates love for her rather than a demand for fulfillment of sexual rights as a husband. She may need more relaxation, seduction or the creation of a certain mood. Maybe soft music, flowers and, who knows? Chocolate-covered strawberries could create such a mood. Or maybe it could be ushered in with just the soft, gentle whispers from her husband with promises of things to come.

21

Men, this is not difficult. In my own homespun version of a wonderful scripture in Psalm 37, I sum it up succinctly for you: "Delight yourself in your wife, and she will give you the sex life your heart desires." I know from letters and conversations with many men that a great "desire of the heart" for many men is their yearning for great sex. Your wife wants to satisfy that desire, and she will do so if you eagerly and habitually delight yourself in her—in public, as well as in the bedroom. That delight is what you want from her, so that's what you must give to her.

Exactly what do I mean by "delight yourself" in your wife? First, nonerotic caresses are very important, enough so, in fact, to be virtually essential to a woman's sexual arousal. Little "honeymoon habits" like holding hands at the movies, the hug and squeeze when you help her on with her coat, pulling her close to you in the car as you softly declare your love—such small touches are not only important, but also fun.

Even if the two of you have been sexually intimate for years, you should continue to exhibit nonerotic touching. It's one of the secret pathways to good sex for a woman, which nearly always translates into good sex for her husband. Start noticing older couples who are still acting like honeymooners. Watch how the men treat their wives with loving care. Start imitating their behavior with your own wife!

Another form of nonerotic caressing is *verbal strokes*—sweet talk prior to the sex act. Use the Song of Solomon in the Bible to give you word pictures to use as you communicate with one another your sexual desires and love for one another. Remember, it is the stirring of her emotions and imagination that helps her to respond. Communicate your feelings to one another as Solomon did to his love.

Your verbal affirmations to her are stored in her memory bank, and they go a long way toward furthering her arousal process. Her ears are an important tool—what she hears from you "sets the stage." Remember, no amount of other sexual stimulation will be truly effective if your wife is feeling distant, remote or silently resentful because you have been mean, critical or harsh to her.

Touch her in ways that are not immediately sexual. Stroking her face, smoothing her hair, rubbing her back or nuzzling her neck are ways to make your woman feel a little "weak in the knees." When you come together for a sexual encounter, try not to place your hands immediately on her genitals or breasts.

Often a man will reach directly for his wife's genitals because that is exactly what he desires her to do with him. A woman, however, will often hold back from such immediate sexual contact or even recoil when her husband does so. This is not what she wants. She hopes that her husband will spend some time first in more general body touching—stroking her arm, rubbing her back or holding her in an affectionate embrace—before he becomes more intimate.

Men, consider a soccer game. There's a lot of back-and-forth running before goals are usually made! Remember to take your time. Only lust and self-gratification are done in a hurry.

When a man moves too quickly to direct sexual touching and she retreats, neither the husband nor his wife is receiving what he or she wants and needs the most! The man is not receiving direct sexual stimulation, and his wife is not receiving the general body touching she needs. It's important for men to realize that women like a little time to "warm up." Don't ever forget that "warm" leads to "hot" on the temperature scale.

> FACT: It's important for men to realize that women like a little time to "warm up."

I'm not saying you need an hour of foreplay. But taking time for a few long minutes of general caresses will be wonderful for your wife. She will note that you are trying to please her—a fact that very often triggers a mechanism in her brain that leads to arousal.

Now, I'll tell you another little secret about women. What "turned her on" last week may not turn her on today. Not that she's a capricious creature, but because her present mood often depends on how her day or week has gone.

For example, I heard the following story on a national radio show. The husband emerged from the shower, wrapped a towel about his torso and presented himself to his wife in grand fashion. Dropping the towel and standing before her in the nude, he asked, "Honey, what do you see?" His wife smiled and became enamored, embraced his warm, steamy body and they had a wonderful sexual interlude. Naturally the happy husband thought he had found a key to great sex with his wife and was eager to try that method again.

Two days later he emerged from the shower, approached his wife in their bedroom where she was reading and repeated his dramatic entrance. Dropping his towel, he asked, "Honey, what do you see?" She glanced up from her book, surveyed him briefly and said, "There's a wet towel on the floor!"

So—what is the answer to her arousal? Every woman I have treated or counseled over the years loves it when her

23

husband pays attention to her. When I advise you to "delight yourself in your wife," this may mean affirming her, becoming playful and affectionate, stroking her in a nonsexual way, complimenting her, talking sweetly, touching her face or hair or anything else she loves from you. These things allow her to relax fully in your presence. Her "self-talk" becomes something like this: "Mmmm...my husband really likes me. He likes my body. I really turn him on. He loves touching me, and he finds me fascinating."

This will relax her, and she will open up. But if her self-talk says, "He's so selfish. What does he want now?", then I can assure you that the sign on her heart will read, "Go Away!", and the sign on her clitoris and vagina will read, "No Trespassing."

When you do not immediately imply sexual intent, it allows her to de-stress without feeling she must "perform." Instead, allow her to become lost in the thoughts and feelings of physical pleasure. Not only does this make her receptive to your sexual advances, but often she may choose to initiate the sexual activity. Because she loves you, she loves this sort of special time and attention. It is very sexy to her, very lovely and nondemanding.

FOR WOMEN—THE MALE AROUSAL PROCESS

Because a man's sexual arousal phase differs in some ways from his wife's, it will be helpful for his wife to learn exactly what happens during male sexual arousal and the erection that follows arousal. This is as important a step as it is for the husband to learn what pleases his wife during arousal. In this way both individuals will better understand not only their mates, but themselves also.

Not surprisingly, the process parallels her own in many ways. Blood travels to his genitalia. The testicles swell, the scrotum tightens and glands within the penis secrete a lubrication fluid that facilitates insertion of the penis into her vagina. In these ways, his series of arousal events mimics hers.

The husband's arousal should result in penile erection, following a marvelously orchestrated set of neural signals that are activated mostly by his wife.

There are actually two neurological pathways leading a man to erection.

First, a man's brain may trigger the event. This can happen as a man thinks about sex, when he sees you in alluring nightwear or as the result of a sexually stimulating comment or conversation. The second pathway is through physical stimuli such as erotic kissing, stroking or touching.

The "signal" affects nerves within the smooth muscle fiber of the penis, allowing the tissue to relax. This allows blood flow into the organ. Arteries dilate, blood fills the shaft's spongy tissues and the penis becomes rigid. Muscles at the organ's base contract, containing the blood within the penis. He now has an erection, which continues until the nerve messages cease.

After age forty, men are likely to report changes in this arousal process. Erection may no longer be achieved as easily as in the past. This is the result of a normal aging process, not the result of a decline in sexuality.

A young husband may experience immediate erection at the very thought of sex or when he sees his wife undressed. In later years his physiological responses slow down—including his sexual responses. When a wife recognizes and understands that this natural slowing is the result of aging, she can assist her husband if necessary by using direct stimulation—light stroking, teasing, lubricating or other ways pleasing to both partners. It is vital to remember that the arousal process changes as both partners mature and age. Lovemaking, however, should remain a wonderful constant within the relationship, despite natural changes through the years.

It is not physical prowess, after all, but emotional, physical and personal intermingling within the act of love that can continue to grow, change and evolve in satisfying and thrilling ways "for as long as you both shall live."

WHAT WIVES SHOULD KNOW

Men achieve erections more easily in the mornings before they become stressed or tired.

TIP: What could be better than an early morning sexual

25

encounter to get his day off to a promising start? True, house-hold logistics might take some working out. For instance, a lock on the bedroom door is a must with children. However, our world is not always an easy place, and many men find themselves "slaying dragons" in the daily workplace. Why not send them off sexually satisfied and feeling well-loved?

Sometimes husbands, like wives, are not in the mood to "go all the way." When stress or extreme fatigue leaves him feeling bushed, ladies, a massage may be in order. Rub his feet for a minimum of ten minutes. Then, starting at his heels, slowly stroke his legs, continuing this leg massage for about fifteen to twenty minutes. By the time you reach the thighs, he may have something else in mind.

Learn to appreciate your husband's erogenous zones. While his penis may be central, his lips, tongue, ears and nip-ples all contain exquisitely sensitive nerve centers you should explore. He would love for you to arouse him in some new and unexpected way.

It is very important to keep your voice soft and gentle around a man. This contributes to his arousal process. I have done extensive studies on male physiology, especially on how a man becomes aroused and how he progresses to an erection. It is through the parasympathetic nervous system. This system requires a quiet female. Loud or brash talking irritates the parasympathetic system.

Just take a look at America's favorite sex symbol—Marilyn Monroe. Her quiet voice and slow speech pattern were half of her winning ways with men. To this day, people talk about her "sexy" voice. The quietness draws men in. Loud voices run men off. Please teach this information to any young woman you know who is loud and boisterous!

INITIATING SEXUAL ACTIVITY

Do you initiate sex? If not, realize that's one important dif-ference between men and women. Many wives feel uncom-fortable at the idea of even discussing sex, much less initiating intercourse with their husbands.

Indeed, many women actually avoid physical affection lest

their husbands interpret the affectionate touch as a signal that sex is desired—and that wouldn't be "ladylike." Or perhaps the wife, who just wants to snuggle for a while, holds back affection because she doesn't want her husband to get the wrong message. If one spouse feels hugs and kisses are given just to obtain sex, it can become a source of great irritation and a way to build up resentment.

> FACT: A distinctly physical approach works well only if it's a positive approach for both the man and the woman.

Women often signal their interest in a sexual encounter with their husbands in ways that are far more subtle than those by which their husbands signal a desire for sex. Wives may put on a particular article of clothing, dab on a favorite perfume or set up a romantic setting in the bedroom. They may also speak in seductive tones or brush against their men in a provocative way. For one couple I know, when he hears her bath water running, he knows what's on her mind!

Men, generally speaking, are much simpler creatures in this regard. A man seems to know only two main paths that lead to initiating sex. The first is simply to ask for it. The second approach involves touching his wife's body in a sexual fashion. These two very direct approaches may work well in your marriage. However, if they are "turnoffs," it's better to find another method for initiating sex in order to get the optimum-quality sex life you desire.

One couple solved the issue this way: They decided to initiate sex by nonverbal means. They keep a pair of figurines in their bedroom. When one or the other desires sex, he or she simply places one of the figurines on its side. If the other partner agrees, sometime during the day or evening he or she lays the other figurine down. It's nonverbal, yet direct. It builds anticipation, playfulness and fun. Another man I know issues a written invitation to his wife for a "night of pleasure." Even if she is in a bad mood, she says it always softens her heart.

Put a little imagination into the way you approach your sexual relations, and your marriage will take on new interest. One caution though: If you don't feel open to a sexual

27

encounter, try meeting your spouse's request with a counteroffer rather than a plain "No!" Sensitivity and diplomacy at that juncture may go a long way toward keeping trust and romance alive and avoiding hurt feelings.

Finding intimate, meaningful ways to communicate your desire for intimacy with your mate can be fun, fulfilling and rewarding. In the next chapter I want to help you find ways to heal a lack of arousal and to restore the intimacy in your relationship.

CHAPTER 4

Healing Nonarousal

B
ut Doctor, I don't get aroused like I used to. What has happened?"

Before we move on to the subject of a variety of medical conditions that can lead to libido loss in husband or wife, let's list other reasons for a shutdown in sexual arousal and desire.

For example, many people express surprise that some of the most common culprits may be ordinary prescription and over-the-counter (OTC) medications—antihypertensives, major and minor tranquilizers, diuretics, antihistamines and birth control pills, among others.

We are blessed to have access to the world's finest medications. However, many drugs or combinations of drugs cause various side effects, including lessened or absent sexual responses. Usually it's possible to substitute another remedy for the one in question—if you realize that it's the medication that is causing the problem! Remember, every synthetic drug, whether prescription or nonprescription, provides not only benefits, but often some less-welcome side effects. Reading the literature that accompanies your prescription, or carefully reading the OTC drug information, can be an eyeopener.

If your spouse or you have medications you suspect may be contributing to libido loss, you should promptly inform your physician and request an alternate medication. This is one side effect I advise you not to ignore.

I'm also constantly surprised at how often my patients report the following:

1. Their previous physicians never inquired about any sexual changes or problems they might be experiencing.

2. If the patient ventured to ask questions about sexual functioning during a routine physical exam, the doctor would either chuckle or move to the next subject. I have even had some patients say that the doctor outright ignored the question.

Perhaps that's why I find most women get their gynecological information from other women, books or media reports on medical issues or current research. By the time individuals query me, they're often surprised to discover that their long-term nonarousal problems could have a very simple non-threatening answer: Get off the libido-suppressing drugs!

Let's review the things that can help you restore libido. Begin by seeking answers to your questions. Be prompt and proactive. Questions about sex should never embarrass either the patient or the medical professional.

Let your physician know that a lagging or absent sex drive is not an option for your marriage. If you do not ask your doctor specific questions, you cannot expect him or her to provide the information you need. When has your physician ever told you, "By the way, this medication may affect your sex drive"?

Lifestyle is often another contributing factor to nonarousal for some patients. So many lives today border on "out of control," with people often so exhausted from being on what I call "the hamster wheel" (going round and round), that loss of sexual desire ranks as a very low-priority issue. Get off that "hamster wheel!" When the sexual oil tank gets low, it should serve as a red-flag warning. By then you can predict some engine problems ahead.

In later chapters we will consider some common medical challenges that adversely affect male and female sexuality. We will consider the positive roles of nutrition, exercise and natural hormone replacement therapies. I will also describe food and vitamin supplements known to enhance libido and improve sexual function.

NONMEDICAL CONDITIONS THAT HINDER AROUSAL

But first, let's address some of the nonmedical conditions that so often hinder or prevent arousal. Some of these will require pastoral or psychological counseling for ultimate resolution. Others may respond to frank and respectful discussions between husband and wife. All deserve your most tender and caring attention, keeping in mind the fact that God intends only the best for you, your spouse and your marriage.

I want to encourage you to step out and claim what is yours. Whatever the sexual difficulty, answers usually are well within reach. You and your life partner can have better sex, and your mutual efforts will be rewarded.

EMOTIONAL DISTANCE

Your body has become relaxed, lubricated and engorged, but your emotions remain in total disconnect. You do not feel sexually aroused... in fact, that's the last thing you feel!

There's a wide range of emotions that can surface in any human being that can interfere with sexual desire and fulfillment. These include underlying feelings of fear, shame, guilt, resentment, hopelessness, sadness... you name it.

Emotions happen. In fact, they happen—and interfere—at some of the very worst times. But when you habitually become angry instead of aroused, weepy instead of intimate, fearful instead of welcoming, you are wrestling not with sexual problems, but emotional conflicts.

Women tell me that when there's a pattern of bickering and strife in the home, the husband's idea of how to resolve the tension may be through sexual intercourse, while the wife's solution may be that of withdrawal.

Unless there is mutual honesty and respect, this impasse will get worse, and the chance of sexual closeness will get

31

more and more remote. Thus the rift gets wider. Definitely, fulfilling sex will not happen.

Healthy people cannot help but feel the weight of lies, infidelity, dishonesty or anything else that precludes the openness and freedom needed for sexual or any other kind of joy. It is important to realize that the price of attaining ultimate marital pleasure is that of achieving a level of emotional transparency and openness with your mate.

Let me share another clinical case with you.

> Edwina told her husband, "We've never bothered to hide our naked bodies from one another, but it seems impossible for us to show one another our naked emotions." Her honest comment led the couple to make greater efforts to communicate their deep feelings, which in turn led them to new closeness and more expressive lovemaking.

When we can bring ourselves to the point where we can tell our spouse what we want—whether our desire is physical, emotional or spiritual—it usually breaks through barriers and leads to heightened awareness, intimacy and pleasure for both. Conversely, those holding "don't-go-there" areas of themselves invariably place distance between themselves and the very person they need and desire above all others.

Ladies, don't blame your husband for not being a mind reader. You must express your desires, needs and even the mechanical tempo of lovemaking that pleases you most. Maybe you need to tell him that you like a slow hand, as the song says.

The answer may be as simple (not easy!) as confessing how much you really charged on the credit card, or as complicated as dealing with overtones from past hurtful experiences having nothing to do with your spouse. However, the bottom line is this:

> FACT: Each partner must clear away as much emotional debris as possible if true openness and intimacy are to flourish.

Always respect your emotions and those of your spouse. Encourage each other to share your feelings, recognizing them as a real and vital part of your personality. I know this is very difficult for many people. Some people would rather attempt to climb Mount Everest than to truly open their hearts with all of their insecurities. If you have a spouse like that, assist him or her by asking gentle leading questions.

Although I am a medical doctor, my experience in dealing with my patients is that we simply cannot separate our emotions from our sex life. If you cannot reveal all your emotional issues at one time, if that would be too much, too soon because of the many emotional withholds in your life, begin by taking baby steps. Share one little revelation at a time. Decide to make it a positive experience. Try saying, "You know, honey, here's something I bet you never knew about me..." Or try the old "a penny for your thoughts" routine. Anything you can do to help open up is not too silly or too mundane. Be brave!

LOW SELF-ESTEEM

I dislike using the nineties' catchall phrase of "low self-esteem," but a positive self-worth is very important. It is actually our biblical birthright: We were "fearfully and wonderfully made" (Ps. 139:14, NKJV). Conversely, a negative self-worth is very destructive.

Let's open my clinical files and find Ginny.

> "No wonder I'm not easily aroused," forty-three-year-old Ginny told me. "Tom's at the peak of his handsome self, but my looks are slipping. He never says anything about my extra weight, but he always pinches my 'love handles.'"
>
> Ginny, former cheerleader and college beauty queen, now sees herself as fat and losing her fresh-faced prettiness. She describes her husband, who is two years older and beginning to see a few flattering strands of gray in his dark hair, as always looking impeccable.
>
> "It's not fair," Ginny said. "Women get older and less attractive, while men just look distinguished."

That may be true, but there's a fallacy in Ginny's thinking. Ginny's problem has nothing to do with love handles or the gray in her hair these days. Pretty Ginny, who should know she's still good-looking enough to turn a few heads, nevertheless suffers from strong feelings of low self-worth for which there is no rinse or cover-up available.

Her husband appears to have a great life—professional success, strong business friendships and interesting law cases with which to occupy and challenge his mind. Ginny's mind, however, is filling up fast with all the self-defeating ideas in the book—self-doubts, self-pity and destructive self-talk. How much can Tom help Ginny with her self-esteem problem? What can create in Ginny the will to find herself, value herself and begin to seek her highest life's purpose?

This handsome, talented and gifted couple seems headed for a proverbial marital collision course. Self-worth deficiencies can escalate into "personality suicide." At the very least, they create serious problems within the marriage, an institution designed to help both partners grow and prosper, individually and as a unit. When one partner encounters such pervasive problems with low self-esteem and dwindling self-confidence to the point that sexual desire becomes erased, certainly the sufferer should seek answers. The spouse should support him or her in that vital search. The spouse who is being supportive will sometimes need to take on the role of "parenting" the weaker partner. You may get mad about this, and steam and say, "I'm not your mother!" or "I'm not your father!" But sometimes in a marriage your "spouse" hat needs to come off and your "nurturer" hat be put on to help your loved one through a difficult time.

As with all challenges a couple may face, this too should result in a new threshold of closeness and cherishing for both. It is amazing how rapidly the love fires restart once you or I decide to seek solutions to our self-identity and self-worth issues.

In the Bible, Solomon said it well. "You are so beautiful, my beloved, so perfect in every part" (Song of Sol. 4:7). "He is lovely in every way" (5:16). You are all fair!

DEPRESSION

Sales of Prozac and other mood-altering drugs are booming these days as more and more Americans are being diagnosed as clinically depressed.

Such drugs can strongly inhibit sexual arousal and functioning—but then, so does depression itself. Depression is a serious libido suppressant. It has a strong negative effect on the ability of the body to become aroused.

Beyond its effects on one's sex life, however, even mild depression, with its accompanying inertia, anxiety and feelings of hopelessness, unshakeable fatigue and sadness, can induce a general malaise that seems to color the sufferer's entire life a dull gray.

We all have down times, of course. Accidents, disappointments and tragedies happen. Even the most optimistic and naturally resilient individual you know doubtless at some time will experience the "black night of the soul."

But when depressed feelings persist for a month or longer, I believe it is time to take the problem seriously. Hormonal imbalance and thyroid problems are among the most common medical conditions that can cause depression and a related loss of libido. A concerned physician who performs not only a thorough physical examination but also considers such factors as diet, sleep disturbances, medications and other related issues very often can pinpoint the cause and soon turn things around for the patient.

However, too many conventional medical doctors are prescribing Prozac, Xanax, Zoloft and other strong prescription medications. These medications can disrupt the serotonin levels in the brain, which contribute to a healthy libido.

Very often upgrading one's physical state, with particular attention to exercise and nutrition—including some outstanding supplements—can solve even apparently intractable depressions without the need of prescription drugs. (Remember, though, that clinical depression is not just a low mood, but a true medical problem that deserves prompt medical attention.)

SOME MAJOR SYMPTOMS OF DEPRESSION

- Loss of energy (Yes, this can mean you are depressed.)
- Feelings of worthlessness (one of the most common symptoms)
- Insomnia
- Loss of interest in life's pleasures
- Loss of libido

There are safe natural remedies (herbal treatments and supplements) that can be tried, often with excellent results. Remember, if you are already on a prescription medication for depression, you *must* wean off that medication slowly and this *must* be done under the advice of a treating physician.

Some of the natural remedies include the following:

- St. John's Wort—works to increase dopamine production in the brain. It is good for mild to moderate depression. Research has shown that St. John's Wort may be even more effective in relieving depression than some prescription drugs, without the undesirable side effects such as reduction in sex drive and drug "hangover." It is also purported to help control appetite, if that is a benefit you are interested in.

- 5-HTP—helps the body increase its natural serotonin levels. Low levels of serotonin can be the cause of depression. It has been used by many as an alternative to Prozac. It appears to work just as effectively without the unpleasant side effects of dry mouth, anxiety and decreased sex drive associated with Prozac. 5-HTP has also been used to treat insomnia because serotonin is the precursor to melatonin, the hormone that regulates our sleep/wake cycles. Like St. John's Wort, 5-HTP has also been shown to suppress appetite and contribute to a sense of fullness.

- L-tyrosine—increases the rate at which the brain produces dopamine and norepinephrine (natural antidepressants). Depressed people often are found to have low tyrosine levels. Some prescription medications for depression work by boosting tyrosine levels in the brain. L-tyrosine effectively treats depression without side effects. It also has been shown to improve mood and sex drive.

Important: If you have a deep clinical depression (feel completely debilitated and have suicidal thoughts), YOU MUST SEEK A PHYSICIAN'S CARE!

I also recommend confessing your sins to the Lord openly—aloud. Depression is usually always accompanied by frustration and hopelessness. Confessing your sins to the Lord can make you feel like a new person! God is faithful to forgive (1 John 1:9). God's Word assures us that "as far as the east is from the west, so far has He removed our transgressions from us" (Ps. 103:12, NKJV).

DRUGS THAT CAUSE LIBIDO LOSS

As we said earlier, drugs found in most bathroom medicine cabinets can sometimes cause libido loss or sexual dysfunction. Almost everyone has used antihistamines, for example, to treat allergies, colds or sinus troubles. The anticholinergic agent that dries up your nose (the reason you take it) may also dry up vaginal secretions or cause temporary impotence. These effects disappear once the medication is discontinued, but older men and women seem particularly vulnerable to such side effects.

Antidepressants can produce somewhat more complex side effects. Taken to offset depression, which itself often causes libido loss, the drugs sometimes create the same adverse effects on a person's ability to become aroused.

Such drugs as Elavil, Endep, Tofranil, Norpramin, Pamelor, Vivactil, Surmontil, Sinequan and Ludiomil can cause sedation and decreased desire in both men and women, as well as impotence and impaired ejaculation in men. If you suspect the antidepressant you take may be suppressing your sex drive, ask your physician's advice about substituting another medication.

The ulcer medication Tagamet, a commonly used treatment for ulcers, has some antihistamic properties and also

37

has antisexual effects on men, since it blocks the effects of androgens (male hormones).

Other drugs that may cause difficulties with arousal include major tranquilizers usually prescribed for serious psychiatric conditions, but also given occasionally in low doses for symptoms such as severe anxiety. These include Thorazine, Stelazine, Trilafon, Mellaril and Haldol. These drugs have sedating effects, which can inhibit sexual desire. They also contain anticholinergic effects, which can interfere with erections.

At times tranquilizers can cause loss of sexual desire, impotence and impaired ejaculation or orgasm. Again, older individuals can be more vulnerable to these unwanted side effects.

Antianxiety medications such as Valium, Librium and Xanax also may decrease sexual desire, especially when taken in high doses. Muscle relaxants such as Flexeril, Norflex, Norgesic and Disipal occasionally may cause sexual difficulties as well. Medications for Parkinson's disease such as Cogetin, Artane, Kemadrin and Akineton are others that can affect sexual performance. Other miscellaneous medications—Lanoxin, Dilantin, Reglan, Flagyl, Indocin and Atromid-S—also may affect sexual response for reasons not fully understood.

38

Remember, taking one of these medications does not mean you will experience sexual difficulties. But if sexual problems begin shortly after you start taking the drug, consider it suspect and notify your physician.

SEXUAL ABUSE

Childhood sexual molestation invariably leaves a scar on the adult's sexual wholeness. When an older person stimulates sexual feelings in a child or adolescent, the child is left confused, and the brain can be damaged. Behaviors meant to engender pleasure become associated with force, coercion, fear, pain and shame. Thoughts of *Why me? Why did God let this happen to me?* begin to surface.

Let's look in my clinical files again:

Julie, married for fourteen years, had been molested at

age four by a trusted adult. She vividly recalls her early marital sexual aversion and inability to become aroused and achieve orgasm. "I couldn't figure out what was wrong with me," she said. "At last, after eighteen months of frustration, I made an appointment with my doctor to find some answers."

With her doctor's help, Julie was able to deal with the issue of molestation, which she had blocked from her mind up until that time. The reason the mind often blocks traumatic negative experiences is because it waits until the person is able to cope with the issue without destroying the life of the individual.

Childhood sexual abuse and incest are not uncommon. They damage marriages because a spouse often doesn't have a clue about what his or her mate is thinking. A husband would never imagine that his wife might be treating him like a perpetrator! For others, the events of the negative sexual experience play over and over in the person's mind, causing great distress and avoidance of all sexual experiences—positive and negative.

I firmly advocate medical and psychological counseling for individuals who must deal with such issues. Why waste precious time as Julie did? I strongly believe in seeking the best possible medical advice when it is needed, but I believe even more wholeheartedly in seeking help from the Great Physician.

Julie underwent counseling, and she also reads Psalm 34 over and over. She reads that "God promises that His children's faces will never be covered with shame." Stories like Julie's reinforce my belief and my practical experience that medicine is an art and a science—but God is truth!

Tragically, Julie's story is hardly unique. Accepted statistics in America now indicate that one girl in three, and one boy in every seven, will experience childhood sexual abuse. The posttraumatic stress effects in these individuals should not be underestimated.

Scientific literature reveals much more about the aftereffects of childhood sexual abuse. The seriousness of the inevitable emotional residue—inability to trust, fear of intimacy, depression, suicidal ideation and other self-destructive behaviors, low

39

self-esteem, guilt, anger isolation and alienation—can be seen in many women. Many severely overweight women had a history of sexual abuse in childhood. Help is available, if wife and husband ask for it. With proper counseling and a patient husband, women like Julie can truly discover and testify that there is nothing wrong with them, sexually or otherwise.

Equally moving stories involving women who have experienced rape, battering, marital rape, psychological aftereffects of previous abortions or sexual promiscuity again reinforce one all-important fact: *God heals*. You can regain your physical, mental, spiritual and emotional health. I urge you to seek the help you need.

Never underestimate the power of the human spirit. As every medical practitioner has occasion to see, that spirit, which has been instilled in each of us by our Creator, can help us be overcomers as provided in His Word. His Spirit can burn fiercely as a "refiner's fire," consuming prior devastating life experiences and reducing them to harmless ashes. God can take the ashes of your life and turn them into a thing of beauty.

Then, healing comes. That wholeness, of course, will include the wholeness of full sexual health.

OTHER LIBIDO INHIBITORS

Bad breath or other body odors, as well as gross obesity, being severely underweight, strong perfumes, harsh lighting, strident voices and untidy surroundings, frequently add up to sexual turnoffs.

The most common turnoff of all, however, is that of simply getting out of the habit of wanting and initiating sex. It's as simple as this:

FACT: Less sex creates reduced desire.

Try not to say no too frequently, because even when sex seems inconvenient or otherwise less than perfect, the habit adds immeasurably to a couple's well-being. No other human stabilizer can compare. Resolve not to "get out of the habit" through neglect, indifference or carelessness. Sex is too important to your marriage!

THE ABILITY TO BECOME AROUSED

Obviously, treating the causes behind one's inability to experience sexual arousal should become a primary responsibility of the couple undergoing difficulties. Marital sex, after all, ranks as a basic need, not an add-on or accessory to marriage.

The inability to become sexually aroused can, as we have shown, stem from numerous simple-to-discover causes. If physical lovemaking at present seems impossible or even lost, you can and should determine why—now—and resume enjoying normal arousal and sexual intercourse. As the renowned novelist Thomas Hardy wrote:

> New love is the brightest,
> And long love is the greatest.
> But revived love is the tenderest
> Thing known on earth.

Never accept arousal difficulties as "the way things are." Initiate treatment, and enjoy the results. I've known women who have been in marriages where they stopped having sex so long ago it would seem impossible to start again because they and their spouses have become sexual strangers. Even they can be helped.

CHAPTER 5

Pleasure Areas:
Men and Women

Science is learning more all the time about the medical and psychological benefits that feelings of happiness, pleasure and joy bring to our lives. The brain-altering chemicals called endorphins, often released during exercise, sexual intercourse or even the hearing of wonderful news, have a definitive effect on one's body and brain waves.

Because of their dynamic power to dampen physical pain, banish depression, release new strength and energy and even heighten the brain's ability to think with exceptional clarity, endorphins and the pleasure they produce deserve our attention.

Just as we cannot separate our sexuality from the rest of our multifaceted lives, we cannot separate pleasure and its potential effects from the rest of our psychological makeup. Some therapists believe pleasure to be so important to our health that they urge us to intentionally structure opportunities for joy into each day or even each hour. Remember, God instructs us to "count it all joy"—even our various trials (James 1:2, NKJV). He knew how important joy is to our physical and mental health.

That's where sex enters the picture. What God has intended for our supreme pleasure often springs from our own personal joy. It's really a chicken-and-egg situation. Does happiness come first, creating a desire for sex, or is it the other way around?

Whichever it is, we literally need to *experience* pleasure—not just *analyze* it. Researchers have explored the profound effects of pleasure on our mind, body and within the hidden complexities of the brain. It is up to us to recognize and give due importance to the place of pleasure and happiness in our daily existence and within the totality of our lives.

The pleasure principles and practices in this chapter can enhance your well-being, sexual and otherwise. In the study of physiology in medical school, and in my more than twenty years of practicing medicine, I have learned much about what brings physical pleasure to both men and women.

WHAT MEN LIKE

What are some ways in which wives can bring pleasure to their husbands?

Men like stronger, deeper caresses, with pressure on the muscles of arms, shoulders and calves. (The hormone testosterone makes men's skin thicker than that of a woman's.) And is there a man on the planet who does not enjoy a back and shoulder rub? Use a nice scented oil or body lotion and long, firm strokes for this. Husbands become putty in their wives' hands when those hands learn how to make him relax-x-x.

43

Long, soft, unhurried kisses remind him of why he married you...and that it only gets better as time goes by. Keep him guessing, one male psychotherapist (and husband) advises. "My wife keeps me just a little off balance," he said. "I never quite know what to expect, and that charms me." My own suggestion is that you kiss him in some unexpected but sensitive place—the neck and throat, for example, where one kisses a baby, or the curve where the neck joins his shoulders. Men love such tenderness.

During sex, husbands become excited when their wives whisper, comment or say sweet things to them as intercourse progresses. The spontaneity, excitement and love messages linger on their minds. I know that this is hard to do for some women, but knowing that many men really like this and find it erotic may help you to want to try it.

Remind him in intimate moments of things you remember from earlier lovemaking experiences. He loves it that he pleases you and that your times with him are memorable.

Romance your man in any way you can imagine, from leaving tiny love notes for him to find in the bathroom the next morning, to reading him to sleep at night. One overly busy city official, tough as nails at the negotiating table, always fell asleep to the soothing sound of his wife's low, musical voice, "Good night, sweet prince..."

Romance him in your own special way. All men, I firmly believe, are potential Great Romantics. They appreciate and respond to a wife who actively woos them.

YOUR LOVE MESSAGE TO HIM

Your bedroom beckons, lovely, tranquil and inviting. Plump pillows, soft bed linens, flattering colors and lighting make this the most alluring room in your house. Now, do one extra thing. Spray the sheets lightly with your cologne, the same scent he senses whenever he hugs you.

He may not notice what you have done, but your scent will impart a subtle message. You are here in this room, and pleasure will follow. The olfactory senses, especially strong in the male, send powerful messages.

Use this as a special way to give him additional excitement, sentimental feelings or anticipated joy.

FOR HER—NONSEXUAL "FOREPLAY"

The more attentive to his wife a husband becomes, the more ready she becomes for sexual intercourse. Such everyday courtesies as opening her car door, standing when she enters or leaves a room or seating her at the dinner table rate high on a wife's response scale. One woman said, "For me, his taking the garbage can to the curb can be foreplay!"

But can it be this simple to romance such a complicated woman as your wife? Yes, for many women it can be. Sure, it may sound old-fashioned or unrealistic, but... You get her full attention. She knows, because you show her, that she is very special in your eyes. And once a woman becomes convinced she married her knight in shining armor, a gentleman beyond compare, you may be amazed at how generously she responds in kind.

SOME TIPS

- ∾ Perfect table manners not only honor her and the meal she has prepared, but also set a great example for your offspring.

- ∾ If you have children, tend to the kids without being asked, and allow her to prepare and serve dinner in a relaxed and happy mood. That sets the stage for later.

- ∾ Pay full attention to her when she wants to discuss something with you. It's a radical idea, but it might pay to turn off the TV and listen.

- ∾ Draw her a nice, warm bath and put on some music for her to enjoy while she bathes.

- ∾ In bed, offer a positive comment or two about her body. (Most women question their looks). "I love being married to a blonde (or brunette)" can lead to explaining why, and things could go on from there. Or ask her what she likes about her body. Her answer may surprise you. Then focus on that area more often as it is obviously a comfort zone for her.

45

Pleasure principle: True intimacy—mental, spiritual and sexual—may begin at a car door, a lively dinner table or even the garbage can. Both husband and wife will thrive on civility, honor and respect. Your sex life will reflect it, too!

FOR HER—GENTLE TOUCHES

Men, be smart enough to learn how to gently caress the woman you love into some weak-in-the-knees moments. Here are a few touches most women like:

- ∾ A light kiss on the side of her mouth
- ∾ Touching her face lightly (softly try not to smear any cosmetics she may be wearing)

- Little kisses on the nape of the neck or along her shoulders
- Your hands along the curve of her waist and hips
- A kiss on the hand (debonair and adoring) or kisses on her fingertips
- Gentle, nonerotic touches on her breasts
- Stroking her hair

Remember, relaxation is essential to a woman's ardor. Take time to offer her your gentle touches, strokes and nonsexual kisses, and she should respond to you in all the ways you love when the time for sexual intercourse arrives.

OBSTACLES TO PLEASURE

Decide with your partner that your mutual pleasure in one another will become a top priority for both of you. Guard that promised pleasure jealously, for the obstacles are many. Decide on ways to deal with:

TELEPHONE CALLS

Find ways to avert evening interruptions via answering services or machines, and stick to your policy. Reinforce the fact that he or she matters more to you than business, parents, telemarketers, the PTA or anyone else during those designated times. Establish an island of privacy and peace for the two of you, and let nothing else invade it.

WORRIES ABOUT APPEARANCE

Don't fret obsessively about your appearance at the wrong time. Simply present yourself as attractively as you can to the person you love. If he's in the mood, you are wise to just seize the moment and do the primping next time!

RESENTMENTS

Lovers don't carry grudges, pout or punish by the silent treatment, withdrawal or other means. Offer your wife or husband your best self. "Do not let the sun go down on your wrath" (Eph. 4:26, NKJV). *Resentment* (the word literally means "re-feeling") blocks new, pleasurable feelings from appearing.

FEAR AND WORRY

The Bible tells us that "perfect love expels all fear" (1 John 4:18). It seems equally true that perfect fear or worry casts out love. Give yourself times when both husband and wife agree to banish nagging worries from the present moment. The discipline of casting worry aside completely strengthens not only your marriage, but each of you individually.

At times like that, peace and pleasure can be restored to the marriage you cherish. And as a bonus, the release from tension often allows promising new solutions to current problems to spring to mind.

By now I hope you have reached this conclusion: Men and women alike need to set the stage for peace, relaxation and harmony in their home life. Decide how you can solve some of your worst obstacles to sexual and other pleasures. In other words, make space for your sex life to grow.

FREQUENCY OF INTERCOURSE

When spouses differ on the frequency of their desire for sexual intercourse, conflict may result—and eventually escalate. If the husband desires sex once a day, and she is quite happy with once a week, the difference usually becomes exaggerated. Over time he may end up complaining that she only wants to have sex once a month, while she is now convinced that he wants it three times a day!—a crisis in the making.

As the misunderstanding escalates, the wife begins to avoid her husband. He, meanwhile, increases his advances, thinking that if he approaches her once a day, she perhaps will acquiesce once a week. This, of course, only makes the entire situation worse.

Diplomacy, not avoidance, is the answer. Honesty, gentleness and love provide the ideal climate for de-stressing the differences and for helping husband and wife to appreciate them. This common conflict need not make either partner unhappy, if handled with love and understanding. Remember, sex by demand or duty sex never becomes great sex. Recall the man I know who issues his wife the written invitation—this scenario presents a wonderful opportunity to get creative with your spouse.

I know couples who actually schedule appointments for "nights of pleasure." It may seem too cut and dried to you, but it certainly works for them. Oftentimes the answer is to indulge your partner even when you are not "in the mood." Some husbands and wives have told me that those times have been some of their best times, emotionally and physically, once they got "into" it. It is surely a combination of the act of "giving" and those endorphins that are released during sex.

For some tips from other married couples, please see chapter fourteen. There may be something there that will be just your "cup of tea" in this regard.

UNEXPECTED PLEASURE

Here is a story from one of my patients that is very poignant and revealing about tenderness bringing about extremely fulfilling sex:

48

While she was walking ahead of her husband as he locked their car, Alice turned her ankle sharply and then fell on her hands and knees on a rocky walkway. The fall was ugly. As Norm helped Alice to her feet, he caught sight of her bleeding hands and knees.

Quickly Norm scooped her up, carried her to the car and drove home. Alice felt amazed at what happened next. Norm placed her on their bed, then fetched the first aid kit and began to doctor her, talking all the time. "Oh, honey, I saw you falling, and I couldn't get there in time. I know this stuff hurts. Baby, I wish it had happened to me. I'm so sorry..."

Norm went into the bathroom to draw a warm bath for Alice, still talking to her as he proceeded, "...so your whole body won't be sore tomorrow. You can keep your knees out of the water so the bandages won't get wet. Here, let me help you into the tub."

Those were defining moments in the life of a super-independent woman, one very unused to being physically cared for. Later, warm, clean, pain-free and snuggling in bed with her sweet husband, Alice thought about the side of Norm she never had seen before—especially his caring, empathetic feelings toward her, and his tenderness and protectiveness.

Mishaps, sadness and even tragedy offer husbands and wives singular opportunities to minister to one another and take pleasure in doing so. Fully accept the responsibility, as did Norm, and you may solidify your marriage as nothing else could do.

"But what does that have to do with sexuality or pleasure?" you may ask. Everything! As Norm and Alice know, tenderness and taking pleasure in nurturing one another are vital keys to experiencing exquisite lovemaking and sex.

P.S. Alice told me that after this episode she and Norm had one of the best sexual experiences of their ten-year marriage.

KISSES

Most women—and men—love to be kissed. Start out with tender kisses. Men, please remember to kiss her at times when lovemaking is not on the menu. Believe me, there's nothing more deadening than knowing a kiss really is a demand for sex.

One couple I know established the "seven-second kiss." When they kiss, they linger for seven seconds. Seven seconds, by the way, allows for a very nice, intimate kiss. A kiss like that in the morning, I am told, produces that warm feeling that can lead to a daylong anticipation of the evening's coming events. Try it!

When a man kisses his wife, he should not move immediately into a deep aggressive kiss. He should explore her mouth. Be tender. Hold back just a little and allow her to become the aggressor. This feels good to a woman, since her husband usually controls the kissing and instigates the foreplay.

But when he surrenders a little of his sexual power, he may be interested to see where it leads. Many women tell me that their husbands become too aggressive too fast, or want to move events along far too rapidly. When a man learns the

49

many nuances of a really intimate, wonderful kiss, his wife will rarely complain that he is "rushing things" along.

TIP: Soft lips. Soft lips are very sensual to a woman—and to her man. Remember, the man provides the spark that lights a woman's fire. Kissing often becomes that spark.

OPPOSITES ATTRACT

One potent and continuous pleasure source in marriage is that of enjoying the ways he differs from her—and vice versa. Back to my files:

> Malcolm, married to Beth, hated her habit of using their bed as an ironing board. She had a habit of hurriedly pressing a few wrinkles from her outfit each morning. An odd habit? An overblown reaction? No, Beth was really beginning to irritate him.
>
> One morning, instead of a disapproving glare at his wife, Malcolm simply asked Beth why she allowed her ironing chores to delay their ride to work each day. Beth, a banker, offered Malcolm several reasons for what he considered her "really weird" habit. Beth valued her professional appearance. Their crowded wardrobe closets crushed her clothing. And finally, she said, "I don't want to waste our precious evenings together on such mundane pursuits."
>
> Malcolm reflected on how he'd nearly made another snappy, disparaging remark to Beth about her ironing habit. He was glad he had asked and was touched by her answer.

50

Women do some rather strange things at times. So do men. About some things, the two will never agree in a million years. And why should it matter? Learning when to speak, when to remain silent, when to tolerate, when to change whatever needs changing (the crowded closet for one thing!) and in general acquiring the wisdom to accept that she (or he) seldom thinks about these things in the same way you do can add enormously to a couple's pleasure in each other.

A dentist told me, "I used Rosemary's (his wife's) car while she was out of town, and noticed her speedometer was broken. I mentioned this to her when she returned home and asked why she had not taken it for repair. She said, 'You broke it!' I asked her, 'How in the world could I have broken your speedometer?' She said (and by now the dentist was laughing), 'I know you drove my car too slowly.'"

(Have you ever noticed how much men seem to love "ditzy-wife" stories?)

The point is that Rosemary, who is brilliant and illogical, knows how to keep her husband laughing. Another man might have become irate, even abusive about such a "stupid" reply, but Rosemary pretty much knows what she's doing. She charms her spouse. Their personality differences seldom seem to matter.

Laughing off the small differences that really don't matter, discussing different viewpoints or teasing about your spouse's endearing habits (his left foot always hangs off the side of the bed while he sleeps) add spice to a marriage. A critical spirit and disapproving attitude only serve to distance two people.

Learn to enjoy your differences in temperament, outlook and habits. After all, they intrigued you initially and were part of the "chemistry" that brought you together. Allowing small, individualistic traits to *please* rather than *annoy* you help boost your love quotient considerably, and hence, your sex drive.

51

> TIP: Try to overlook at least one personal annoyance by your better half each day. Laugh it off whenever possible.

FOOT MASSAGE

Rubbing or massaging the feet can reduce neck pressure, stress, eyestrain, tension, nervousness and anxiety. This is a therapy practiced for thousands of years in China. It also can improve your spouse's (or your) mood, regulate breathing, relax muscles and increase circulation.

Whether or not these medical claims prove true, there's no doubt whatsoever that a foot rub or massage can soothe and relax like almost nothing else (with the possible exception of a Caribbean cruise). Do this for your wife (or husband) and watch her or him melt into perfect bliss.

Here's the way to massage your loved one's feet:

1. Both of you should find a comfortable position so you can easily access both feet.

2. Use a body lotion to give greater ease to your stroking motion. Drape a towel over your knees so lotion doesn't land where it shouldn't.

3. Your goal is to release the tension on tiny muscles and ligaments, which hold the small foot bones in place. Your thumbs are perfect tools for the job. It is best to use small, circular strokes from heel to toe, using your thumbs the way a masseur would move up your spine. Caution: Do not use a two-handed squeeze from instep to toes, since any compacting, crushing motion pushes tiny foot bones together, and that hurts.

4. Follow these pathways to ultimate foot joy:

- Be gentle. (If a woman is about to begin her menstrual cycle, the outer side of her feet below the ankle may be quite tender.)

- Release toe pressure by gently pulling each toe in an upward motion.

- With thumbs together at the center of the bottom of the foot, using an outward stroking motion with both thumbs, firmly stroke across the ball of the foot. Use that same stroke down the entire foot, top and bottom.

- Use the heel of your hand on the heel in a circular motion. Then switch to thumb or index finger, bent like little knees, for more pressure. According to some, the foot holds a number of erotic trigger points, which, when pressed, create sensations in a woman's genitals.

FOOT PRESSURE POINTS

- Massage the big toes with thumb and fingers.

- Massage three inches alongside the bone running from the back of the heel toward the calf of the leg.

༄ Use a circular massage to connect the three points that run in a line from the end of the heel to the sole of the foot to the middle toe.

Massaging these points, based on reflexology, will reduce anxiety. Both men and women say a foot massage relaxes their entire bodies, gives them tremendous pleasure and makes them feel loved. Try it and see!

USING YOUR SENSES

Pleasure lifts our senses to wonderful new heights. In our hurry, we too often forget to pay attention to these five important messengers: sight, smell, taste, hearing and feeling. Sensory messages can alert and arouse sexual desire. Perhaps that's a primary reason these keen and exquisite senses have been created in us in the first place. It seems amazing that a woman can detect the scent of her husband—an amalgam of after shave lotion, his favorite wool jacket, bath soap, well-worn denims, paint from his boat-painting project and much more—even if she were blindfolded. In the darkest cave, she could recognize his hands among dozens of other hands, because she has memorized their size, texture and their imprint on her body.

Our senses identify many things—the particular color of her hair when she stands in full sunlight, the timbre of his booming laugh, the texture of our spouse's skin, the taste of a kiss, the sound of his footstep or her lilting laugh. Our sensory perceptions, sharp, clear and incredibly reminiscent, powerfully recall to our minds so many earlier passions and familiar comforts.

But we tend to dampen down those signals as years pass and our lives speed up. Of course, we can't always live at the height of alertness and stimulation, but neither should we drift into complacent unawareness of the complex and beautiful life around us. It is a fine balance that is often disturbed by the negative effects of our pressured lifestyles. The benefits of massage, the soothing effects of candlelight and music and the use of essential oils are attracting more and more

53

attention and acceptance even from those in the medical community. Taking time for some sensory pleasure enables us to stop and reflect on the wonders of our lives, our mates and our marriages.

There is nothing new about the place of intense pleasure and physical relaxation in mankind's search for healing and optimum well-being. In fact, the inability to experience pleasure often precedes the opposite of well-being—an imbalance, anxiety or dis-ease. Give yourself more pleasure.

Have a conscious goal of enjoying some sensual delight each day of your life. It may be as simple as an attitude "overhaul." It's the difference between cursing the rush hour traffic or sitting quietly and enjoying some "enforced down time," time to think or pray or listen to a tape. It's the difference between grumpily spending a weekend on heavy housecleaning or reflecting that you are making every room in your home beautiful for your family. We need to consciously enjoy, even if the circumstances are less than perfect.

A man told me, "All any husband wants is for his wife to be happy." Just as everyone's definition of happiness may differ, the conditions we place on happiness also are our own. "When he stops dropping his clothes on the bedroom floor..." "When she loses fifteen pounds..." "When we find some way to earn more money..." Such thoughts are big pleasure quenchers. And loss of the pleasure quotient in life robs an individual of sex drive and sex appeal.

Those simple truths too often escape us. As any physician knows, the woman who "can't stand her in-laws" or the man who blames his wife for "never making him happy" eventually is likely to report in with medical symptoms. And the doctor probably will discover, if he or she bothers to ask, that the disgruntled, dispirited and sick individual being treated also has some degree of sexual dysfunction.

The role of pleasure in your life is a vitally important one. A shift in attitude can almost totally correct your lack of pleasurable moments. The world around us will not always be filled with sweetness and light. Daily pleasures help us accept others (and ourselves) as we are. The long soothing bath or the good workout at the gym provides buffer zones, support and stabilization for our emotions.

Pleasure, in essence, is a booster shot, a vitamin supplement and a vaccination against the effects of a lifetime of personal and professional body slams. It also helps you to participate in the goodness of life in its entirety—and in your own life in particular. Pleasure also increases your appreciation for your spouse and your marriage.

The result of the presence of pleasure in your life is a well-balanced, usually happy, highly appreciative lifestyle, providing the basis for a lifetime of mutually satisfying sex and a cherished, nourishing marriage.

Note to men: These techniques may seem more centered on the husband's giving pleasure to the wife. This is because if you bring her pleasure, she will be a "tiger in your tank." The Bible tells us that what we make happen for others, God will make happen for us. (See Ephesians 6:8.) As the husband becomes the head of the relationship, he loves his wife as Christ loves the church. The husband, like Christ, should be the first to lay down his rights for the health of the relationship. As you take the time to communicate and bring pleasure to your wife, your own sexual fulfillment will increase. I know this from the satisfied women I counsel. They often cannot do enough for their loving men.

55

CHAPTER 6

From Sexual Arousal to Orgasm

Many women—and men—lose interest in sex because they begin to have feelings of "it's not worth it" or "I never really get anything out of it." If this is a problem in your marriage, this section is for you. However, if you find the somewhat explicit material regarding the functions of the body during intercourse contained in this chapter offensive to you, feel free to skip this chapter. I would be very grieved if I offended you. For others, the information and materials may be steps to restoring a fulfilling, intimate sexual relationship with their spouse.

Let's pull another case history from my files:

> Slender, brunette Liza, married for twenty-plus years, told me she had never experienced sexual orgasm. In fact, she wondered if she ever would. Though she loves her husband, Hal, and described him as "considerate," their infrequent lovemaking for years had obviously missed the mark—big time!

You probably know at least one woman like Liza. I have spoken with thousands—intelligent, attractive, healthy and feminine—and most seemed bothered, even bewildered, with being a partner in a marriage where orgasms somehow just weren't happening. "What's wrong with me?" was the great, unspoken question.

Liza, at last, had plucked up her courage and contacted me. She wondered if there was something more she could or should be doing. And did this something really matter? She explained that she never felt the supreme sensations she read about in women's magazines or sometimes heard her sister and friends allude to.

"I feel kind of stupid even asking," she told me. "I don't know if it's possible for you to help me, or if it would be wise for me to rock the boat. Hal and I have always been satisfied with things the way they are."

Liza had a lot to learn about herself. First of all, we discovered that Liza, like so many other women, had little idea of how the female body moves toward orgasm. She simply did not understand how she was meant to achieve sexual pleasure—much less how Hal's body had been designed to interact with hers for their mutual joy.

To complicate things further, Liza also learned that she was actually blocking herself from ultimate pleasure sensations—and that her inability had nothing to do with her husband's performance.

WHAT MEN AND WOMEN NEED TO KNOW ABOUT THE FEMALE ORGASM

All women's bodies are designed by God with the ability to achieve orgasm. In fact, a landmark sex study published in 1981, the Starr-Weiner Report, found that a healthy woman's frequency of orgasm increases each decade up through her eighties![1] I am sure this is a surprising finding for many—perhaps for you—who think a woman's sex life only diminishes with age.

After many years of practicing medicine and counseling female patients, as well as my years of hosting *Doctor to Doctor*, I have compiled a great deal of data on female sexuality. This information can help men to be aware of the very specific ways they can give their wives a delightful sexual experience. Many women have expressed to me the fact that their husbands don't know how to focus on these specific areas of pleasure.

So, here is a lesson in Female Pleasure 101. Women actually can reach orgasm from two sources—the clitoris and the vagina. The greatest single source of sexual pleasure for a woman, which contributes to orgasm, is derived from pressure or touch on the clitoris. It is very interesting to note that, unlike the penis, which is used for urination, the clitoris has no other known purpose than to provide sexual pleasure for a woman.

Similar to the physiology of an erection, when a woman becomes aroused, the venous spaces around the clitoris fill with blood, and the clitoris increases in size. Most women do not enjoy immediate direct stimulation to the clitoris. Direct stimulation on the head of the clitoris can be too intense and therefore quite painful. Women prefer to be stimulated or touched around the clitoral area at first. A light, "feathery" touch is best.

It is best to wait until your wife is lubricated before applying too much touch to this area. Start by applying a rhythmic, bouncing pressure on the vaginal lips. Then apply gentle pressure to the outer vaginal lips. When her vagina begins to lubricate, you can apply some of this lubricant to her clitoris with your fingers.

Hormonal changes can influence the way a woman likes to be touched at different times of lovemaking. The optimum solution is to ask your wife how she likes to be touched. For some women, this is a difficult subject to discuss. You may have to simply try some different techniques and observe how she responds. There is a technique that will bring your wife a great deal of sexual pleasure. Your assignment is to find it.

More than half the women I have examined or talked to have told me that they are unable to reach an orgasm without some direct clitoral stimulation in addition to intercourse.

As a woman becomes fully aroused and ready for intercourse, vaginal lubrication begins and the inner two-thirds of the vagina expand, lifting the uterus and cervix up and away from the end of the vagina. The outer inch and one-half of the vagina becomes engorged, which narrows the opening.

That is why, in a fully aroused woman, penis size is unimportant—her vagina will grip the penile shaft even if her husband's penis is very short or thin.

At this point she may feel added pleasure in the vaginal area, a grasping feeling, accompanied by a desire to be penetrated. Her heart rate increases, her blood pressure may elevate and her skin may flush over the neck and chest area. The clitoral glans pulls itself under the little hood that protects it from too much stimulation. Her body has become ready to experience orgasm.

SELF-SABOTAGE

Here is where orgasms go wrong and where women sabotage themselves. The arousal process I just described is controlled by the *passive (parasympathetic)* branch of the nervous system. However, just before orgasm occurs, the body switches its control to the *active (sympathetic)* nervous system.

Active responses to heightened sexual sensitivity can include:

- Increased breathing
- Involuntary thrusting
- Contraction of the facial muscles, causing facial contortions
- Involuntary vocal sounds such as gasping and moaning
- Rigidity of the entire body

59

If you fear or feel averse to these reactions, it is likely that you will decide, consciously or subconsciously, to remain passive and close down. If so, as I explained to Liza, you will not experience the active responses, thus placing a solid roadblock before any real possibility of orgasm.

Facial grimaces, gasping, moaning and heavy breathing are involuntary sexual responses programmed into your body by your Creator. Brain wave patterns actually change during orgasm. In both men and women, heavy breathing has been shown to be necessary in order to reach orgasm.

Let yourself go! When you inhibit these responses, you inhibit your ability to achieve the fullness and completion of orgasm. In other words, participate in your climax. Trying to be quiet, passive or "ladylike" will diminish the orgasm or, worse still, block it entirely. So be brave—let yourself go.

If this "just isn't you," I suggest you start small. Allow your facial muscles to relax or allow yourself to moan softly. Try this just once, and you'll see how it works. Bring your hips to meet your husband's strokes. This movement is vital, since it allows maximum genital stimulation—so different from simply lying in an accepting position. I suggest you experiment just once with "letting yourself go," knowing that if you don't like it, you always can revert to your passive ways.

I believe that when a woman is adequately stimulated, opens herself to her husband and allows herself to feel "out of control," sexual experiences become much more intense and orgasms almost invariably occur. This may not work for all women, but I stress that the more active you become during intercourse, the more likely it is that your body will respond with an orgasm.

A woman may experience orgasm from stimulation inside the vagina by the penis or from stimulation applied directly to the clitoris. Most women say there is a difference in these two types of climax. With the penis in the vagina, orgasms are described as very deep, more diffuse and more whole-body involving. Many women find them more satisfying because of the intimacy of the penis within the vagina. Orgasms that occur when the clitoris is being stimulated without the man's penis inside the vagina are often described as much more intense in physical nature because during these climaxes, the PC muscle contracts rhythmically with nothing to block its movement. Some women report that these contractions last longer, although this is not true in all cases. Both types of orgasms are nearly always described as totally satisfying.

Most women have told me that they needed some outward clitoral stimulation in order to achieve orgasm. I believe this is because many women have never learned to thrust up to meet their husband's strokes, which brings the clitoris into contact with the male pubis. This movement is vital because it lifts the woman's body up for maximum genital stimulation.

Following orgasmic release, a woman usually feels a great sense of fulfillment and tenderness toward her husband. The husband's emotions correspond to hers, because the wife he loves has entrusted herself to him without fear or reservation. Only God could have devised such demonstrative, spontaneous, giving and wholehearted love.

Why participation matters

Openness to active participation in sexual intercourse makes most women discover that their sex drive increases. God made women capable of experiencing great sexual pleasure, not only to encourage us to procreate, but also for our enjoyment. Once having experienced this sort of sexual intensity, most women desire more. After all, God is no respecter of persons. He did not create such glorious sexual pleasures for other women and not for you. My experience has shown that women patients who have sexual intercourse regularly are more likely to have a higher sex drive than those who have sex infrequently. They also are more likely to be orgasmic due, I believe, to several factors.

The woman who enjoys sex more frequently becomes more in tune with the rhythms of her body and how she likes to be touched and stimulated. She then knows how to move her body accordingly. She lubricates more readily. She also is much less likely to be shy or embarrassed with her husband, and will freely give herself over to allowing her nervous system to switch from the passive to the active stage without holding back.

Like Liza, other women who learn how their own body and that of their husbands are meant to "work" soon discover that the amazingly orchestrated stages of mutual stimulation, arousal and full orgasm become natural, joyous, fully experienced events.

Question: "Dr. Pensanti, I don't know if I have ever had a real orgasm."

Orgasm comes from the Greek word *orge,* meaning "excitement." It has been described as a temporary feeling of suspension and warmth. Contractions of the vagina follow this feeling for a few seconds. Sometimes a woman may not know if she has experienced an orgasm. If your vagina contracts involuntarily, if you feel excited and then feel calm and satisfied, you can take that as evidence that you have had an orgasm, even though it may have been a weak one. A mild orgasm may consist of about five contractions, and an intense one will have about twelve to fifteen contractions. You can fall anywhere in between.

Question: "Dr. Pensanti, what about the multiple orgasms I've heard about? It has never happened to me."

Some women have found that they are capable of more than one orgasm during a session of intercourse. At times these women do not move from orgasm to the resolution state. Instead they return to the plateau phase where they remain in a state of arousal and can be almost immediately stimulated to orgasm again. Despite the plethora of magazine articles on this topic, most women achieve one orgasm during lovemaking. Many say that their clitoris is too sensitive right after a climax to go immediately to another. Sometimes a woman will have a vaginal orgasm and then have her husband stimulate her clitoris for one or more subsequent orgasms.

Some might say trying for multiple orgasms is putting too much emphasis on the "functionality" of intercourse rather than the psychologically fulfilling aspects. You must be the judge of whether this is a sexual goal for you.

Question: "How important is it to a man that his wife's orgasm coincides with his?"

My advice is that you do not waste time or energy striving for simultaneous orgasms. It is not common that this happens by chance, and it is something that you will have to work to orchestrate. This, of course, takes some of the recreation out of sex and can place pressure on either spouse, which is not desirable in my opinion.

For many couples, an important part of sexual pleasure is watching and experiencing their partner's orgasm. This particular pleasure is diminished if a person is having his own climax at the same time.

Question: "Dr. Pensanti, what is the 'G-spot,' and what is it for?"

A German doctor, Dr. Grafenberg, first suggested the presence of the "G-spot" in 1950, hence its name. Since that time and to date, there is ongoing debate as to whether there really is such an area as the "G-spot" in women. I definitely agree that the G-spot exists, and furthermore that its stimulation can result in a new kind of climax for many women.

If you would like to locate your G-spot, use your finger to massage or explore the upper front wall of your vagina (the side that is toward your belly button). The G-spot is a small mass of tissue about two inches inside the vaginal opening. With your finger you will feel that there is an area that is rippled and non-smooth. This is *not* the G-spot. The G-spot is hidden inside the wall between the non-smooth surface and your urethra. It feels smooth in contrast to the rough feel of the tissue around it. It is the size and shape of a small bean.

The G-spot is highly sensitive to stimulation, and when it is stimulated it becomes larger and swells to a small lump about the size of a dime. The best way to stimulate it is with a back to front motion with rather firm pressure. It will begin to swell and firm, much like the erectile tissue of the man's penis. Firm pressure and a lot of friction can lead to a G-spot orgasm, which has been described as incredibly intense.

Some women get a feeling of the need to urinate when the G-spot is stimulated, so it is best to empty your bladder before you begin lovemaking.

Many women experience an ejaculation when the G-spot is stimulated. The areas swells with fluid, and you may experience anything from a few drops of liquid to a large "gush." This ejaculate actually comes from the urethra, but it is not the same makeup as urine, even though it may feel as if you are urinating. The fluid is usually clear and odorless. This ejaculate is perfectly normal and should not be a source of shame or embarrassment.

Many women have told me that they have found it easier to have multiple G-spot orgasms than to have multiple clitoral orgasms. For some women, the G-spot does not become an active area of orgasm until some weeks after they first start to experiment with it.

The best position for achieving a G-spot orgasm is the missionary position with the wife beneath the husband and her pelvis tilted upward. This assists the penis with coming into contact with the G-spot. You can facilitate this by placing a pillow beneath the wife's buttocks.

Again, this may not be a "goal" for every couple, and I include this information only to provide a comprehensive look at all aspects of sexuality within the marriage bed.

WHAT MEN AND WOMEN NEED TO KNOW ABOUT THE MALE ORGASM

Question: "Dr. Pensanti, I read that a man's orgasm is different from his ejaculation. I never knew that. Am I doing something wrong? It all feels the same to me."

Many wives are surprised to learn that in men, ejaculation and orgasm are two separate processes. Interestingly, the male is like the female in that as he approaches sexual climax, his adjoining organs lift away from the penile shaft. His testicles lift high into the scrotum, which is pulled up and presses close to his body.

Meanwhile, prior to ejaculation, the prostate gland and seminal vesicles contract and force seminal fluid into the vas of the urethra (the tube that leads to the end of the penis). Fluid containing sperm may leak from the penis at this time. The sphincter from the bladder closes down so no urine can be expelled during orgasm. Ejaculation now becomes inevitable, and the man feels virtually helpless to stop it. This dramatic two- or three-second interlude, often termed "coming," describes his sensations of inevitability, the feeling and knowledge that his semen and sperm are about to be delivered to his wife's vagina and uterus.

Immediately afterward the man enters his next stage—orgasm. His penis and urethra contract rhythmically, forcing semen out of his penis. The sphincter muscle in the anal area also contracts rhythmically as he ejaculates, with these contractions occurring in exactly the same rhythm as a woman's. As with a woman, intensity of orgasm differs from man to man, and often from one time to the next. At times his orgasm may feel "low-key," only a slight throb in his genitals; at other times, his entire body may stiffen and thrash in near seizure-like responses.

64

The man's bodily responses during orgasm also are remarkably similar to his wife's. His nipples harden, his heart rate increases, his blood pressure elevates and a flush may spread over his chest and neck. His breathing becomes heavy and gasping, his feet may spasm, and he generally will exhibit facial contractions.

WHAT HAS HAPPENED

Can a wife feel her husband's ejaculation within her body? The penis will pulse as semen is expelled, and you may be able to feel this in the outer one-third of the vagina. The inner two-thirds has few nerve endings, so it is unlikely the sensation could be felt there. Many women like to place their hand near the base of their husband's penis, to caress him and feel the contractions of his orgasm during this most intimate moment.

Men's orgasms, like women's, range in intensity. For husband or wife, orgasms generally become more intense when the arousal stage preceding it was more intense.

Many women ask me what semen consists of. Semen is composed of protein, fructose, citric acid, sodium and chloride. It also contains trace amounts of ammonia, calcium, ascorbic acid and phosphates. Needless to say, it is a completely natural and safe substance.

65

THE POSTCOITAL PHASE: DIFFERENT FOR EACH GENDER

Following orgasm, as the body returns to its normal pre-arousal state, men and women differ greatly. A man returns to his precoital state in only one or two minutes, whereas a woman may require up to thirty minutes.

If she had an orgasm, this phase is much shorter. If she has been aroused but has not experienced sexual release, it can take much longer, and she may experience some back pain.

Whether or not she has climaxed, however, these moments can be a very intimate time for husband and wife. It is very helpful for a man to understand the physiology involved with his wife's response. It takes up to thirty minutes for the clitoris, labia minora and labia majora to return to their normal size and position. Her uterus returns to its precoital position quite quickly.

Some women cry during the resolution or postcoital phase, probably because crying is the body's mechanism to release unresolved sexual tension or to help her relax. Men should not interpret this as disappointment or frustration, but should realize that her body uses tears as a natural tension-release mechanism.

This postcoital phase is a time for affection and intimacy. For the husband, the period following orgasm is known as the "refractory" period—the space of time necessary before he can once again ejaculate. The refractory period usually lengthens in time as a man ages, and can range from minutes to hours to days. A man in his twenties may be able to attain a second erection within minutes. In his thirties, the average time is twenty minutes, and in his forties, one to two hours. When a man reaches his sixties, the refractory period may be as long as a day or more.

66

Wives should understand that male physiology, not his feelings for you, determines the length of his refractory period. Following orgasm, during the resolution phase men lose penis rigidity almost immediately, though it may take some time to return to its completely flaccid state. His genitals may become extremely sensitive, especially the glans of his penis. His muscles relax, and he may become extremely sleepy. This rapid resolution response, so much faster than that of his wife, can lead to feelings of rejection if she does not understand the biological difference between them.

I recommend that the husband try not to withdraw from his wife's physical presence immediately following orgasm. Try lying next to her with your penis inside her for a few minutes. Remember to touch and caress her to help her relax. These moments are a very important time for intimacy for your wife, though it means denying your own desire for sleep for a few minutes.

Undeniably, her postcoital or resolution phase will take much longer than your own. If you simply cannot stay awake, try lying in the "spoon" position with your arms around her.

Remember to whisper some little endearment before you doze off. It is up to the two of you to find some common ground that brings mutual satisfaction. The proper handling of your postcoital phase of lovemaking goes a long way toward enhancing the intimacy of your marriage bed.

Many Christians ask about oral sex or the use of the mouth and tongue in lovemaking. Consider this thought in your choices for enjoying your spouse. If it is wrong to use the tongue or mouth to bring pleasure to your spouse, then it might follow that kissing is also wrong. I personally do not feel that using what God has blessed us with to bring pleasure to our spouse is to be considered taboo. You and your spouse must make this decision. Never force your spouse into something. That would not be love, but lust.

SUGGESTION: Thank God for your sexual feelings. Ask Him to bless your sexual times together.

67

CHAPTER 7

Women at Midlife

Menopause, hormones and hysterectomy are the Big Three medical midlife issues most likely to confront women from their midforties and throughout their fifties. But these issues should no longer stop a woman in her tracks. You are not your mother's menopausal persona. Generally more knowledgeable, more proactive and more physically fit than women in previous generations, today's woman has learned to expect far more from her physician and herself than her forebears did. And that is healthy!

These days, as researchers learn more and more about the mysteries of male and female hormones, their findings should encourage and delight us. Women at this stage can take on a new lease on life. They can become more assertive, more comfortable with themselves and generally enjoy sex and marriage with newfound zest. You've probably read this declaration before—it has become a popular topic in women's magazines, but perhaps you are still thinking, *Fine, but what happened to ME?*

A woman's physical experiences into her forties and fifties can be fascinating as well as sometimes challenging. And as we shall see, they also can be wonderfully rewarding. For many of us, the forties, fifties and sixties and beyond can offer the steady comfort of especially satisfying sex as we enjoy well-established marriages, successful career and community status, children reared and on their own, time for such personal rewards as travel and the joy of grandchildren. By this time we have also come to full acceptance of our bodies—the fight is over. Sex lives should be able to flourish at this time of life!

At this point in life many women have quite a lot going for them. But physical and emotional disruptions do happen, and we will consider some of them in this chapter. We will take a look at Premenstrual Syndrome (PMS), the aftereffects of hysterectomy and controversies surrounding Hormone Replacement Therapy (HRT). No doubt you have encountered some of this information before, but if you have passed your fortieth birthday, it won't hurt to have another overview. With all the new breakthrough studies I have at my disposal, there is much that is new for you to learn.

HORMONE POWER

Throughout our lives, hormones exert powerful effects over our physical and mental development and have a dramatic influence on the workings of our brain. In light of that, when we speak of our teenager's "raging hormones" or describe our boss as "hormonal," we may be right on target.

But we should not be careless when addressing the importance and distinctives of the hormonal functions of our bodies.

I have noticed that more and more people are becoming very frustrated with the "vitamin revolution." Patients say to me, "Doctor, I have been taking handfuls of vitamins every day. I exercise, eat right, don't smoke and only drink in moderation. Why do I still feel like I'm starting to fall apart?"

Yes, you have been doing the right things. However, for many individuals, there is a serious flaw in their health routines. In my opinion, many women have not been giving their bodies' hormonal panels their due respect! Nothing will really work well if your hormones are out of balance or deficient and sending signals to your brain that your body is no longer vibrant and strong.

A woman dealing with lost libido, PMS or hot flashes may hate the way her hormones are behaving, but she needs to become proactive. She needs to learn as much as possible about why her temporary or chronic hormonal imbalance exists, and how she can help regulate it. Let's face it: Women are incredibly complicated creations. The wonder is not that our hormones may get out of whack at certain times, but that over the long haul, most of the time they serve us marvelously well.

Physicians who specialize in endocrinology help us to fully appreciate just how much these built-in chemicals design our lives. As mental and physical beings, we utilize our hormones as chemical neurotransmitters, which create our emotions and guide our thought processes and physical responses. Their delicate balance affects the health of every system in the body, but most especially of the reproductive (sexual) organs.

HORMONAL MAKEUP

70

The introduction of *testosterone (male hormone)* into early-stage fetal development forms the fetus into a male. Like his estrogen-endowed fetal sister, his body chemistry also includes some *estrogen (female hormone)* and always will. She, in turn, will have a weak level of testosterone in her body.

At puberty, sex differentiation dramatically increases. Boys' testosterone levels become ten times stronger, resulting in physical changes (body and facial hair, deepening voices, broadening shoulders, longer bones and developing musculature, genital and other changes).

Girls develop budding breasts, pubic and other body hair, the onset of menstrual periods and other more subtle changes. Hormones create the bridge between childhood and our eventual maturity into the full physical, mental and emotional attributes of adulthood. Both the female and the male body contain the hormones estrogen, testosterone and progesterone, but in different proportions.

HORMONES AND SEX DRIVE

Estrogen loss alone is not responsible for diminished sex drive.

Physicians now know that it is a combination of lowered or unbalanced progesterone, estrogen and testosterone that can wipe out a woman's libido at menopause. Some women do not know that testosterone, the hormone largely known for its role in male muscle development and aggression, normally exists in a small but important proportion to the estrogen in a woman's body.

Testosterone is one of the hormones known as an *andro-gen*. Androgens are hormones that have a masculinizing effect on the body. In women they are made primarily in the adrenal glands and ovaries; in men they are made in the adrenal glands and testes. The two most commonly known androgens are testosterone and DHEA. In the ovaries, androgens are converted into estrogen, which is why we look feminine instead of masculine despite the presence of testosterone.

All of the hormones in the body exist in a very intricate balance. At menopause, ovarian function decreases and hormonal balances change. If hormones shift so that estrogen dominates, there are many subsequent changes that occur. The testosterone balance in a woman's body is very delicate. When it is disrupted, it is very evident from side effects that occur. The side effect of importance in our discussion here is the dramatic loss of libido that occurs in some women as they get older.

It seems reasonable to assume that because libido has dropped, the woman is suffering from a lack of or imbalance of testosterone. But according to my many conversations with John R. Lee, M.D, whom I like to call the "Father of Natural Hormones," most of the women he treated for libido loss actually were not deficient in testosterone, but rather they lacked progesterone, the hormone that some researchers call the "feel good" hormone. Dr. Lee is the author of the best-selling books *What Your Doctor May Not Tell You About Menopause* and *What Your Doctor May Not Tell You About Premenopause*.[1]

I agree with Dr. Lee. In the woman's menstrual cycle, it is the surge of progesterone midcycle that gives her the urge to have sex (and sometimes lots of it!) because that is her fertile time. I have prescribed progesterone for thousands of women who have experienced a successful increase in libido as a result of using progesterone. In fact, I actually have had husbands call and thank me!

Consider this example from my case histories:

> Mary is a fifty-seven-year old lady who complained of a total loss of libido for the past three to four years. She was at the point where she felt like telling her husband to "just go find another wife; I can't function anymore." She also had mood swings, insomnia, depression and feelings of despair. She had been in menopause since the age of fifty-one, and had been on and off synthetic hormones, mainly because she cannot stand the way she feels on them. She has a history of fibrocystic breasts.
>
> I started Mary immediately on natural progesterone to restore her hormone balance, telling her that we could not begin with phytoestrogen due to her fibrocystic breast condition. However, we might think about adding the phytoestrogen in the future if her breast tissue returns to normal as it often does with natural progesterone therapy. After determining that she had no history of other medical problems, due to the long history of loss of libido I started her on a natural testosterone booster, Testron SX, with a dosage of two pills daily for thirty days, which I reduced to one pill daily thereafter.
>
> It took about six months, but I am happy to report that Mary improved. She began to notice a gradual rise in her feelings of well-being within three to four weeks of using natural progesterone. Within the next two months, she noticed a spark returning when she thought about her husband and how much he loved her and how patient he had been for the past many years. Within six months Mary was once again enjoying sex, and told me she had even gone so far as to initiate it—something she used to do only on their anniversary!

This approach runs contrary to what most physicians have been taught for many, many years. When I was in medical school, a myth was circulating among women and some doctors that continues to make the rounds today. This myth

72

states that it is estrogen that keeps women from turning into shriveled old ladies who can no longer seem attractive to their husbands. Women have been told, "Without estrogen supplementation you will end up looking like a man (and maybe even grow a beard)."

That is simply not true. It is the estrogen, testosterone and progesterone "mix" that creates and sustains your femininity. Unfortunately, many women suffer from hormone imbalances that run from mild to severe and that compromise their health and well-being, especially in the years directly leading up to and including menopause.

> FACT: It is the estrogen, testosterone and progesterone "mix" that creates and sustains your femininity.

Here are a few interesting facts about estrogen:

At menopause, estrogen levels in a woman's body may lower by 50 percent, but they do not fall to zero.

Sex drive derives from all three major hormones: estrogen, testosterone and progesterone. If a woman receives estrogen replacement without progesterone, she will have trouble regaining her lost libido.

Premarin, the synthetic estrogen replacement usually prescribed, is derived from horses' urine. It can actually lower libido, cause substantial weight gain and can, in some cases, lead to thrombophlebitis and stroke. I deeply regret that I ever wrote even one prescription for Premarin. It is far safer and more effective, in my opinion, to opt for natural hormone replacements.

My new slogan is "It is a Syn to take Synthetics." I also appreciate this statement from one of my television viewers: "You were created in a garden, NOT a laboratory." I believe we should look to God and natural remedies first. If that fails, then we may need to go to man and mainstream medicine.

HORMONAL IMBALANCE
AND LOSS OF LIBIDO IN WOMEN

"What has happened to my sex drive? I've lost it." I have told you already that this is, without doubt, the number one

73

question I have been hearing for the past twenty-one years in my medical practice, from my television viewers and, quite frankly, even from people I meet socially. Women are desperate to regain this lost part of their lives.

And why not? Sex is important to our mental and physical well-being.

Much of the time the culprit is the hormonal shift associated with menopause or perimenopause. Gentlemen, believe me, it is not that your wife has suddenly found you unattractive or uninteresting. Rather, she may be experiencing something ranging from a dramatic to a subtle shift in her hormone balance.

The pattern of a woman's monthly hormone secretions actually begins to change at some point when she is in her forties. These years before periods stop forever are called perimenopause. Many women are surprised to learn that the perimenopause phase can last as long as ten years.

During this time, some periods may be heavier or lighter than others. Cycles begin to be irregular or to be skipped completely in some months. The hormones of a woman's menstrual cycle shift out of balance during the perimenopausal years and become more erratic in the following years.

Here is a list of symptoms reflecting the body's response to its changing hormone balance.

- Hot flashes
- Night sweats
- Insomnia
- Vaginal dryness and thinning of the vaginal area
- Decreased libido (sex drive)
- Anxiety, anger and mood swings
- Forgetfulness or "fuzzy brain" syndrome
- Depression and feelings of despair
- Vaginal and bladder infections
- Short-term memory loss
- Joint and muscle pain
- Rapid skin aging and loss of tone in breasts
- Fatigue and heart palpitations

Do you recognize yourself (ladies) or your wife (men) in these symptoms?

No wonder a woman begins to turn from feeling desirable and sexy to feeling tired, frumpy and even resentful when her husband approaches her. Her entire body chemistry is changing, and she may not even be aware of it—she only knows that her sex drive is gone. This can lead to guilt, frustration and anger—not conducive to a romantic interlude! Even if you do make love, the experience can fall quite short of former times due to dryness, pain and fatigue. So she may become less and less interested as time goes on, leading to total cessation of lovemaking. Can this be helped? YES!

THE ROLE OF ESTROGEN

What is estrogen? What happens to estrogen levels at menopause?

The word *estrogen* generally refers to the group of hormones produced by the ovary, all of which have similar actions. The three most important hormones of this estrogen class are *estriol, estrone* and *estradiol.* In popular writing, however, each of these specific members of this class are communally referred to as *estrogen.*

Please note that I will be referring to *phytoestrogens* throughout this book. These are plant-derived hormones. They are made from substances extracted from wild yams or soybeans, specifically *diosgenin.* Phytoestrogens refer to plant compounds that produce estrogen-like activity in the body. They are generally weaker than your own estrogens. They also have a protective effect by occupying estrogen receptors and competing with more potent or excess estrogens found in the body or that come from the environment.

If you (your wife) are already on a synthetic or chemically-altered hormone, this may fall far short of the "cure" you have expected. In fact, it could be making the problem of lost libido worse! The most commonly prescribed synthetic estrogen is Premarin. (The Estraderm patch is a close second.)

There is a lot of confusion among women who actually think Premarin is a natural hormone. Doctors like to tell women that Premarin is "natural." This is because the makers of Premarin like to refer to it as "natural" because it is made from the urine of pregnant mares. It is produced by collecting the urine from artificially inseminated horses that are kept in stalls with collection bags strapped over their anatomy. The urine is then made into the drug. The generic name for Premarin is conjugated equine estrogen.

Only two of the female hormones contained in the human body are present in Premarin: estrone and estradiol. The rest of the estrogen in Premarin is extracted from horse urine, which is not natural to the human body! If the consumption of horse urine is natural, only then is Premarin natural!

The hormone estriol is completely missing from Premarin (as well as from other forms of conventional hormone replacement therapy). This is quite appalling to me, because in the human body, estriol is the estrogen that is found in the greatest amount compared to estrone and estradiol. Over 80 percent of our natural tri-estrogen is estriol. Many researchers and physicians dismiss the importance of estriol because it is the weakest estrogen. However, studies have shown that estriol protects the body from the more carcinogenic estrone and estradiol and is especially protective against breast cancer.

In addition, the percentages of estrone and estradiol found in Premarin are much greater than the levels your body produces naturally. Therefore it is no surprise that women on Premarin develop symptoms of hormonal imbalance. The estrogenic effects of Premarin on a woman's body are much stronger than those produced by natural human estrogens.

This explains why so many women taking Premarin tell me that they "don't feel right" or "I don't feel like myself anymore." It is important for you to understand that the pharmaceutical companies are using the term "natural," but any product that requires a prescription is not natural. Natural products cannot be patented; therefore, they are not of interest to the drug companies. Instead, they have taken natural substances and altered their chemical structure so that they can be patented. Thus, these are really man-made substances, which are foreign to the human body.

Let's look at the side effects listed in the *2000 Physician's Desk Reference* (PDR). These are also listed on the package insert that comes with your prescription.

SIDE EFFECTS OF PREMARIN

- Endometrial cancer
- Fluid retention
- Loss of hair
- Breast cancer (high doses for prolonged periods)
- Edema
- Hirsutism
- Enlargement of benign tumors of the uterus
- Blood clots
- Uterine bleeding/uterine fibroids
- Changes in libido (AHA! Why are a record number of women having libido problems? Could it be due to the millions of Premarin prescriptions that are written yearly?)
- Candidiasis
- Gallbladder disease
- Breast tenderness and enlargement
- Nausea, vomiting, abdominal cramps, jaundice
- Chloasma (abnormal pigmentation of skin)
- Increase or decrease in weight, bloating
- Reduced carbohydrate tolerance
- Headache, migraine, dizziness
- Mental depression[2]

In addition to these disturbing side effects, let me tell you another startling fact: *The American Journal of Obstetrics and Gynecology* now states that not only long-term, but also short-term use of the number-one-prescribed synthetic hormone Premarin carries a 40 percent risk of acquiring breast cancer.[3]

Another estrogen commonly prescribed by mainstream medical doctors and called "natural" is the estrogen patch. The patch contains 100 percent estradiol, which is the most potent of all the estrogens found in the female body. This estradiol is extracted from the wild yam, but aside from that, I do not believe the patch can be called natural. It contains no

77

estrone and no estriol. This creates an extremely unbalanced, unnatural estrogen state in a woman's body.

In June 1995, one of the largest studies done, the Nurses' Health Study, showed that women taking synthetic estrogen alone had a 36 percent increase in their risk of breast cancer. Those on synthetic estrogen plus progestin had a 50 percent increase, and those on progestins alone had a 240 percent increase in breast cancer.[4] Women who at the time of the study had been taking estrogen and progestin for five to ten years had a 45 percent increase in their risk of breast cancer.[5]

The older the woman, the higher the risk. Women between the ages of sixty and sixty-four who had been taking synthetic hormones for five years or more had an increased risk of developing breast cancer by 71 percent.[6] This is important when you look at the way hormones are being marketed to prevent osteoporosis and heart disease. Women are placed on synthetic hormones at around age fifty and told to continue them for the rest of their lives. That is why it is so important to switch to truly natural hormones. Unlike synthetic estrogen, phytoestrogens do not increase the risk of breast cancer. They also do not promote fat storage. The average weight gain I saw in women who were placed on synthetic hormones was between twenty to thirty pounds, sometimes even more! Furthermore, in April 2000, a federal study of twenty-five thousand women indicated that HRT may put women at a higher risk of heart attacks and stroke.[7]

By now you should have a very good understanding of why I urge women to get off synthetic hormones and switch to natural hormones. I cannot take lightly this opportunity to talk to you and not mention such potentially life-saving information. Your precious husbands do not want to lose you or see you suffer with cancer (not to mention your families, friends and brothers and sisters in Christ).

WHAT HAPPENS TO ESTROGEN LEVELS AT MENOPAUSE?

During and after menopause, your body will continue to make some estrogen from androstenedione in your fat cells, so your estrogen levels will never actually fall to zero, as is commonly thought. These lower estrogen levels, it has been determined, have a limited effect on sexual desire. The role that estrogen does play in regard to sexuality is more like that of a protector. It provides general protection to the woman's sexual nature. It can increase blood flow to the clitoris and therefore enhance sensitivity. Estrogen supplementation lessens night sweats, improves sleep, diminishes fatigue and thereby helps restore sexual energy and sexual desire. When estrogen levels get too low, the vaginal mucosa often shrinks and becomes thinner. In addition to the discomfort of dryness, the loss of resistance and resilience of those tissues predisposes a woman to other problems. She may develop vaginal inflammation or vaginitis, and she may get frequent bladder infection or cystitis.

The following are some of the symptoms of low estrogen:

- Hot flashes (sometimes with dizziness)
- Night sweats
- Vaginal dryness
- Shortness of breath and palpitations
- Sleep disorders, insomnia
- Dry hair, hair loss
- Anxiety
- Mood swings
- Headaches
- Depression
- Frequent urinary tract infections

Men, would you feel like making love if you had these symptoms? Perhaps now you have a better understanding of what may have happened to your wife's sex drive. However, men and women, take heart. In these cases supplementation with *natural* estrogen is indicated. As I have said, I do not advocate synthetic or chemically altered hormones for women who need estrogen.

Many of you may have heard about some new "designer estrogens" that are supposedly "natural." Although I am pleased to note that more and more drug companies are beginning to talk about natural alternatives, these "designer" estrogens are manufactured by major drug companies from materials not found in nature and still are synthetic to our bodies. As far as I am concerned, we just do not know enough about the effects and side effects of these drugs. Why should you be the guinea pig when you can use estrogen that you know is natural?

WHAT IS NATURAL ESTROGEN?
WHO NEEDS IT?

Natural estrogen consists of all three estrogens—estriol, estrone and estradiol, which are derived from a plant source, the wild yam *(dioscorea composita)*. This specific variety (Mexican wild yam) contains active estrogen- and progesterone-like substances very similar to those produced in the human body.

These substances are called *phytoestrogen* and *phytoprogesterone*. In the 1950s, it was discovered that these substances could be easily converted by biochemists into estrogens and progesterone. Their molecular structure is so indistinguishable from the structure of those hormones found in the human body that phytoestrogens will actually bind to your body's estrogen receptor sites and produce estrogenic effects. They were found to function the same as our own natural hormones. More recently, soybeans have also been found to contain the diosgenin found in wild yams, and they are also used in natural hormones.

Although natural progesterone is effective for most menopausal women, there are three main symptoms that indicate natural estrogen is needed. These are severe hot flashes, night sweats and vaginal dryness. My research and patient trials have indicated that these symptoms require more than progesterone alone. (We will discuss other remedies for hot flashes, night sweats and vaginal dryness a little further along in the book).

Alleviating these very distressing conditions will certainly go a long way toward making you more receptive to lovemaking. After all, these are very debilitating conditions to many women.

I also believe that estrogen plays yet another role in regard to libido. Although some doctors may differ with me, I have worked with enough women with diminished sex drive to see that natural estrogen makes a difference. Estrogen receptor activity is highest in the cells that line all blood vessels in the vascular network. That means that when your estrogen levels are low, your body may take much longer to respond to the sexual stimulation that results from increased blood flow to the vulva and clitoris. In my experience, women have reported an increase in the level of sexual desire and sexual activity after using a phytoestrogen cream for three to six months. It is very interesting to note that none of these women received testosterone supplements.

HOW DO I FIND NATURAL ESTROGEN?

For many years I have used natural hormones to help women with PMS, menopause and decreased sex drive. However, I do not advocate that any woman take estrogen only. Doing so can lead to problems ranging from estrogen dominance (which we will discuss later) to a higher risk of breast cancer and uterine cancer.

81

From all of my research and patient trials, I have formulated a special blend of natural hormones that contains both phytoestrogen and phytoprogesterone in the proportions found in the human body. This promotes the hormonal balance that menopausal women are usually lacking. It is called Menopause Relief Cream. This cream contains the tri-estrogen combination in the proportions of 80 percent estriol, 10 percent estrone and 10 percent estradiol, closely mimicking the ratio found in nature.

Many naturopathic physicians and, I am pleased to report, some mainstream medical doctors prescribe triple estrogen creams in the 80/10/10 ratio for their patients. These creams, usually called tri-estrogen or tri-est, are available from compounding pharmacies in the United States—they are usually not available at standard pharmacies.[8] If you cannot locate a doctor who is knowledgeable in the use of natural hormones, please see the back of this book for information on how to order a topical phytoestrogen cream. I also have available the topical phytoestrogen cream, Ostaderm, which is often recommended by my dear friend and mentor, Dr. Julian Whitaker of the Whitaker Wellness Clinic in Newport Beach, California.

HOW TO USE NATURAL HORMONE CREAM

I advise women who use a natural estrogen/progesterone cream to apply one-fourth teaspoon twice daily to soft skin areas such as the neck, breasts, buttocks, inner thighs and inner arms. It is absorbed transdermally. However, once the fat cells just under the skin are saturated, absorption will be compromised. For that reason, you should vary the areas to which you apply the cream over a three-day period to allow time for the absorbed estrogen and progesterone to be used by your body. Breasts have enough fat cells for daily application.

During hot flashes, use one-half teaspoon every fifteen minutes until you feel relief. Many women say that it helps to put the cream on their neck during hot flashes. For vaginal dryness, use one-fourth teaspoon daily, applied intravaginally with fingertips, until symptoms subside.

If you cannot use estrogen because of a history of breast or uterine cancer, or do not wish to use an estrogen product, try natural progesterone for three or four months. This may be enough to sensitize receptors to the lowered levels of estrogen still present in your body. I have patients who suffer from hot flashes and vaginal dryness who report favorable results using progesterone only, and it may work for you. At least it should alleviate symptoms enough so that you will feel more like your old self and be more receptive to lovemaking.

WEANING INSTRUCTIONS

If you are already on estrogen replacement therapy, a slow weaning process is necessary. If you are on the combination of Premarin and Provera (Provera is a prescription progestin, or synthetic progesterone), after you begin using the natural cream, you may drop the prescription progestin (Provera) immediately. Take your estrogen pill (it may be a synthetic other than Premarin) every other day the first month. The second month you will take your estrogen pill every third day while continuing to use the cream. The third month you will take your estrogen pill every fourth day. During the fourth month you will be off the prescription product entirely. Alternating days like this works better than dividing the tablets because they are difficult to split.

For women on the patch, you can wear it for shorter periods of time, gradually diminishing the duration of the application over three months. Or you may do it another way: Cut the patch in half for the first month, using paper tape or gauze bandages to hold the partial patch in place.

The second month you will cut the estrogen patch in quarters. The third month you will cut it in eighths, and the fourth month you will go off it entirely.

> IMPORTANT NOTE: You should not go off synthetic estrogen suddenly as you may experience resultant crying jags, irritability and emotional mood swings. Don't do it!

PERIMENOPAUSAL (OR PREMENOPAUSAL) HORMONAL IMBALANCE

The period leading up to menopause is called perimenopause, and for some women it can last five to ten years. This can be an extremely trying time hormonally for many women due to something called *estrogen dominance.*

What is estrogen dominance? John R. Lee, M.D., a Harvard graduate and medical doctor who has studied the hormonal problems of women extensively, coined this phrase to describe the hormonal imbalances he found again and again during his private practice and research in the field of women's hormones. *Estrogen dominance,* according to Dr. Lee, is actually a result of progesterone deficiency.

Dr. Lee states that a hundred years ago women did not have the same early menopausal problems, osteoporosis problems and cancer rate that we have today—all of which are appearing to get worse. Why? Women in nonindustrialized cultures had more traditional diets, did not eat much processed food and were not exposed to the levels of pesticides and toxins that we are exposed to today. Their progesterone levels did not drop off as dramatically as women of this generation.[9]

Dr. Lee explained that progesterone is a product of ovulation, and more and more Western women are experiencing ovulatory difficulties at an earlier age. This leads to lower and lower progesterone levels.

WHAT IS PROGESTERONE AND WHY IS IT SO IMPORTANT?

Progesterone is a steroid hormone that is manufactured by the corpus luteum of the ovary at ovulation. It is also made in smaller amounts by the adrenal glands. Progesterone is a precursor to most of the other steroid hormones—cortisol, androstenedione, estrogen and testosterone.

One of its most important roles is to balance the effects of estrogen in the woman's body. It also stimulates the building of bone and is a valuable protection against osteoporosis. As you can see, it is a very vital hormone.

If our ovaries have stopped making progesterone prematurely, the adrenal glands are forced to produce most of the progesterone we need in order to produce our other steroid hormones. This leaves little or no progesterone to balance the estrogen in our bodies.

By the time a woman reaches actual menopause, her progesterone level has fallen to nearly zero. There is nothing to balance out the estrogen in her body, which continues to be manufactured by her fat cells.

Factors that contribute to estrogen dominance are substances in the environment with the ability to attach to estrogen receptor sites and act as estrogens. They are known as *xenoestrogens*. They include pesticides, plastics, industrial waste, car exhaust, hormones found in meat and even soaps. Dr. John R. Lee believes that if your mother was exposed to xenoestrogens during the embryonic stage, your follicles may have been damaged, leading you to have menstrual cycles during which you do not ovulate. This, as previously explained, causes estrogen dominance. Stress induces anovulatory cycles, due to the fact that the body protects against a possible pregnancy during times of stress. According to Dr. Lee's studies, the combination of anovulatory cycles and xenoestrogens produces estrogen dominance in many women.[10]

The signs and symptoms of estrogen dominance are water retention, breast swelling, fibrocystic breasts, PMS mood swings, depression, loss of libido, heavy or irregular menses, weight gain, cravings for sweets and fat deposits on hips and thighs.

These symptoms occur if you have too little progesterone in your system in relation to your estrogen level. Since almost all of the progesterone in your body is made from the corpus luteum of the unfertilized egg, even if you are having a regular monthly period, if you are not ovulating, you are NOT making progesterone. Therefore estrogen dominance is a syndrome that affects women who suffer from PMS as well as women who suffer from perimenopausal or menopausal symptoms. The synthetic substances in birth control pills also cause estrogen dominance.

Most importantly, in terms of our subject matter, the surge of progesterone in a woman's body at the time of ovulation is the source of libido, the urge to procreate, the urge for sex.

85

WHAT SHOULD YOU DO IF YOU HAVE ESTROGEN DOMINANCE?

According to Dr. Lee, supplementation with *natural progesterone* will alleviate most of these symptoms by restoring your body's natural hormone balance.

No matter how valuable estrogen is, when unopposed by progesterone, it is not something to be wholly desired in the female body. Many of estrogen's undesirable side effects are blocked by progesterone.[11]

The following list shows the effects of the use of progesterone on symptoms of estrogen dominance:

Estrogen Dominance Symptom	Result of Progesterone Use
Weight gain	Utilizes fat for energy
Decreased sex drive	Increases libido
Insomnia	Restores normal sleep pattern
Fatigue	Restores cell oxygen levels

Memory loss	Helps with concentration
Irritability, mood swings	Normalizes blood sugar levels
Fibrocystic/tender breasts	Protects breast tissue
Breast cancer risk	Helps prevent breast cancer
Depression/anxiety	Natural antidepressant
Fluid retention (bloating)	Natural diuretic
Thyroid imbalance	Assists thyroid hormone action
Blood clots	Normalizes blood clotting
Migraine headaches	Prevents/protects against migraine
Risk of miscarriage	Maintains secretory endometrium
Hair loss	Normalizes zinc and copper levels
Acne	Aids in skin disorders
Irregular menstrual flow	Normalizes periods
Osteoporosis	Stimulates bone mineral density

SYMPTOMS OF LOW PROGESTERONE

- Anxiety
- Moodiness
- Loss of libido
- Fuzzy thinking
- Depression
- Irritability
- PMS symptoms

You can see that progesterone is extremely important to a woman's healthy hormonal balance. Many doctors put patients on birth control pills for symptoms of low progesterone. I do not advocate the use of synthetic progestins. They do not have the same molecular structure as the hormones your body makes. That is why you will develop side effects from these drugs. Your body recognizes that they are foreign substances. I advocate only natural progesterone, with the transdermal cream being the first choice with oral as a second choice only.

WHAT IS NATURAL PROGESTERONE?

Today natural progesterone is mostly produced from wild Mexican yam plants and soybeans.

You may be wondering, *If natural progesterone helps increase sex drive, can't synthetic progestins do the same thing?* No, but I don't blame you for being confused. Many physicians are confused by the definitions of the words *progesterone* and *progestin*. Progestins are synthetic progesterones. The pharmaceutical industry purchases the natural progesterone, which comes from wild yams and soybeans, and then changes it to make the non-natural substances called progestins. Progestins do not undergo the same chemical reactions in our bodies as natural progesterone, and they are not as safe to use because of their side effects.

Do not confuse natural progesterone with synthetic progestins—the form of progesterone usually prescribed by physicians in birth control pills or as part of menopausal hormone replacement therapy.

When a woman is treated with synthetic progestins, her body becomes confused. Cells that bind progesterone will receive this false progesterone known as progestin, but because it is a different shape, it will not function properly. Side effects could include salt buildup, fluid retention or edema, hypoglycemia, mood swings, migraines, cardiac or kidney dysfunction, interrupted sleep patterns, loss of libido, depression and possible stroke.

Natural progesterone, on the other hand, has no unpleasant side effects.

PROGESTERONE AND SEX DRIVE

Probably one of the greatest enemies of a woman's libido is the estrogen-dominant condition we have just discussed. My perimenopausal patients would complain of feeling bloated, depressed, tired and irritable with sore breasts and dry skin. Menopausal women who were taking conventional synthetic hormone replacement prescribed to them by another physician would complain of a total lack of sex drive in addition to weight gain and insomnia. Some were so miserable they would begin crying hysterically the minute I began to take their medical history.

I am sorry to say that many conventional medical doctors

mistakenly think that a woman's libido comes from estrogen. I believe this is a direct result of pharmaceutical companies who make synthetic hormones and lobby the doctors to use their products. These companies send sales people to the doctors' offices to court them with lunches, dinners and attendance at seminars in exotic locations, where they are inundated with literature proclaiming the benefits of drugs like Premarin, Estrace and Prempro. The myth is perpetrated that lack of estrogen causes a woman to shrivel up, lose her sex drive and begin to look like a man. This myth has been circulated in the medical community for years. Physicians then try to do what they think is best for the patient and prescribe estrogen.

Unfortunately for countless numbers of women, our mothers included, this had just the opposite effect. The side effects of synthetic estrogen and excess estrogen can absolutely destroy libido. I have seen women in my office who have been on estrogen for their lack of sex drive, often for years with no results. As a matter of fact, countless other women told me they lost their sex drives only after they were put on synthetic hormones!

In reality, it is the hormones progesterone and testosterone that enhance sexual libido and sexual energy.

Progesterone can affect libido positively—often in a very dramatic way. Progesterone is often called the "feel good" hormone because it is most abundant at times in a woman's life when she is most interested in sex. Progesterone levels rise during the week following ovulation, the time in a woman's menstrual cycle when she is most fertile and when many women experience a surge in libido.

Because women who are perimenopausal or menopausal produce decreased or nonexistent levels of progesterone respectively, it is reasonable to believe that supplementing with progesterone will have a positive effect on sexual interest and libido.

Corroborating evidence of progesterone restoring libido is found in medical literature involving animal studies.[12] Several of my colleagues who are naturopathic physicians have also told me of an island culture where it has been reported that the women have a very high sex drive during the entire month. They say that researchers believe this may be due to the fact that one of the primary foods on this island is yams, which contain high amounts of natural progesterone.

Progesterone plays a role in pregnant women because it is required for survival of the fetus. Therefore high levels are produced during pregnancy and are believed to be responsible for the "glow" of the pregnant woman and her heightened feelings of well-being.

I am not surprised that many of the women whom I place on progesterone supplementation report that they have never felt so good and have a renewed interest in sex. The safety of natural progesterone has been confirmed by extensive testing, and the FDA has had no adverse reports when progesterone is given in doses up to and including 800 milligrams per day.

HOW TO SUPPLEMENT WITH NATURAL PROGESTERONE

When I talk about the use of natural progesterone, as with natural estrogen, I am talking about transdermal application. Progesterone is fat-soluble and is much more effective when applied transdermally (through the skin). It is readily absorbed into the underlying fat layer and then goes into the capillaries where it is released into the blood. By contrast, up to 80 percent of the effectiveness of progesterone can be lost when taken orally, as it must pass through the liver tissue before entering the blood stream.

Transdermal application is easy and quick. I recommend that the woman apply the cream anywhere the skin is thin and capillaries are plentiful—especially the upper chest, face, neck, inner arms or palms of the hands. Rotate areas every three days or so to keep receptor sites from getting oversaturated. The goal is to administer a dosage equivalent to normal body functions. This is called a *physiologic dose*.

GENERAL GUIDELINES

ॐ Absorption will be greater if you spread the cream thinly over a larger area.

෨ Do not get too worried about both daily doses—or even doses from day to day—being exactly the same size. The hormone will release steadily into the blood stream even if the amount of the dose varies.

෨ Some women who have insomnia like to use a smaller dose in the morning and a larger dose at night, as progesterone can help with sleep patterns.

෨ Remember, all creams are not created equal. If the base is not of a good quality, you will not get good absorption. Buy only from reputable vendors.

෨ Do not apply other skin creams in the same area where you are applying your hormone cream that day.

SPECIFIC INSTRUCTIONS

PERIMENOPAUSAL WOMEN WHO ARE STILL MENSTRUATING, EITHER REGULARLY OR IRREGULARLY

Count the first day your period begins as day 1. Beginning on day 12, apply ¼ teaspoon of cream (natural progesterone) both morning and night. Continue until day 26. If your period starts before day 26, stop using the cream and begin counting again. Start using the cream again on day 12. If you have irregular periods, it will probably take about three months before you have a more regular cycle. If you cease menstruating entirely despite trying to cycle the cream, follow the instructions for the menopausal woman.

Remember to use the cream only two weeks of the month. Using the cream improperly will interfere with your cycle, and your periods will become irregular.

WOMEN WITH PMS

Follow the instructions given above. For the first month or two, be generous with the cream. It is OK to use up to ½ teaspoon twice daily during the initial months. This may mean that you use a full 2-ounce jar per month initially. This should relieve your symptoms more quickly. Then cut back to ¼ teaspoon twice daily.

If you are very low in progesterone, you may experience some initial symptoms of estrogen dominance when you begin using the cream. These may include headaches, swollen breasts and a bloated feeling. This happens because your body, sensing it has no progesterone, has "turned down" its estrogen receptors to try and avoid estrogen dominance, which is very undesirable. Once progesterone is added to your body, these estrogen receptors will tune back up, and you may notice these distinct symptoms. Persevere—the symptoms disappear in as little as two weeks, although in some women it may take two to three months. Breast tenderness seems to be the most common complaint in my patients, but it will pass.

WOMEN WHO MENSTRUATE AND SUFFER FROM MENSTRUAL MIGRAINE HEADACHES

Use natural progesterone during the ten days before your period. For example, if you are on a twenty-six-day cycle, use the cream from days 16 to 26. Use ¼ teaspoon twice daily. When you feel the "aura" that indicates you are about to get a migraine, apply ¼ to ½ teaspoon of cream every three to four hours until symptoms cease (probably after one or two applications). Many women have found that it is very helpful to apply the cream directly to their neck or temples.

MENOPAUSAL WOMEN

Women who have had a hysterectomy, with or without ovaries removed (this is known as surgical menopause), should follow these instructions. Choose a day of the month and count it as day 1. For the next twenty-five days, apply ¼ teaspoon of cream (either natural progesterone or your natural progesterone/natural estrogen blend) both morning and night. On days 25 through 30 (or 31) do not use any cream. This is designed to prevent your body from building up an immunity or tolerance to the phytoprogesterone and/or phytoestrogen. Most women like to keep it simple and will choose to take off either the last five days of the month or the first five days of the month off. It is entirely up to you as long as you remember to discontinue use of the cream for five days each month.

If you experience an extreme recurrence of symptoms, or

if you get headaches during the days you are not using your cream, you can take as little as three days off. Otherwise, try to go the full five to six days.

If you are a woman who has just had your hysterectomy, you might want to double the dose for the first month. If you are a woman with strong symptoms of estrogen dominance, begin with the cream that contains only progesterone. For the first month or two, double the dose, using ½ teaspoon twice daily until symptoms subside. Later, if you have severe hot flashes or vaginal dryness, you can switch to the cream containing both estrogen and progesterone.

If you have had a hysterectomy but still have your ovaries, please know that a hysterectomy causes the blood supply to the ovaries to be dramatically reduced, and they quickly stop producing progesterone. Within two years, the estrogen level also drops off to postmenopausal levels.

IMPORTANT ADVICE FOR ALL WOMEN

You will fall somewhere into this "normal" pattern of dosing. However, observe your symptoms and patterns carefully to be sure you are getting a true physiologic dose. If your symptoms are improving and you are feeling great, you probably have received the dose your body needs. At that point you can try reducing the dose to see if you can find the minimum dose your body requires to keep you balanced.

If you do not notice any improvement after one or two months, you are probably not getting enough progesterone.

If you begin to feel drowsy, you have probably received more progesterone than you need.

MY ADVICE TO HUSBANDS

My patients who use the natural progesterone cream faithfully report that they notice a definite increase in libido. I strongly advise that you assist your wife in complying with her daily regimen. This is often the downfall or reason for the program being unsuccessful. The woman will either forget to order the cream, stop the program or be sporadic in its application. Because the cream requires transdermal application, you can make this part of your support system to your wife while at the same time using it as an opportunity for intimacy. Each evening you can bring her the cream or help her rub it onto her arms, temples, neck, breasts or thighs. Not only will you be helping her with balancing her hormones for healthy living, but who knows where the process will end up?

And by the way—for men over fifty-five, try rubbing a little progesterone cream on your perineum. My male patients report a stronger sex drive and stronger, longer-lasting erections.

NATURAL HORMONES—A GUIDE

My medical practice has led me to develop combinations of natural hormones specific to various groups and clusters of symptoms.

For example, for those age forty to forty-eight, in natural menopause, perimenopause or PMS with symptoms such as regular or irregular menses, irritability, anxiety, depression, breast tenderness, headaches, fuzzy thinking and low sex drive, without vaginal dryness, night sweats or hot flashes, I "prescribe" a 960 to 1000 milligram dosage of natural progesterone cream. My personal choice is called Pro HELP.

93

For ages forty-eight to ninety-eight, and all surgical menopause cases, with symptoms such as hot flashes, night sweats, insomnia, vaginal dryness, low sex drive, anxiety, depression, mood swings, headaches, short-term memory loss, frequent urinary tract infections, dry hair or hair loss, I advocate using a phytoprogesterone/phytoestrogen product that is balanced in the proportions produced and utilized by the body. My favorite is called Menopause Relief Cream.

For women who have had a personal history of breast or reproductive cancer (uterine or ovarian), I recommend using only the natural progesterone cream. Some doctors believe that any estrogen, even phytoestrogen, can exacerbate the growth of cancer cells. For this reason, I urge you to use natural progesterone only.

ALL HORMONE CREAMS ARE NOT CREATED EQUAL

There has been an explosion of companies that are offering

"yam cream" to alleviate PMS and menopausal symptoms. *All creams are not created equal!* You need to purchase your cream from a reliable source to insure that what you buy contains real progesterone in a high enough concentration to be effective. Look for "USP Progesterone" on the label.

My colleague, John R. Lee, M.D., a pioneer in the field of natural hormones, warns that:

1.   A cream will not be effective if it is not suspended in the proper medium.

2.   Products containing mineral oil can prohibit absorption.

3.   Some products have not stabilized the progesterone properly and it deteriorates rapidly. Therefore, some of the creams you may purchase can be almost useless.

4.   Not all products claiming to be "wild yam extract" actually contain any progesterone.

94

For your further edification, I have included a chapter in which I answer your most frequently asked questions about the use of natural hormones. Please see chapter fifteen.

WHAT ABOUT THOSE HOT FLASHES? WHAT CAN BE DONE?

ATTENTION HUSBANDS: It is important for you to read this information! Hot flashes are really the hallmark of the perimenopausal and menopausal years. Studies have shown that about 60 to 80 percent of menopausal women experience hot flashes for up to five years after menopause begins. Some women have reported having them for more than twelve years, although this is a very small group.

Unmanaged hot flashes can completely change a woman's personality, her outlook on life and her sense of well-being. Sleep is interrupted, and even when she does sleep, REM (dream) sleep is often reduced so she does not awaken refreshed. She becomes fatigued, irritable and perhaps depressed, and she usually loses a huge portion of her libido.

Hot flashes start prior to menopause in about 60 percent

of women. They become more intense and more frequent at the time of menopause. Some women suffer from them for only a few months, and in others they can continue for five to ten years following her last period. Without going into an elaborate description, what is essentially happening is the woman's decreasing estrogen level has caused changes in her hormone signaling system. Her body (through the brain's hypothalamus) is trying to signal her ovaries to ovulate. There is no response from the ovaries, which are shrinking and shutting down. The brain then has to go into "high alert" to try and get the message to the ovary. This signal then affects the area that triggers dilation of surface blood vessels—the body's thermostat, so to speak.

There are also external factors that may cause hot flashes. These include alcohol consumption, coffee, spicy foods, stress and sometimes warm weather.

What are hot flashes like? Try to picture a blowtorch aimed directly at you for three to six minutes, and you will have an idea of what a hot flash is like for some women. Some women report hot flashes that last up to thirty minutes. Others describe waves of flashes. All of a sudden a comfortable room temperature feels like 90 degrees. It may feel as if her skin is "crawling." She may feel dizzy or faint, and her heart will start racing. There may be a feeling of suffocation and a period of profuse sweating. Then, as if this is not bad enough, the next minute she may be shivering uncontrollably as her body rapidly cools after the flash. Now imagine that you are out in public when this happens.

When this happens during the day we call them *hot flashes*. When a woman awakens at night with flushing, this is called a *night sweat*. She may wake up so drenched with perspiration that she has to get up to change her clothing and sheets. In severe cases this can happen several times in one night.

Night sweats can be even worse than hot flashes because of the psychological aspect of being awakened out of sleep with your heart racing and body temperature rising. Some women with night sweats become extremely depressed. Is it any wonder that lovemaking will often fall by the wayside during these roller-coaster years?

Hot flashes and night sweats can be debilitating, and some women become emotionally exhausted trying to "maintain" normalcy. My female patients have told me that episodes of hot flashes have literally changed their personalities. Picture now how she might feel if you come alongside her and make a sexual advance. Can you identify with her lack of response? I am sure you can. But take heart; we are going to provide ways and means of relief for her, and you can assist your beloved wife with some of the following remedies.

There is no "cure" per se for hot flashes and night sweats, but they can be relieved so that a woman can get her "old self" back and husbands can have their lovers back. Try some of the following remedies:

1. Both progesterone and estrogen can alleviate hot flashes. It is common for mainstream medical doctors to prescribe synthetic estrogen for menopausal women who seek help, but I do not agree with this because of the dangerous side effects. Also, some studies have shown that not all women with hot flashes respond to estrogen therapy. Menopausal women whose blood shows normal estrogen levels may still have hot flashes.

2. We know a woman is still making estrogen even after menopause, but she is not making progesterone. Therefore, I give my patients a blend of phytoestrogen and phytoprogesterone, either my Menopause Relief Cream or Ostaderm. One recent study confirmed my belief that progesterone can affect hot flashes. In the study women who used ¼ teaspoon of progesterone cream daily reported an 83 percent improvement or resolution in hot flashes.[13] You can also use progesterone directly following the first flash to prevent a wave of flushing. Use ¼ teaspoon every fifteen minutes for one hour following the episode.

3. High doses of vitamin E (800–1000 IU a day) have been

extremely effective for many women. Take it with meals, as vitamin E needs fat for absorption. Reduce dosage to the lowest effective dose as flashes decrease. Do not exceed 1200 IU daily. Be sure to use the natural form of vitamin E, which is d-alpha tocopheryl—not the synthetic form, which is dl-alpha tocopheryl.

4. Keep rooms cool at home (65 degrees) and avoid hot environments.

5. Take essential fatty acids in the form of borage oil or evening primrose oil. These contain gamma linolenic acid (GLA), which increases prostaglandin production and seems to relieve frequency and severity of hot flashes.

6. Eat soy. One study indicated that 60 grams of soy taken daily decreased hot flashes by 45 percent after twelve weeks. Soybeans are a good source of soy, as are tofu and tempeh. (Use an amount that equals 60 grams daily.) This diet is linked to reduced incidence of hot flashes in Japanese women.

7. Try a good woman's herbal formula. Products containing some combination of the following have been used to reduce hot flashes: dong quai, black cohosh, licorice and ginseng. They all have mild estrogenic activity and may help compensate for decreasing estrogen levels.

8. Dong quai has been shown to increase both estrogen and progesterone levels in women with insufficient ovarian function, decrease hot flashes, increase circulation to the genital area and improve decreased libido. It is usually not taken by itself but is found in formulas in combination with other herbs, especially black cohosh. If you have high blood pressure or asthma, do not take any formula that contains ginseng.

9. Black cohosh has been shown to help prevent hot flashes and also to relieve depression caused by lowered hormone levels.

97

10. Take a good B-complex vitamin.

11. Deep breathing (deep from the diaphragm so that you can see your abdomen rise) may shorten or even stop a hot flash.

12. Get regular exercise. Exercise improves circulation and also helps increase the amount of estrogen circulating in your blood. Women who exercise do not seem to have as many episodes of hot flashes as women who don't.

13. Keep a thermos of cold water close by to help your body cool down during hot flashes.

NIGHT SWEATS

Use a natural hormone for night sweats, just as for hot flashes. Use all the techniques above as well as the following:

1. Keep bedroom temperature cool. If possible, leave a window open.

2. Use only cotton sheets and nightgowns.

3. Keep a bowl of tepid water and a sponge on your nightstand to help cool yourself. Let the water evaporate on your skin as a cooling mechanism. (Husbands, perhaps you can help with the sponging.)

4. Discontinue all hot baths or hot showers before bedtime.

You should try as many of these remedies as possible. Some combination of them should work for you. Ladies, I strongly urge you to talk to your husband about these physical feelings and let him help you. From your phone calls and letters I know that too many of you are simply withdrawing from your spouse. This will be interpreted as rejection, and you will do even further damage to your sex life. These hot flashes and night sweats will pass, but the hurt of rejection is hard to overcome. Please give him the benefit of the doubt. He probably does not understand the depth of your suffering and may need you to confide in him.

VAGINAL DRYNESS

Of all the symptoms of menopause, vaginal dryness is the one that has the most negative, detrimental effect on a couple's sex life. Over the years, I have had many women weeping in my office over their lost days of lovemaking. I know how they suffer because I saw how thin their vaginal tissues were when I did their Pap smears. For some women, a Pap smear was so painful that they would actually scream.

With vaginal dryness, women begin to dread sex, and even arousal, due to the anticipation of pain and because they have no expectation of pleasure. Perhaps the saddest aspect of this problem is that men cannot identify with it as they have nothing in their direct experience with which to compare it. I know that some men have come to believe that their wife's pain is "all in her head." Often the wife would feel too guilty, ashamed or inadequate to discuss it with her husband. I certainly enjoy that ladylike quality that some women have where they will not discuss anything they think is "indelicate." I have a very close friend who is just that way. But, ladies, some things NEED to be said. This condition has been responsible for doing great damage to many marriages.

So, on behalf of all women, I want to tell you husbands that any inflammation, irritation or swelling of female genitalia, internal or external, causes pain in those tissues whenever they are touched. The pain associated with having sex with a dry vagina can be excruciating. Your concern for your wife will go a long way toward encouraging her to find the solution to this problem, which should be a shared problem.

The same drop in estrogen that causes vaginal dryness also leads to vaginal atrophy (shrinkage).

Women with vaginal atrophy experience a dramatic decrease in sexual desire. When the vagina is irritated, dry or atrophied, the penetration and friction of intercourse can cause such discomfort that women begin to avoid sex. Even women who enthusiastically enjoyed sexual relations with their husbands will curtail activity in these cases.

I am going to tell women how they can return moisture to

their vaginal tissue, but it would not hurt to go out and stock up on some lubricants. Put them somewhere close at hand in the bedroom where they can be easily reached if you begin some spontaneous lovemaking—for instance, in the top drawer of a nightstand.

WHAT CAUSES VAGINAL DRYNESS AS A WOMAN AGES?

When estrogen levels drop at menopause, the walls of the vagina respond by becoming thinner and dryer. The dryness is caused by a decrease in mucus secretions. Although these changes vary from mild to severe, depending on the woman, the truth is that the vagina does become more prone to abrasions. The glands that provide lubrication are reduced, and the mucosa (cell lining) of the vagina becomes very thin and easily irritated. Vaginal lubrication takes longer, and vaginal soreness often occurs during or after intercourse because the vagina failed to lubricate. In some women the vaginal lining may actually crack and bleed.

In addition, because there are fewer cell layers, the pH level of the vagina is often changed, becoming more alkaline. Bacteria and yeast now have a much more favorable environment in which to grow. (Yeast loves a high pH or alkaline state.) You may experience itching and frequent vaginal infections, another deterrent to a normal sex life.

Research has shown that menopausal women who continue to have sex once or twice a week will still lubricate adequately when aroused. Yes, it really is true: Regular sexual activity will keep your sex organs healthy and will help to prevent vaginal dryness and atrophy. You may groan and say, "I just can't; it hurts too much!" I am very sympathetic to your condition. However, my job here is to show you that there is hope for your sex life despite these unwelcome physical changes.

You may also be saying, "Why can't I just give up sex? I've had my 'salad days,' to quote Shakespeare." This is not an acceptable attitude if you want to keep your marriage healthy. Husbands often interpret the woman's response to these menopausal changes as rejection by their wives. As the women become less responsive, the husbands try harder and harder to arouse them sexually. When the women adopt the attitude of "I can take it or leave it, and I'd rather leave it," the husbands grow more and more anxious about the adequacy of their own sexual performance. Eventually, according to my colleagues who specialize in urology, many husbands go on to develop problems with erectile dysfunction, a very sad result.

However, there is help for you. A vaginal cream containing estrogen, particularly estriol, is an excellent way to treat vaginal dryness, thinning vaginal walls, vaginal atrophy (shrinkage) and even the dry, cracked vulva that some of my patients have endured. Estriol is the estrogen most beneficial to vaginal tissue. Use only a natural, plant-based formula designed for intravaginal use so it will not irritate the already sensitive tissues.

For many women, after they have been on a regimen of natural progesterone or natural estrogen/progesterone externally, they will notice that vaginal moisture is regained.

By the way, natural hormones also help after menopause when uterine contractions during orgasm are painful or weak due to lowered estrogen levels, an added benefit. If after using transdermal cream for three months you have had no real improvement intravaginally, or if you have a very severe case of vaginal dryness, you can ask your doctor to write you a prescription to take to a compounding pharmacy. There the pharmacist can compound a natural estriol cream (the weakest estrogen). You can place about ¼ teaspoon directly into the vagina two to three times per week. I advise that you do this in addition to using your regular natural hormone.

A phytoestrogen/progesterone cream called Ostaderm V is a wonderful product, and I give it to all of my patients with vaginal dryness (except those with a history of breast or repro-ductive cancer). It works quite rapidly to increase moisture and elasticity in vaginal tissues. Once tissue health is restored, you can use it about three to four days each month to main-tain moisture. Ostaderm V is currently available only through naturopathic physicians. I have listed a source of Ostaderm V for you in the back of the book.

For women who have had a history of breast or reproductive

cancer—for whom any form of estrogen is contraindicated—natural progesterone may be inserted into the vagina. Use ¼ to ½ teaspoon once daily or as needed, applied with your fingertips. It is not necessary to try to place it deep within the vagina, as your vaginal tissues will absorb it at the entrance.

Although I always recommend Ostaderm V or natural estriol cream for women who have no history of cancer, I have a great number of patients who cannot use estrogen products due to a past history of breast or uterine cancer. I have been extremely gratified to observe that, for many, their vaginal tissue has returned to a moist and resilient state after about four months of progesterone use (daily transdermal use with two to three intravaginal applications per week). The mechanism behind this may be that the natural progesterone works to sensitize vaginal tissue receptors to the lower levels of estrogen in menopausal women.

In most cases of vaginal dryness that I have treated, it takes about four weeks of natural hormone therapy before the vaginal tissue begins to improve.

OTHER REMEDIES FOR VAGINAL DRYNESS

While you are waiting for the natural hormone cream to restore some moisture to your vagina (and even afterward), there are several other remedies for your dryness.

1. Take vitamin E (natural please, no synthetic forms). You should take it orally every day because it is such a powerful nutrient, particularly as protection against heart disease and heart attacks. However, for vaginal dryness it will be much more effective to puncture a capsule and insert it into the vagina. This little tip has been a godsend according to many of my patients.

2. Include essential fatty acids (EFAs) in your diet and/or take them as a supplement. Essential fatty acids help nourish the vaginal tissue mucosa. They are also a key to the body's natural hormone production, and thus they help to increase hormone levels after menopause. Make sure you get Omega-6 (found in evening

primrose oil and borage oil) and Omega-3 (found in fish and flax). The best source is salmon, but halibut, mackerel, tuna and swordfish are also excellent sources. Omega-6 is also known as linoleic acid. (Omega-9 is olive oil.) Because it is difficult to eat enough fish to obtain enough of these vital nutrients, you may wish to supplement with a capsule. Products are available that conveniently combine the 3, 6 and 9 fatty acids.

3. I'll say it again—have regular intercourse. This increases blood flow to the vagina and helps to keep tissues strong and healthy.

4. Use a water-soluble lubricant before or during inter-course. This will not thicken the vaginal tissues like estrogen, but will provide some relief. Some good ones are Astroglide and AquaLub. Never use products containing petroleum jelly, mineral oil or baby oil. Avoid them because they are not healthy for vaginal walls. They are difficult for the body to absorb or discharge and can cause allergic reactions.

5. There is also a product called Replens that is long last-ing, with a single application lasting up to seventy-two hours. Studies have shown that Replens favorably low-ers the vaginal pH and also increases vaginal secre-tions. The downside is that it is rather expensive.

DRY VULVA

Some women suffer from severe dryness and irritation of the vulva, which is the external area of the vagina. As we age, the skin in this area can become thin. If you are using natural estrogen cream for vaginal dryness, you can rub some on the vulva area as well.

However, there is a product that I have found to be extremely effective for dry vulva called Vital Vulva. It is for-mulated precisely for this problem and contains wild yam, vitex (chasteberry) and vitamin E oil. Because it is in a salve

103

form, it is extremely lubricating. It is specifically designed to promote healing and protect this very sensitive area. Used outwardly, it will relieve painful dryness. It is also wonderful as a lubricant and safe for use during intercourse.

Vital Vulva also contains essential oils and flower essence, so it is excellent for masking odor in any woman who has a leakage problem. It is made by Moon Maid Botanicals.

Of course, the use of soap should be minimal, as it will simply make matters worse. When you do need to use soap, use baby bath soap, and even then dilute it. Rinse liberally. It is fine to simply use water and a very soft cloth or brand of tissue. This delicate area does not need to be scrubbed with strong cleansers. Also, choose cotton underwear only.

PAINFUL INTERCOURSE

There are several reasons for painful intercourse. As you can imagine, this condition has a powerful, negative effect on libido. Normally the walls of the vagina are very elastic, marvelously able not only to accept the husband's penis during intercourse, but also flexible enough to allow stretching and the safe passage of a baby during childbirth. Loss of normal elasticity can cause the vaginal opening to narrow, making sex more difficult and painful.

Tears in the opening of the vagina or small cuts (fissures) inside the vagina usually cause very sharp and specific pain, which helps a woman pinpoint the exact spot that hurts when touched or thrust against. The vagina's moist environment, coupled with continued sexual activity, causes slow healing of fissures and tears. These should be treated immediately.

If deep sexual thrusting causes a sharp, stabbing pain, it is most commonly due to a tipped or retroverted uterus, which allows the cervix to be thrust against during deep thrusting. Since the cervix is sensitive to pain, each thrust produces a sharp, stabbing pain.

For immediate relief, shift positions slightly or place a small pillow or folded towel under the women's upper buttocks if she is in the underneath position.

Other internal pathologies, such as endometriosis, ovarian

cysts or pelvic inflammatory disease also can cause pain upon thrusting. For these and other types of female pain, talk first to your husband, then to your doctor. Do not allow pain to continue. Sexual activity regularly associated with pain is not the norm, and you should seek help to get the condition treated and cured. Some yeast infections such as trichomonas or gardnerella can cause severe inflammation and soreness and will not respond to over-the-counter medications. They should be diagnosed and treated by a physician.

GENERAL OBSERVATIONS

Occasional painful intercourse is normal. After several strokes, discomfort usually subsides.

- Learn to relax vaginal muscles around the vaginal opening, which can spasm (vaginimus) when touched by the penis. This involuntary reflex can be cured by relaxing consciously.

- Endometriosis (uterine tissue growing outside the uterus and into the pelvic cavity) can cause pain when a woman has intercourse just prior to her menstrual period.

- The uterus may be more sensitive as a woman nears her monthly period.

- Shallow, gentle thrusting is more pleasurable for many women after menopause.

- Utilize sexual positions that allow the woman to "take charge" of penetration and depth and help her to avoid pain.

CAUTION: After the reason for the pain is gone, you may find yourself pulling away or tightening up to avoid the painful sensation—a conditioned response you need to identify and consciously break by using relaxation techniques and allowing sexual pleasure to return.

CYSTITIS/URINARY TRACT INFECTIONS

Estrogen is very vital to the health of the woman's urinary tract. Estrogen receptors are found in the bladder and the lower urinary tract.

After menopause, hormonal deficiency causes thinning of

105

the urogenital system, and many women become very susceptible to urinary tract infections.

It would probably be very difficult for a man to know how agonizing the symptoms of a bladder infection can be. The pain is like a flame in the urinary tract. There is also back pain, and the woman feels as if she has to urinate constantly, but cannot pass the urine. In my practice I have seen women doubled over in pain and agony with cystitis.

Causes are related to bacteria that have ascended the urethra. Treatment involves a course of antibiotics. During the acute phase, sex will probably be next to impossible due to the pain. If you do try, be sure to use lubrication. To prevent recurrences, always urinate sometime shortly after intercourse, and always be sure to wipe your perineum from front to back using unscented white toilet paper.

Natural hormone cream applied to the vaginal area will help prevent this condition. The estrogen absorbs through the vaginal wall and reaches the urethra where it works to keep the tissue healthy and infection-resistant.

106

For temporary relief of a urinary tract infection, try this herbal remedy of parsley tea: Take two bunches of regular parsley. Boil in 3–4 inches of water for twenty minutes. Let cool, then drink the tea.

It is soothing to the bladder!

"NOT TONIGHT, DEAR, I HAVE A HEADACHE"

How many men have heard this refrain from their wives, and how many have actually believed it? Well, gentlemen, the chances are very likely that you were not being rejected, that she really did have a headache. The changes in estrogen levels that take place in a woman's body during perimenopause, menopause and premenstrually can trigger headaches and/or affect the frequency of headaches. Women who have migraine headaches just prior to their menstrual cycle are usually estrogen dominant, because estrogen causes blood vessels to dilate. These enlarged vessels are believed to be the cause of most migraines.

The good news is that natural progesterone helps

counteract the dilation of blood vessels and restores them to normal. If you consistently have premenstrual headaches, use natural progesterone during the ten days prior to your period each month to restore hormonal balance. My patients have reported that in three to four months the headaches completely disappear.

If you are having a migraine headache, apply ¼ to ½ teaspoon of progesterone cream immediately, and then every three hours until your symptoms have subsided. You can experiment with the dosage to find what works for you.

Many women who are placed on synthetic hormones such as Premarin report increased incidence of headaches. Once again, this is probably related to estrogen dominance. Natural progesterone can be used to restore balance.

I would like to say that I strongly advise you against using this excuse if you truly do not have a headache. Instead, be honest with your husband if you don't want to have sex. Most women tell me that they end up feeling very guilty when they use the "headache excuse," almost as if they have "defrauded" their husbands. Satan will use that guilt as a weapon against you to come between you and your spouse. Remember, your goal is to protect and nourish your sexual life with your husband, and there is no room in godly intimacy for even "little white lies." Be honest with your husband because we are promised that we will reap what we sow, both good and bad.

Remember: The Bible indicates that it actually is a form of fraud when we (both men and women) refuse to give physical pleasure and satisfaction to our mate. (See 1 Corinthians 7:3–5.)

CHAPTER 8

Life
After Hysterectomy

Why do so many women dread the idea of having an unhealthy uterus surgically removed? What exactly do they fear? Sometimes other women who have experienced a hysterectomy describe post-op depression followed by months of libido loss. Reports like that can lead a woman to fears that libido loss or depression could become permanent. Other women's experiences with childbirth, menopause and hysterectomy can often be highly colored by their own imaginations and expectations. Take such well-meaning advice with several grains of salt. None of these things have to happen with you if you absolutely must have a hysterectomy due to a serious medical attention.

Let me take you back to my medical files:

> My patient Elinor had all the usual trepidation about the hysterectomy she had been told by her surgeon she needed to have. All else had been tried, and it was now a medical necessity. How much would this surgery detract from her body? Would she lose her allure or her sexual desire? Would she become less feminine? Could she still satisfy her husband sexually?
>
> Obviously, Elinor needed some facts. I explained

that her uterus, with no pregnancy to enlarge it, actually was a rather small organ the size of her fist. Losing it would not make her feel "empty." I also advised her that she should not gain weight or lose her good looks. The surgery should affect neither her sexual desires toward her husband nor her ability to please him.

Like Elinor, if you are facing a hysterectomy and wonder exactly how it may affect you, ask your doctor. Even so, I'd advise you not to take every generalization he or she offers as gospel. One surgeon told my patient Sandra that she would be hospitalized at least seven days, would be given pain medication and fed intravenously for a few days. After that, she would have to be weaned off some heavy drugs. She could possibly be back to normal in about six weeks.

However, three days after surgery, Sandra's surgical incision was completely healed, so she was discharged from the hospital. She had received no pain medications and no IVs, and normal meals had been permitted. Sandra walked quite often during her three-day hospital stay and remained completely pain free. Her recovery, according to her doctor, was astoundingly rapid and uncomplicated.

In my experience, although the surgery itself may be somewhat traumatic, within several months following the surgery, most women I saw reported that they were just about totally recovered. Although some women worry excessively about the aftereffects, especially depression, most of the post-hysterectomy patients I have met or treated were pleased—probably about 90 percent of them—and almost as many said that they would encourage a friend who needed to have the procedure. Only a very few said they were depressed once their healing was complete.

I have had patients who have gone immediately on to natural hormones following their surgery tell me that their energy has increased, their mood improved, and there has been little or no adverse effect on their sexual desire and responses.

YOUR EXPECTATIONS
AFFECT THE OUTCOME

Your approach to a hysterectomy procedure plays a big role in how you will feel after it. If you expect your femininity to decline, that your husband will find you less desirable, or even "old," or that your own sexual desires will vanish, you likely may become depressed and actually have sexual difficulties following the surgery.

Approach hysterectomy as a positive answer to such uncomfortable symptoms as dysfunctional and heavy bleeding, urinary incontinence or painful intercourse, which you may have been suffering due to your severe medical problem. If you do so, you are likely to be pleased after the operation. Natural hormone replacement can help keep your sexual desire undiminished.

If you have had a hysterectomy and now have doubts about whether it was the right thing to do, do not allow your negative thoughts to depress you. Look on the positive side, and remember that once your uterus and ovaries have been removed, you will never have to worry about ovarian or uterine cancer. OK, it's done—one less thing to fear and think about. Don't look back and allow it to depress you.

Husbands, your encouragement plays a big part in how well your wife does following this surgery. Your reassurances about her sex appeal and your future lovemaking with her make this just one more excellent opportunity for the two of you to bond, support and encourage one another. Many women have reported that the intimacy that transpires after she and her spouse go through a major surgery together leads to even better sexual expression.

INTERCOURSE
IMMEDIATELY AFTER HYSTERECTOMY

It is natural to have a little apprehension and even some soreness when you first resume intercourse following surgery. Your apprehension may even cause a lack of vaginal lubrication and some involuntary flinching of your vaginal opening.

However, your labia and clitoris were not affected by the surgery. They should not be tender, and you should enjoy clitoral stimulation, which, in turn, will relax and help arouse you. If those "first-time feelings" of anxiety cause you not to lubricate, it is best to use a sexual lubricant, but please, no petroleum products, which can have a backlash of dryness.

Your husband can help to ease your apprehensions and help you to resume lovemaking in a gentle, gradual fashion. Suggest that he gently caress your clitoris, which will help your natural lubricant to return. The pleasurable feelings should help restore your sexual confidence.

The next step is to guide first your husband's finger, then his penis, into your vagina in a slow, controlled way. Ask him not to thrust until you are sure you are comfortable. (By this time you may find yourself reassuring him.)

When you feel comfortable and secure, the usual desires begin to return. You are in control, able to enjoy the feeling of his penis in your vagina, and you then can choose to continue from that point into full intercourse. The experience should reassure both you and your husband. Should there be any discomfort or pain despite all your precautions, of course consult your gynecologist.

111

If lack of vaginal lubrication occurs after hysterectomy, it should be only a temporary problem. If your ovaries were removed, however, estrogen loss can cause a lasting decrease in lubrication. You can use a sexual lubricant for immediate relief, but you should go on a treatment program of natural hormones to maintain hormone balance, especially if your ovaries were removed.

I advise patients to use a natural hormone therapy of phytoestrogen and phytoprogesterone for three weeks of the month. I suggest Menopause Relief Cream. (Remember, a hysterectomy is considered surgical menopause.) This will restore vaginal lubrication and maintain your vaginal tissue's health as well as supplement your body with the progesterone and estrogen that are normally made by your ovaries.

SEXUAL DESIRE AND FULFILLMENT

About 75 percent of women discover their level of desire is unaffected by a hysterectomy. Some 20 percent, in fact, say they have more desire after the procedure—probably because the surgery corrected previous sexual discomfort or other gynecological problems.

Those who report a decrease in desire, however, usually had their ovaries removed as well as the uterus. The ovaries produce most of a women's testosterone, which is the most active androgen. Removal of the ovaries may thus cause a fall in testosterone levels, which may produce a loss of sexual desire because of an imbalance of the estrogen-progesterone-testosterone ratio. This can be corrected by natural hormones and natural testosterone products as well as a libido-enhancing androstenedione spray, discussed in chapter thirteen.

Will I enjoy intercourse as I did before? Will I be able to climax? These often become the two big questions for women who enjoy lovemaking and want it to continue. The answer is yes and yes. Those women who formerly experienced orgasm deep within the pelvis, however, may experience difficulty in achieving orgasm, since the cervix and uterus have been removed. The ability to achieve orgasm is not gone, but simply requires relearning via clitoral stimulation, which many consider an even more intense experience.

Your sexual health and desire need not suffer after a hysterectomy. In fact, there is a chance that your level of desire may actually rise to new heights and sexual intercourse become even more fulfilling. There is no reason to let diminished hormone levels dictate your sex life when there are natural treatments available today to free you from the necessity of taking synthetic hormones, which can actually diminish desire.

Do not accept a prescription for estrogen only, simply because you do not have ovaries. This will increase your risk of breast cancer dramatically. Even if your ovaries are spared, begin a regimen of natural hormones. Within two to three years after a hysterectomy, most ovarian function has ceased, and the ovaries are no longer producing hormones.

SOME THOUGHTS ON
MIDLIFE MEDICAL ISSUES

Hormones, menopause and perhaps a hysterectomy may seem like quite a bit to deal with during this time of a woman's life. The truth is, menopause and hormonal changes are normal, and a hysterectomy often corrects conditions that affect your sexual confidence and health.

I want to assure you that whatever changes may occur in your body during your forties and fifties, you should never assume you are sexually changed. Don't get into a mind-set that tries to convince you sex is too much trouble and no longer necessary or that you just "aren't up to it any more."

These years can be some of the happiest, sexiest, most rewarding times in your life! If there is anything about your body or in your thinking that tells you otherwise, I urge you to consult a physician or other therapist and learn the facts. As you know by this time, I believe in natural hormones and certain herbal supplements that can enhance your body's ability to maintain hormonal stability, a strong sex drive, high energy and a general sense of well-being.

Decide to maximize midlife in every way possible. If you have never done it before, begin to nurture yourself with more rest, relaxation, exercise, vitamin supplements, dates with your husband or anything else that pumps life up a notch. Make a date with your nutritionist, masseur or hairdresser. If you feel life is missing something, go ocean cruising or ballroom dancing. Take up tennis or anything else you've always wanted to do.

Get those hormones going, and you'll discover new worlds. They may include college classes, tea parties, resuming flirting with your husband and arranging secret meetings for lunches or weekends. Or you may want to just kick back and relax, journal, visit friends or enjoy your family. Whatever it is, don't let one minute of your precious life slip away. You are still a girl, and always will be!

Rx: God created you a feminine soul. Enjoy it!

113

CHAPTER 9

Men at Midlife

Typically, men at midlife certainly don't forget about sex, and they don't go crazy. Happily married middle-aged men generally feel understood by their wives and satisfied with marriage. This stage of life, most agree, offers some rare rewards and experiences.

Around the age of fifty-five, most men will begin to notice some of the following physical and psychological changes: decrease in muscle strength and endurance, becoming more easily fatigued, some aches in joints and muscles, changes in skin tone and perhaps some short-term memory loss or insomnia. Some men panic at these signs, but overall they are normal and not a reason for panic or depression. Most active men can keep going at the same old pace, and those who do it best are those who have a positive and proactive attitude about keeping their bodies healthy.

After the age of forty or so, some reduction in sex drive may occur in men, although each man is different and his body will have a different timetable. He may be in his fifties or well into his eighties before his interest in sex lessens. Most men do better when they recognize that this is a universal phenomenon and not their own separate problem. You may not feel the same urgency to have sex as often as you did when you were younger.

However, I will advise you that the more active you stay sexually as you age, the more sex your body will want—the same thing I have been telling the women. The firmness of your erections may diminish, but the level of pleasure you are capable of giving your wife has probably increased.

Your climaxes may undergo some changes—you may not climax as easily or as often as you used to. This may be frightening if you look upon this as a sign of impotence. It is NOT. Studies have shown that most men over sixty require only one to two climaxes a week to feel completely satisfied. Most women actually enjoy this time in their husband's life because lovemaking may last longer and the entire experience may feel more sensual and intimate.

When you engage in sexual intercourse it is best not to push yourself to have a climax. Relax. Enjoy the loving feelings. The positive side of this effect of aging is that you can enjoy intercourse for longer periods of time as your body is not as focused on the need for ejaculation. Remember, your wife requires a longer period of stimulation for full arousal and orgasm. Once a man ages, it is often a very satisfying time for her sexually. If you do not manage to ejaculate every time, it is important to remember that there is probably nothing wrong. Also, the force of ejaculation may have diminished.

What is the cause of these changes? The entire male sexual system is very complex, but is fueled primarily by the male hormone testosterone, which is needed in adequate amounts to keep the system working without error. You may also have some hardening of the arteries in the vessels that supply the blood flow to the penis. A diminished blood supply affects the speed at which your erection occurs. Also the effects of aging on the venous system may cause some blood to leak back out of the penis, which affects the firmness of the erection. All of these changes are compatible with aging and are within normal limits.

There are many natural substances that can be used to enhance a man's sexual function at this time of life, and I have included them in a special section in chapter thirteen. They include some natural supplements as well as a libido-enhancing androstenedione spray.

115

MEN'S PROBLEMS

Though the number of women in their forties and fifties who experience a total loss of libido is high, it is highly unusual for men in those decades to lose it completely. Rather, it is more likely that men will begin to experience premature ejaculation or erectile difficulty than total inability to perform.

A man's erection difficulties can occur at various moments during sexual intercourse. There may be no erection at all. He may lose his erection during the sex act, at the point of penetration or during the act of thrusting. Though none of these situations are necessarily permanent, almost invariably the husband will greet the moment with some degree of dismay or even begin to dread making love to his wife.

These feelings may be misplaced. Even men who deal with some severe medical problems and whose doctors inform them that their prescribed medication will cause impotency should accept that advice with some skepticism. The fact that these drugs cause impotency in some men does not predict the same outcome for all. Further, the idea itself can become a self-fulfilling prophecy.

IMPOTENCY PROBLEMS OR ERECTILE DYSFUNCTION

The term *impotence* has traditionally been used to describe a condition in which a man cannot achieve and maintain an erection that is sufficient to permit intercourse. The term *erectile dysfunction* is more precise and was coined in 1992 during a National Health Institute Consensus Development Conference on Impotence. It is commonly referred to as "E.D." The panel defined *E.D.* as "the inability to attain and maintain an erection sufficient to permit satisfactory intercourse at least 75 percent of the time."

It has been estimated that 26 percent of men over forty-five suffer moderate or severe erectile dysfunction. Age alone is not the cause of E.D. Men in their eighties are able to have erections. In older men, though, physical illness usually underlies E.D.

In some men, especially younger men between thirty and

fifty years of age, psychological factors such as depression, stress and performance anxiety are more likely to be the culprit. However, at any age a number of things can interrupt the delicate balance inherent in a man's sexual process. Anger toward his wife, guilt, depression, marital health and the state of the relationships between individuals in the marriage can be a cause of erectile dysfunction.

As most physicians will testify, however, remarkably few men have much understanding about the cause and treatments for E.D. A majority of men probably do not seek help. Part of this may be the old "head-in-the-sand" or "ostrich" approach—ignore it, and it will go away.

It won't. Some men faced with episodes of impotency suffer fear, embarrassment and general denial. Others blame their wives. Too few do the sensible thing—first consult their physician to check for possible underlying causes of E.D.

This is absolutely your best course of action. Erectile dysfunction can definitely be related to poor health. Approximately 90 percent of all cases are estimated to be due to an organic or physiological (related to the body) condition. Proper diagnosis is vital, because the next step is to correct any underlying organic factor in order to restore sexual function. In many cases a thorough physical, vascular or neurological exam, medical history or laboratory tests can lead to a diagnosis. In others, a simple noninvasive test may reveal the source of E.D. The diagnosis and testing is best performed by a urologist.

117

WHAT CAUSES E.D.?

The most common cause is a reduction in the blood flow to the penis. A man's erection is a vascular response to sexual stimulation. Vascular disease may be due to hypertension or heart disease. Diabetes can cause damage to nerves responsible for the erection reflex. Other causes include medications, high cholesterol, prostate disorders, Parkinson's disease and multiple sclerosis. A lack of testosterone can be a cause, but certainly is not the cause of all E.D. Beta-blocker medications and antihypertensive medications are two of the worst culprits in the drug category. High levels of stress, poor diet (too much sugar and high amounts of caffeine, in particular) and alcohol consumption can also increase the incidence of erectile dysfunction. Smoking lowers vascular capacities, so it is not surprising that studies show that smokers are twice as likely to develop E.D. as non-smokers.

> FACT: Less than 10 percent of the estimated 30 million men in the United States with E.D. ever seek medical help.[1]

The remainder of men either assume that nothing can be done or are too embarrassed to talk about it, even to a physician. Our culture tends to treat sex as something for the young, and it is often thought of as unseemly in older men.

The good news is that a poor health picture almost always can be changed for the better. And even if one's condition does not clear up completely, a good sex life need not be lost forever. In fact, E.D. can serve as a valuable signal that a man's health needs upgrading—a far more sensible and conservative approach than attempting to find a quick fix, medically prescribed or otherwise, such as Viagra with its life-threatening side effects.

The average woman's life expectancy at this point in history is six years longer than that of her husband. Therefore I strongly advocate that wives urge their husbands to make good personal health a top priority, so men will learn how to live as long as their mates.

Wives, persuade your husband to visit his doctor! In a matter-of-fact way, without warning, nagging or expressing apprehension, schedule an appointment for your husband with his physician. Chances are he needs a checkup anyway. Gently remind him to be sure to tell his doctor about his sexual problem, since his physician may not ask.

Receiving a good medical verdict does something wonderful for clearing up a man's fears and worries and encouraging him that, in fact, his sexual lapses were temporary. But if he is dealing with type II diabetes, a prostate problem or any other serious physical disorder, you need to know it now.

Researchers believe there will be a million new cases of E.D.

each year as baby boomers age—the group that encompasses some seventy-six million Americans born between 1946 and 1964. While boomer women want to continue to maintain active sex lives, they will experience difficulty as their husbands suffer health problems that could lead to impotency. The answer is obvious—head off poor health in your husband.

The smart wife—one too smart to nag her husband about his health—learns to use whatever strategy she needs to make his good health (and her own) a priority. One couple I know sets aside two to five days a year to "go through the clinic" together in their hometown, reviewing each other's medical reports and conferring with each other's physicians. Such "preventive maintenance" has become a ritual, bringing them closer in their marriage, with no medical secrets between them. If future problems should strike, each has a good understanding of the other's health picture and can participate in their partner's healing.

> It would be interesting to know how many sexual problems men could avoid if they considered their own good health scores as important as their football or golf scores!

119

YOUR DOCTOR AND YOUR E.D.

If a man can produce an erection by a particular lovemaking technique, awaken with a morning erection or achieve erection by masturbation, he probably does not need to see a doctor—unless continuing problems make him suspect the possibility of some underlying illness. It is definitely time to consult a doctor if he cannot achieve erection at all, or if E.D. is becoming noticeably worse.

Should the physician dismiss your husband's complaints by saying something like "It's all in your head," or writes a psychiatric referral without first conducting a physical exam, get yourself to another doctor who will examine him.

Use the following guide to be certain you receive a complete and thorough examination and assessment:

1. Describe the situation in detail: how long the problem has existed, when and how it began, whether the

onset was gradual or sudden and whether or not it ever improves. Recall what was going on in your life when E.D. began. How has the problem affected you and your relationship?

2. Review your medical history. Do you or your family have a history of diabetes, heart disease, high blood pressure, stroke, sickle-cell anemia, prostate problems or other major illnesses? Are you exposed to toxic substances at work? Have you had any other genital health problems? An endocrine system disorder? Have you ever suffered a serious back or spinal injury? Do you smoke?

3. Never visit your doctor for an erection problem without taking all your prescription medications with you. List all the over-the-counter drugs you use. Discuss any combination drug taking, or the amount of alcohol you use. Combinations of drugs, or alcohol-plus-drugs, can create serious side effects. In fact, drugs of all types are a leading cause of non-erection.

4. Have your blood pressure checked. Even young men these days discover some seriously elevated pressure readings. High blood pressure is associated with stress, diabetes, arteriosclerosis and other conditions that contribute to non-erection.

5. Get a complete physical, including a digital examination of the prostate gland and PSA test, which should be a yearly event.

OPTIONS FOR TREATING E.D.

The majority of cases of E.D. are not cases of permanent impotence. As we have discussed, it is normal for men to experience occasional problems. But if a man often cannot maintain an erection long enough to have intercourse, he should visit his doctor and seek help for his condition.

However, even if a man does receive a diagnosis of severe E.D., there has been some very advanced research into treatment. Some of the latest options available to men with erectile dysfunction include:

- A vacuum pump that draws blood into the penis, producing an erection. An elastic band is placed at the base of the penis to hold the blood in. As long as you remove the band after thirty minutes, this device is quite safe.

- Inflatable penile implants have been implanted in tens of thousands of men who usually express great satisfaction with the results. Such procedures no longer are considered experimental, and the various implant models have good success rates. Some 75 percent of men who have elected to receive penile implants are between the ages of forty and seventy, although men in their eighties and a few in their twenties have received them.

- One form of implant involves surgically placing two cylinders (comparable to the corpora cavernosa) in the penis and attaching them to a reservoir of liquid placed within the abdomen. A pump is inserted in the scrotum, which pushes the liquid into the cylinders and produces an erection.

- Injections of a drug called alprostadil, sold as Caverject or Edex. The injections are self-administered and produce erections quite rapidly. They last approximately one hour.

- A variation on the injection in which a pellet of alprostadil is inserted into the tip of the penis with an applicator.

WHAT ABOUT VIAGRA?

Viagra, the male sex drug introduced in 1998, unfortunately has not lived up to men's (and women's) expectations. Viagra has been found effective in helping men to have erections, but it does not affect libido. There are some strong side effects, too.

Viagra does not cause an erection; that part is up to you and your wife. What it does is increase blood flow to the penis, so that when a man is sexually aroused he can get and keep an erection. When the sexual encounter is over, the erection goes away. However, Viagra carries many grave side effects. For men with heart disease, in fact, Viagra can prove fatal.

121

You absolutely should not take Viagra if you are on certain medications, specifically nitrate drugs like nitrogylerine. This combination can make your blood pressure suddenly drop to unsafe levels. (Nitrates are found in many prescription medications that are used to treat angina.) Viagra has been known to cause heart attacks and also strokes in men.

I would be very reluctant to see anyone I loved taking Viagra. Instead there are natural remedies that we can try. For the most part, the "natural" substances include herbs that improve hormone production and vascular function. They include L-arginine and VIP Gel, which is a topical source for the production of nitric oxide, the principle behind Viagra. We will discuss these herbal and natural alternatives further in chapter thirteen.

DETERMINING THE CAUSE: IT MAY BE SUBTLE OR COMPLEX

Back to my medical files:

It took a little detective work, but forty-eight-year-old Albert finally discovered an all-too-common reason for his impotency.

When he asked his doctor for a prescription to help him with his job-related stress (Al worked as a sales executive on a job with long hours, high pressure to achieve quotas and regular travel throughout the United States), his doctor failed to mention that there might be E.D. consequences from taking the drug.

Faithful to his doctor's advice, Albert meanwhile cut back on his work hours, resumed playing golf, conscientiously attempted to lower his stress levels and took his medication. Ensuing non-erection problems, however, created even more worry and stress. This caused his physician to prescribe even stronger antidepressant medication, which created even more serious erection problems, plus additional anxiety and depression.

At last, when Al decided he had had enough of his prescribed drug anti-anxiety routine, he slowly weaned himself away from the treatment with his physician's help. After that, Albert eventually found that his erectile problems had resolved.

PREMATURE EJACULATION

When ejaculation occurs before the man wishes it to happen, the condition is described medically as "inhibition of orgasmic control."

William H. Masters and Virginia E. Johnson, in their book *Human Sexual Inadequacy,* defined the condition as the inability of the man to "control his ejaculatory process for a sufficient length of time during intravaginal containment to satisfy his partner in at least 50 percent of their coital connections."[2]

In layman's terms, it means that a man, once sexually aroused, arrives at orgasm very quickly. Some men ejaculate prior to entering the wife's vagina, while others ejaculate only seconds after entry. Most men and women who complain about the problem say that it causes him to be unable to last more than one or two minutes after penetration. The problem is, that is not enough time for him to satisfy his wife. The aggravation of repeated premature ejaculation affects both husband and wife. Inability to maintain sexual control may make a man feel humiliated and doubt himself as a sexual partner. His wife eventually may experience enough sexual frustration due to his "ineptness" that she becomes angry, disinterested or loses confidence in herself as a partner. It is also true that many married men have bodies long conditioned to quick sexual response, perhaps because they feel this is "good enough sex." Their problems may be that they focus not on good feelings and pleasure during sex, but on release alone.

Often an explanation of the mechanics of premature ejaculation and simple advice can alleviate or even cure the problem. There is a technique called the "squeeze" technique that has been universally used to help men control their early ejaculation.

SQUEEZE TECHNIQUE

Men who deal with premature ejaculation can use the following technique to learn to control the timing of their ejaculation. It is called the squeeze technique.

123

The squeeze technique works most efficiently when a man has a full erection but before he is close to "the point of no return." Men, once there is a full erection, your wife should grasp your penis in the following way: Her thumb should be on the underside of the coronal ridge and her forefinger above and middle finger below the coronal ridge on the upper side of your penis. She should squeeze firmly for about ten seconds.

Wives: Do not squeeze too hard, and do not use your fingernails.

Men: This may or may not result in the loss of your erection. Do not worry if it does; just enjoy your wife's touch and revel in it.

Wives: Move your attention to other parts of his body, caressing him in a more general way. Then move back to penile stimulation. Once he is fully erect, apply the squeeze again.

Men: Enjoy the arousal, but do not physically pursue ejaculation. Learn to build and enjoy sexual arousal without ejaculation. If premature ejaculation occurs, do not be disheartened; just be more aware that your wife must apply the squeeze a little sooner.

Wives: The next step is to manually stimulate your husband to ejaculation. Do not rush. Build it up in intensity, apply the squeeze, back off, stimulate, squeeze, back off.

Men: Focus on and enjoy the penile stimulation. When you do ejaculate, hold your wife and delight in the new level of control you have achieved, no matter how small.

Repeat this procedure until you feel confident (or somewhat confident) that ejaculation will occur only when you both decide it will.

Next, move on to intravaginal intercourse. Once your wife applies the last squeeze, she should move to the top position and guide your penis into her vagina. Lie quietly without moving. If your penis gets flaccid, she will stimulate you back to erection. Do not get anxious. Let your wife control this exercise.

Wives: Begin to move gently. If he signals to you that he is about to ejaculate too quickly, move off and apply the squeeze.

Repeat this exercise. You will gradually achieve a higher level of awareness of your body's sensations as you approach orgasm and will achieve a greater level of control over ejaculation. Work up to periods of thrusting that equal five to ten minutes. Do not be worried about ejaculating after this amount of thrusting. This is normal and is how your body is designed.

Finally, if you have come this far in the process and your wife has not achieved an orgasm, and if you and she desire, you can manually stimulate her for her further pleasure. Or even better, I recommend bringing your wife to a climax first before you penetrate. That way she has been satisfied, her endorphins have surged, and she will feel great—not be left hurt, angry or feeling unloved.

PROSTATE PROBLEMS

Keeping the prostate healthy is vital to sexual function and to prevent erectile dysfunction related to prostate problems. Unfortunately prostate disorders are extremely common among American men. As men age, the prostate gland can begin to enlarge. More than half of all men in their sixties experience this condition. An enlarged prostate can choke the urine tube, causing such problems as frequent, urgent urination, a weak urine stream, leaking or dribbling and incontinence.

BPH

The condition known as *benign prostate hypertrophy* (BPH) simply means enlargement of the glandular, fibrous and muscular tissue inside the prostate capsule. It does not spread elsewhere, is not invasive and is not cancer.

Though BPH presents no danger in itself, it can obstruct the urinary passage and even eventually block urine flow. It can cause painful urination, and small amounts of blood may appear in a man's urine or ejaculate. Other symptoms are increased urinary frequency, nighttime awakening with the feeling of needing to urinate and reduction in the force of the stream of urine.

Despite such signs, which may seem alarming to the man with BPH, it usually does not interfere with sexual activity, except perhaps for a slight decrease in ejaculation.

Some doctors believe zinc deficiency may be a factor in causing BPH. The mineral zinc is often called "the man's mineral"; it is the most important nutrient of the prostate gland and an important element in seminal fluid. Older men tend to develop zinc deficiency. Some studies have shown that getting sufficient zinc relieves BPH. Researchers have said that supplementary doses of zinc of 50 milligrams per day may help prevent or reverse prostate enlargement.

The usual treatment for BPH is a drug called Proscar. However, it takes about six months before any improvement is usually noted, and it does not work for about 50 percent of patients. Clinical trials have shown that an herbal remedy known as saw palmetto, or *serenoa repens,* is much more effective without associated side effects. Saw palmetto has been shown to be effective in almost 90 percent of patients within about four to six weeks. It is natural and is dramatically less expensive. See chapter thirteen for a discussion of saw palmetto.

Another natural remedy for BPH is to eat ¼ to ½ cup of pumpkin seeds daily. Pumpkin seeds are high in zinc and essential fatty acids, which appear to have a positive affect on BPH.

Prostate infection (prostatitis) occurs commonly in men of every age. In an acute onset, it causes fever, chills, nausea, vomiting, inability to begin urination or painful, burning sensations during urination and sometimes penile discharge. Obviously these symptoms are serious and require a doctor's attention. The usual treatment is a course of antibiotics.

Chronic recurring prostatitis can become frustrating for doctor and patient alike, since symptoms are often vague but uncomfortable—low back pain, aching in the area between the scrotum and rectum and burning feelings with urination. These symptoms may disappear for a while, then recur.

For good genital health, as well as overall good health, BPH and prostatitis must be addressed promptly and treated as soon as possible. Once treated, they should cause no permanent effect on one's sex life.

P ROSTATE CANCER

Prostate cancer is slow growing and often easy for a man to ignore. In recent years it has become a high-profile medical issue as various male celebrities have undergone successful prostate cancer treatments and alerted the nation to the need for research that can lead to a cure.

This publicity has encouraged thousands of men to have their prostates checked who otherwise would not have done so. This is a huge breakthrough for men's health!

The prostate-specific antigen (PSA) test is a blood test, is easy to take and offers relatively accurate results. That test, together with a digital examination of the prostate gland, should be taken once a year after a man reaches the age of fifty to assure early diagnosis and treatment. Prostate cancer treatments still pose some possibility of future impotence or incontinence, but techniques are being studied that may render these aftereffects obsolete.

There is a natural herbal treatment for prostate cancer that is called PC SPES. It is named for prostate cancer (PC) and the Latin word for hope (SPES). It is a blend of eight Chinese herbs and has been found in clinical studies to suppress the growth of cancer cells in the prostate.

127

Studies have been published in two well-known medical journals, including the October 2000 issue of the *Journal of Urology,* and reported in major newspapers all over the country stating that PC SPES shows striking results in treating patients with advanced prostate cancer. It has also been shown that it could lower prostate-specific antigen levels in most men with prostate cancer.[3] There are potential side effects, including breast enlargement and an increase in the risk of blood clots in the legs. It may also decrease sexual desire. PC SPES is available from many urologists, and although it is very expensive (between $200–$400 per month depending on dosage), it may be the answer for many men in the future.

> Protect your sexual health and future sexual drive by having a prostate examination and PSA test every year if you

are over the age of fifty. Give yourself and your partner that extra peace of mind.

MIDLIFE RENEWAL

I will say it one more time: Sexual problems are never just physical. As any physician knows, we humans indeed are "fearfully and wonderfully made." In discussing so many of the common sexual problems males can encounter, we have all but overlooked perhaps the most potent weapon a man has in fighting against sexual dysfunction—his wife.

She is the one who should remind him continually of the pleasures—not the obligations—of sex. She, better than anyone else in the universe, knows how to soothe his anxieties, help him dump some of his load of perpetual stress and talk out his worries and fears.

For men and women, midlife becomes an excellent time to renew one's self and one's marriage. Instead of tensing up over sexual difficulties, decide to consult a doctor and resolve them. And meanwhile, focus on the good things in your marriage and in your life. Concentrate on how to become more romantic toward your spouse, more committed, more loving, generous and kind. Remember that midlife men, because of a drop in testosterone, need more romance and nurturing. These tender mercies produce miracles. Even sexual pleasure and the most earth-shaking orgasms take a back seat to the exquisite and memorable moments of pure affection, complete with the kissing, fondling and sweet talk you have both enjoyed from the first.

Amazingly enough, such personal renewal in marriage often leads to a new kind of passion—one much like the old days, but now augmented by so many added years of trials, experiences, laughter, funny memories, proud moments and rich, mostly happy living. Maturity holds many advantages.

Rx: Wives, delight yourself in your husband.

CHAPTER 10

Enjoy Sex Forever

People so often call themselves "too old" to experience sexual desire, but many recent studies and anecdotal evidence show that men and women in their seventies, eighties and beyond enjoy sexual interludes on a regular basis, which proves you can reverse your "I'm too old" thinking. Sex among older people is not a new phenomenon; it just may have been a well-kept secret until the baby-boomer generation brought it out into the open. My own parents were married fifty-six happy years. My precious father died at age eighty-seven, and my mother shyly (and father proudly) admitted that their sex life was alive and well until he died. (I remember one funny incident where my mother threw out her hip, and we had to call 911!)

"Love conquers all," and that is why I think the reasons behind lagging libidos during one's forties and fifties more likely relate to hormonal changes, loss of energy and lax attitudes rather than to sagging breasts, protruding tummies, waistline thickening and gray hair.

Concern about sex, pleasure and our sexuality as we age is as old as the Bible, where Sarah wonders about her life with Abraham: "After I am waxed old, shall I have pleasure, my lord being old also?" (Gen. 18:12, KJV).

Millions of men and women today still wonder, as did

Sarah, whether sex will vanish once they reach their sixties and beyond. For healthy individuals, the answer is that basically healthy people can enjoy an active sex life for many more years than most people believe. Such factors as good health, hormonal balance, weight control, fitness and state of mind remain largely within our personal control.

I know many of you are going to ask me, "But Dr. Pensanti, couldn't it be that I am getting older and am not supposed to have much of a sex drive at my age?"

Yes, aging does have some effect on our sexual behavior, but most of the downturn is due to illness and medication. I believe you can have a wonderfully satisfying sexual relationship with your spouse at any age if you want it.

However, as you age, you cannot count on sex happening exactly the same way it did when you were younger. As I said, physical changes may have occurred, which can affect your body's responsiveness. Specifically, arthritis, high blood pressure, heart conditions and diabetes can affect sexuality. Medications you are taking also can affect your sexuality. And what about physical changes that may occur, even aside from illness or the effects of medication?

Let's address those changes and show you how normal such changes are. You are not alone. Often a feeling of isolation can make you think, *This is happening only to me.* That attitude leads to a depressed state of mind, which is not conducive to intimacy and closeness. I will give you some facts that will assure you that you are quite normal and every bit as capable of being a good sexual partner as the next person.

YOUNG AT HEART

Fairy tales can come true—for you—if you maintain a youthful outlook and believe anything is possible. How much, really, does your age have to do with how you think and feel? And how much does age affect your perspective?

Most of my psychologist guests on *Doctor to Doctor* have told me that as they evaluate individuals as they age from sixteen to sixty-two, productivity, behavior and relationships are found to improve after age thirty—a fact most of you probably

130

have observed. This should provide you with hope that your sexual health does not have to fail as you age!

Looking, feeling and acting vibrantly alive is, like everything else in life, very much up to the individual. We make our own choices. We determine much about our health and fitness levels, and we certainly control our own thinking. As a growing number of current studies show, even in fairly recent times most people held ideas about aging that often seem extremely limiting—or wrong.

Think about it. You probably remember when women of forty wore dark dresses with little lace collars, sensible shoes and carried sturdy pocketbooks large enough to accommodate their knitting. In those days, if a man or woman became widowed and decided to remarry, it created quite a stir. Yes, only a few decades ago, old age came early, by today's standards.

The trouble is, some still carry around the old-fashioned ideas about aging and human sexuality that date back to their grandparents' day.

> FACT: The over-eighty-five population has become the fastest growing group in America.

131

Consider this, Sarah and Abraham's ability to experience sexual pleasure in their eighties and nineties is precisely what our Creator intended for them—and for us. According to *Prevention Magazine,* by the year 2050 age eighty will be considered middle age and eighty-year-olds may look as though they are forty. It follows that those future eighty-year-olds won't expect to give up sex at middle age! It may sound implausible now, but it's true—we have many years ahead of us, and we must seize the day and "count it all joy," each and every day. We were designed to give and receive pleasure.

Health and desire become two key factors in determining how long and how well you and your partner will enjoy the many benefits and satisfactions great sex can bring to your marriage. A third, perhaps most crucial factor in your sexual longevity is your mind-set. How you think about your partner, yourself and your lovemaking makes everything possible (or impossible) at any point in your life. A partner who is interested in you is probably the most important factor for satisfying sex at any age. The decline in hormones as we age, and their effect on our bodies, may pale alongside the value and importance of a fulfilling relationship with our spouse.

MATURE WOMEN

Libidos often do dwindle as women approach menopause, and lessen even more for women past that stage. As we said earlier, these facts are not necessarily "natural," but signal instead that a woman's health, interests, thinking, hormonal activity and sense of herself as a woman have changed. A balancing factor for menopausal women is that they usually have a spouse who is experiencing changes in his own libido and body. I cannot overestimate the importance of familiarizing yourself with the changes that occur in men in their fifties and beyond. This understanding will go a long way toward a more intimate relationship that will be conducive to the continuity of sexual closeness.

132

A woman over fifty may also be experiencing emotional changes that include guilt over her lack of responsiveness to her husband's advances. Or perhaps the sight of her husband's paunch, sloppy dress or other irritating habits simply "turn her off," but she withdraws rather than discuss it. Whatever the reason, if it results in a woman's sending off fewer or no sexual signals, her man is less likely to make advances, which reinforces her unconscious lack of belief in her femininity and desirability and begins the so-called vicious cycle.

It is no secret that some women use menopause as an excuse to end sex lives that have become emotionally or physically unsatisfying to them. One woman in my office joked, "Bring on the concubines!", but I could tell she almost meant it seriously. Consider that perhaps you have rushed to judgment, so to speak, and shut down your receptiveness to your spouse's advances too soon. I want you to give it another chance.

I can tell you from my many years of practicing office gynecology that women in their fifties and beyond who engage in sexual intercourse one or two times a week continue to lubricate well and quickly and also have good vaginal expansion despite some cases of thinning vaginal walls. The age-old maxim really holds true here, *Use it or lose it.* I do not want you to lose it. You were designed by your Creator as a sexual being, and it saddens me when I hear that women give up hope for a satisfying love life. Because I am a medical doctor, I know that physiologically this does not need to be true. And I don't want it to be true for you.

BETTER SEX FOR MATURE WOMEN

As a more mature woman, there are things about sex that should become better, not worse. After all, the average married woman by this time has acquired better, sometimes even expert, sexual skills. She knows by intuition and experience what pleases her husband and herself.

Hopefully, she has overcome earlier sexual inhibitions and can release herself to the utmost pleasure she can give to herself and her husband. And by now, she knows her own sexual needs and preferences and those of her beloved.

Yes, I know that the desire for sex can wane at this stage of life, but it can wane at any stage for various reasons. Do not be willing to give up what God designed as one of life's greatest pleasures. It is a medical fact that less sex leads to reduced desire and, ultimately, to a loss of libido. This downhill spiral and vicious circle is not desirable. I repeat, *Use it or lose it.* Fortunately, solving this problem should not be overly difficult. The answer is to return to a higher level of sexual activity. I know that you can do it because I have talked to many women who tried and succeeded and gave me their testimonies.

133

BEGIN AGAIN

You are older and wiser now, and smart enough to think long term. You understand the benefits and desirability of good sex for your latter years, and now you intend to keep yourself and your partner youthful, sexually active and intimate.

But if the two of you are busy and perhaps suffering physical difficulties or other challenges of daily life, it's possible you may have gotten "out of the habit." How do you resume an active and joyful sexual relationship? Who starts it, and how?

As you know, boosting one's libido depends a lot on mood. Obviously, you can set the mood. A man can do a few attentive, thoughtful things for his wife—open doors for her, hold her hand, kiss her like he means it. A woman can take time for a splash of perfume, a new hairdo or to write her husband a love note. Even these small, ordinary actions make you notice one another more and lead to remembering that chemistry that once surged between you.

Reestablishing intensity and excitement doesn't come automatically. If your relationship has dulled, rekindling the fire may take time and effort on your part. It is crucial that you see yourselves as lovers, and not just husband and wife. Marriage roles can squelch romance over time (if we let it) so that it's easy to see one another as un-sexual. As one woman told me, "Quite frankly, when it comes to sex with my husband, I'd rather just read a book."

That comment seems just about as far from the Song of Solomon as it is possible to go. Don't let the marriage roles, valuable as they are, change you from lovers into much less interested or interesting individuals. You will then be at the point where you are trying to run the car (your marriage) without the spark plug (your sexual life). It is time to regain your lover and restore the allure, passion, excitement, fun and, of course, the romance the two of you deserve.

REKINDLE THE ROMANCE

Begin by showing him or her more affection with caresses, hugs and kisses, especially at times when it is not a prelude to lovemaking. Remind your spouse of those things you always have loved about him or her. Maybe you know a grumpy old man who says, "Why should I tell her I love her? I told her that thirty-five years ago. She knows it." Or a woman who says, "He loves himself enough for both of us. I don't bother to say those words any more." Should you ever find yourself in that category, force yourself to open your mouth and say those three potent little words—I love you. No man or woman ever hears those words too often or tires of hearing them. Any bitterness needs to be sweetened.

"I love you" written in a note or card, and especially when spoken aloud, holds incredible restorative power. Don't ever underestimate the power of those three words, even if they seem to go unacknowledged. And don't expect anything in return. Just give, and let yourself feel the joy of giving. That too has restorative powers. As I have said before, you will reap what you sow; that is God's promise.

Turn off the television and begin to do other things with your evenings. It's easy for "habits" to become "ruts," and "ruts" to become "trenches" until you find yourself watching *I Love Lucy* reruns late into your golden years. So what if you have to be the one to suggest a glamorous evening out, a weekend trip to some beautiful place or even a simple hand-holding stroll around the block. The point is, get out of the habit of allowing dull routines and habits to lead you around by the nose!

Some of the other ideas I have heard from my patients and television viewers include dancing, discovering a new restaurant, eating out at least once a month, sending flowers to his office or treating her to expensive chocolate she'd never buy for herself. The gesture doesn't need to be expensive. Even just surprising him or her by washing the car or volunteering to do the grocery shopping can be important. The idea is, don't let your spouse take you for granted. A little surprise from time to time keeps you young, continually interesting, fun and romantic.

Encourage yourself. You don't have to ask him or her if you still "have it." To your husband or wife, you probably are as beautiful or handsome as ever, according to those who study such things. One report says that among forty-five- to forty-nine-year-old men, 59 percent gave their partners the highest possible rating for physical attractiveness. For those seventy-five and older, the figure was 63 percent! Among women, the proportion who described their husbands as highly attractive was 57 percent at age seventy-five and older.[1]

At an age when physical beauty, as measured by younger standards, is declining, older lovers see one another through different eyes. One of my patients said about her husband,

135

"He is always the best-looking, most exciting man in any room." My neighbor always describes his wife as "the most elegant woman I have ever met." Another patient sums it up even more succinctly: "Larry still 'sends' me." Those lovers are in their late seventies and early eighties.

Studies also show that two-thirds of those who have regular sexual intercourse during their sixties and beyond say they are extremely or very satisfied with their physical relationships. When you resume lovemaking, those same benefits can be yours. You will become more excited about life, better toned physically and, most importantly, better attuned to your spouse. Best of all, you will rediscover that sexual intercourse blunts the "slings and arrows" of everyday life equally as much for older lovers as for those who, in their youthful fervor, believe they just invented sex.

OVERCOMING OBSTACLES

Sexual slowdown generally happens as we slow down physically. As I have said, health obstacles such as diabetes, coronary heart disease, arthritis, prostate problems, obesity and other libido-lowering major diseases deserve our full attention. Painful intercourse, erectile dysfunction, aftereffects of cancer treatments, hormonal imbalances and other sexual inhibitors should be addressed as well. Try working through these life episodes with the idea of becoming closer.

Discuss these issues with your spouse, and seek ways to continue your sex life, which encourages ailing bodies and spirits to heal. As many individuals report, even the pain of arthritis and similar maladies can disappear for a time as sexual intercourse releases a rush of seratonin from the brain.

One of my patients tearfully told me about the night she resumed sex for the first time following her mastectomy. "His tenderness and love overwhelmed me," she said. "All we had gone through as we fought for my life was distilled into those precious moments I'll never forget. That night reminded me that our love, through trials, fear and pain, has become far more powerful and important to both of us than we had known, and no illness or misfortune could damage or affect it."

Sex, which she had dreaded facing following her surgery, became the final chapter in her healing—and their victory. As she underwent reconstructive surgery, she said, "Our marriage is more sexy these days, not less. I have learned that love really means far, far more than just the physical!"

Please...make your lovemaking a high priority. It has to rank above discouragement, aches and pains, negativity and all the other minuses of life. Your sexuality, in later years, may be far more potent than you think.

RECAPTURE YOUR INTENSITY

Does that sound impossible? One of my patients, a fifty-eight-year-old woman, met a sixty-eight-year-old man, fell in love and described their emotions as being "like two loaded freight trains colliding." They went on to describe the intensity of their love, the twenty-four-hour-a-day fervor and, as she termed it, "the absolute ridiculousness of falling in love so hard."

As we talked, she recalled the need to hear his voice and the "weak-in-the-knees" sensation she felt whenever he walked into the room. She said, "We were like two teenagers during our courtship." Now married for sixteen years, they claim that little has changed.

137

If older people can meet, fall in love and experience the same thrilling feelings as twenty-year-olds, then that is equally possible for long-married individuals. Why secretly long for the excitement and newness of what you once had? Medically and psychologically speaking, an active sex life contributes tremendously toward keeping a couple's closeness and happiness intact. The continuity sex provides, that magical thread that binds together so many life experiences—the good and the bad—makes the marriage of two otherwise quite ordinary people into something rare and extraordinary. This does not have to decline as we age.

Ask those in long, contented marriages how they stay sexually interested in one another, and they offer a variety of suggestions:

> ∾ Hug one another a lot, both in and out of bed. Touching

brings old passions to the surface. Hugging and snuggling in bed can be nearly as thrilling as sexual intercourse itself. As a matter of fact, many women tell me that they love the fact that older men cuddle more. This is probably due to lower testosterone levels, which make their lovemaking more mellow than younger men's.

∾ Don't start something (tidying the living room or washing a load of clothes, for example) just before bedtime. Instead, turn off most of the lights, play some music, sit together reading or have a quiet chat, giving one another your full attention.

∾ If you can fit it in, a short afternoon nap helps a woman guard against being "too tired." In fact, one woman says any tasks such as housework, errands or lists of phone calls not accomplished by 2 P.M. get put on tomorrow's list. She reserves her afternoons and evenings for her husband, and she lets him know it.

∾ Snuggle a bit every night before falling asleep, even if just for a minute or two. Let him or her drift off to dreamland after hearing you say, "I love you."

∾ Try making love at different times of the day. I know you may be groaning at this and saying, "Dr. Pensanti has been reading too many women's magazines," but remember, men enjoy lovemaking in the morning when their libido is very often at its peak. Others like to sneak home for a "quickie" during their lunch hour. Women often prefer to make love in the evening when the day is done and the lights are off. Don't either one of you be selfish—mix it up!

∾ Be open to spontaneous lovemaking. One of my friends admits that she really dislikes spontaneous, out-of the-blue lovemaking, but she wanted to please her spouse, who loves it. To force herself to be open to the idea, she made up coupons that entitled him to one session of lovemaking on any day, at any time. She dated the coupons and gave him a number of them. She good-naturedly honors the coupons when he "redeems" them and says it has turned out to be a lot of fun, and he, of course, is very happy.

∼ Be more adventurous and playful. Give yourself permission in the bedroom to be funny or silly. Lovemaking doesn't always have to be serious, and it certainly isn't work.

∼ Begin lovemaking with no particular set of expectations, no pattern or agenda. If he cannot achieve an erection, which sometimes happens, don't let that stop you from enjoying yourselves. It isn't just intercourse that counts toward a satisfactory love life. It's the sum total—everything—that you have and do together.

Later love, for many couples, actually becomes more intense and often distills into an intimacy more potent than that experienced by younger couples.

WHAT YOU
SAY IS WHAT YOU GET

Think about the power of your words. In sexual intercourse, as in everything else, at times a single word or a certain tone of voice can ruin the experience. The words we habitually use, innocent as they may seem, actually color our lives to amazing degrees. Think old and talk old, and you actually will become old. I have seen it over and over again in my older female patients. Also remember to watch the tone of your voice as I told you in chapter three. Men like a nice, soft voice. It caresses their parasympathetic nervous system, which contributes to arousal.

139

In the bedroom, no one should talk about what used to be. Sexually, you are in the moment—past experiences need not be recalled just now, and certainly not as a measuring device. If anything should be measured, it is the power of our words and the voice in which we speak them. The bedroom should be reserved always for love, not for paying the bills, working or above all, deciding to disagree loudly.

The happiest people are mature enough to realize what they have and to take care to see that they preserve their treasured relationships. They save their best selves for their beloved husband or wife. Their bed becomes a sanctuary for both of them, a haven for restoration and the place where lovemaking continually and always receives proper honor.

Sexual changes are one of the most challenging aspects for a couple in their midlife years. However, I believe that this is a wonderful time of life to deepen your relationship rather than becoming estranged. Be sure that both you and your partner commit to focusing on a healthy body. Use some of the exciting nutritional supplements available to sustain your optimum health and sexual relationship.

I don't want to exclude couples who may be in bad marriages. Please go for counseling or behavior modification and seek the Lord. Your husband's or wife's bickering, meanness, withdrawal or cruelty may be a symptom of very deep emotional problems that you cannot help him or her solve. If this is the case, seek professional help, please. Nothing is impossible with God. Sometimes when dark areas are brought into the light, healing can be achieved. Do not be ashamed that there are some things you cannot do by yourself.

Be brave enough to make that first step. Do it for yourself and for your marriage.

> Rx: Do whatever it takes to help yourself and your spouse to age beautifully.

CHAPTER 11

Don't Let Stress Destroy Your Sex Life!

I t is no secret that prolonged stress causes disease, and it is a definite libido killer. Chronic stress, with adrenaline and cortisol being constantly released, begins to negatively affect the endocrine system. This puts stress on the adrenal glands, testes, prostate and ovaries, and you have now begun to set yourself up for disease. When the body is stressed continuously, the damage will show up at the body's most vulnerable point. For many, that is your sexual organs, and thus your libido and sexual function begin to go into a decline. Many doctors believe that one of the prime elements contributing to the prostate's progression from inflamed, to enlarged, to cancer is stress.

Yet chronic stress seems to be a fact of life. I am sure most of you are at the point where you take the existence of stress in your lives for granted. Stress manifests itself in a multitude of forms—emotional, career, nutritional, toxic and lifestyle stresses. Like you, I have been through it. I can relate to the necessity of working long, unrelieved hours during my years as a young woman attending medical school. I can remember plenty of "all-nighters," too. Even today it's easy for me to get overloaded with nonstop professional duties plus the demands of running a household and rearing three lively and uniquely different children.

But "nonstop" is the operable word. This has to change! Let me tell you why. Perhaps I can shock you into putting the brakes on, so to speak. Stress is not just mental—it has definite physical ramifications and causes definite physical changes, many of which can become very serious.

When I am stressed, I can actually feel the adrenaline in my back in a large circle like a bull's-eye. It is affecting me physically. Women and men simply must find ways to ease up on themselves. Let me educate you on this very important subject by following along with this question-and-answer session.

WHY IS STRESS TODAY DIFFERENT THAN IN THE PAST?

Our ancestors encountered and dealt with stress, but on a short-term level. They usually encountered a problem, dealt with it and moved on to normal life. In current times we have what I call long-term stress—financial problems, job-related stress, deadlines, time constraints, divorce, legal problems, taxes and more. The types of stress—and its duration—have changed dramatically. However, the human body has only one mechanism for handling stress, and that is the same mechanism our ancestors had—the production of adrenaline and cortisone by the adrenal glands (the fight-or-flight response).

We are no longer using the stress hormones quickly as the body is meant to do. Instead, we are using tremendous amounts of stress hormones over a longer period of time. The stress hormone was not designed for long-term use. The longer we rely on our adrenal glands to produce the cortisol and other chemicals we need to handle stress, the more fatigued the adrenal glands become and the less adequately we handle stress. In addition, continuous high levels of cortisol are very destructive to the body.

WHAT DOES STRESS DO TO THE BODY?

Chronic stress can lead to adrenal exhaustion, which has many negative effects on the body. The adrenals are two small glands located on the top of our kidneys. They produce or contribute to the production of about 150 hormones necessary for our optimal health. The adrenals release adrenaline to cope with stress. To do its work, adrenaline needs cortisol. Under conditions of chronic stress, you will have chronically elevated levels of cortisol. Chronic excessive secretions of cortisol are associated with obesity, blood sugar imbalances, muscle wasting, heart disease, hypertension and memory loss. After years of trying to "keep up" with cortisol production, the system that controls the secretion of the adrenal hormones can become unbalanced. The adrenals literally become fatigued or exhausted. This is also called *adrenal insufficiency.*

Symptoms of adrenal exhaustion are constant fatigue, confusion, irritability, decreased thyroid function, inability to concentrate, irregular menstrual cycles, loss of libido, headaches, poor memory, inability to cope with stress, insomnia, low metabolism, anxiety, cravings for sweets and depression. As you can see, if you are chronically stressed, you are living on the edge of a breakdown in health and emotional well-being.

143

Extended and chronic stress leads to weakened organs, especially the heart and blood vessels. Prolonged stress seriously damages the body's ability to resist illness. Heart disease, high blood pressure and cancer have all been associated with heavily stressed lifestyles.

Stress also accelerates aging of the organs, and stress hormones have a decidedly negative effect on the brain. Prolonged stress has been shown to damage the areas of the brain involved in memory and learning.

Prolonged and chronic stress can also lead to depression, which, as we have already discussed, has a profoundly negative effect on the libido.

HOW DO I KNOW
IF I'M GETTING TOO STRESSED?

Check to see if you have any of these physical signs of excessive stress:

 ∾ Chronic feeling of tenseness; inability to relax

- Heart palpitations and/or elevated blood pressure
- Getting sick often due to lowered immune function; continuing episodes of colds and flu
- Menstrual irregularities in premenopausal women due to lowered progesterone and testosterone levels. Loss of muscle energy and strength (fatigue) in both men and women
- Low sex drive
- Gastrointestinal symptoms (irritable bowel, upset stomach, indigestion)
- Decrease in muscle strength and endurance due to lack of DHEA and testosterone
- Memory and attention problems
- Insomnia

HOW CAN I COMBAT
STRESS AND RESTORE ADRENAL HEALTH?

A recent survey showed that "less stress" and "more free time" are the top things forty-five- to fifty-nine-year-olds say would most improve their sex life.[1] Perhaps I cannot give you more free time, but I can certainly tell you what you can and must do about your stress levels.

Cortisol and the other stress hormones have a natural rhythm. Their levels are designed to peak in the early morning so that you have energy, feel focused and are able to take on the events of the day. These levels begin to decline slowly throughout the day so that you are prepared to rest and sleep in the evening. If, in the evening when you are designed to begin resting, you are running errands and beginning projects and new activities, you are disrupting God's natural design for your body. Your cortisol levels are not meant to remain steadily high throughout the day!

Tips to restore adrenal health

1. Change your circumstances if you can, or change your attitude about your circumstances.

This is probably the most important step. It is what we call stress reduction. It is very difficult to do in our society.

However, after our review of what stress can actually do to your body, perhaps you can understand why I am so serious about this. Begin by trying to avoid new stress. Evaluate every new situation or project and ask how stressful it will be. Do not take on new stressful activities.

Then begin to work on the areas of your life that are already stressful. My patients have found it very helpful to get away from their immediate environments for a one-day vacation or a long weekend. You will see that it is hard to be anxious about the same things when you are away from the daily routines and circumstances that normally cause anxiety. Try to utilize your free time to do something that you find relaxing. If you find gardening stressful, that is not the place for you to be in your spare time—no matter how relaxing other people find it to be. If you are a person who previously has felt guilty by just sitting down to read a book in the middle of a day off, remind yourself that your life may depend on this relaxation. Stop feeling guilty about the things that are essential for your health—rest and relaxation. The single most important thing you can do to restore fatigued adrenal glands is to rest. This means getting plenty of sleep in addition to pursuing less stressful activities.

145

I am a firm believer that for six days you labor, then for one day you rest!

2. Take essential vitamins and minerals to support your adrenal glands.

Be sure that you include vitamin C. The adrenal gland is found to contain a significantly high amount of vitamin C, which is vital to its function. The level of vitamin C diminishes under stress when the adrenal cortical activity is elevated, so supplementation is very beneficial.

Use a B-complex, especially vitamins B_5 (pantothenic acid), B_6 (pyridoxine) and B_3 (niacin or niacinamide) daily. B_5 plays a key role in the synthesis of cholesterol and steroid hormones. It is known as the "anti-stress" vitamin because high levels positively affect the adrenal glands. Pantothenic acid, or vitamin B_5, helps the adrenal glands manufacture hormones, helps fight stress and fatigue and provides support for exhausted adrenal glands. Low levels can significantly affect the adrenal cortex. Vitamin B_6 supports adrenal gland health and function. B_3 is necessary for adrenal gland health and function. It is essential for synthesis of estrogen, progesterone and testosterone.

You also need magnesium, potassium and zinc. These substances are essential for your adrenal glands in order for them to manufacture the hormones that your body needs.

Calcium (taken in conjunction with magnesium) exerts a calming effect on the body. Together they have been shown to reduce blood pressure and relieve stress.

3.   Take adrenal supplements.

I like to recommend taking some organic adrenal glandular extract from a sheep source. This helps your body by giving you small doses of cortisone and other hormones that were contained in those adrenals. These are processed in a very safe and beneficial way and have been found to be free of any side effects.

There are some very good products available in health food stores. Be sure to purchase a reputable brand. I like to emphasize the sheep source over the bovine source, although both are purported to be quite safe. My favorite is a product called Isocort, which comes in pellet form and is highly absorbable. Isocort contains freeze-dried adrenal cortex from sheep. The sheep used for this product are raised in New Zealand and graze on land that is free of chemicals. The dosage I recommend is two pellets three to four times daily.

4.   Use natural progesterone to support adrenal hormone production.

The high cortisol levels associated with stress can invade the progesterone receptors in the body and render them unavailable to progesterone. This can result in estrogen dominance. Progesterone is manufactured in the adrenal glands as well as the ovaries. If the adrenal glands are exhausted, they are unable to make progesterone. Women with adrenal exhaustion usually have an extremely low libido. Natural progesterone will help support and "heal" the adrenal glands, counteract estrogen dominance related to stress and help restore sexual desire.

5.   Take pregnenolone as a supplement.

Pregnenolone is a hormone made primarily in the adrenal glands and also in the brain. It is a precursor to DHEA and other steroid hormones. Pregnenolone works to prevent and reduce stress by blocking the effects of cortisol in the body. Pregnenolone can also be metabolized into progesterone. The fact that it is converted into DHEA and progesterone may contribute to the reason that pregnenolone is often called a "feel good" hormone. Patients who take it report restored youthful vigor and vitality in terms of energy, improved mood and a general feeling of well-being. Like DHEA, pregnenolone levels decline with age. Just five to ten milligrams daily can do much to combat stress and increase energy in those who are fatigued. If you take pregnenolone, take occasional breaks from using it. Because it is a hormone, do not use it if you have any history of reproductive or prostate cancer.

147

6.   Take ginseng as a supplement.

Ginseng belongs to the group of herbs known as *adaptogens*. Adaptogens work to help the body return to a balanced state. Ginseng has been shown in many studies to reduce the negative effects of stress on the human body. Ginseng contains phytochemicals known as *glycosides,* which support the adrenal glands and help to normalize the adrenal response to stress. It has the ability to help the body inhibit the overproduction of cortisol. Ginseng also boosts energy levels, improves mental stamina, improves mood and boosts libido. You may use either Panax ginseng, American ginseng or Siberian ginseng. American and Siberian ginseng have a more calming effect on the body, so I believe they should be your first choice. I also recommend that you take ginseng in a cycle—take it daily for two to three weeks, then take a one- to two-week break before beginning again. The usual dose for Panax ginseng is 75–100 milligrams daily; for American and Siberian ginseng, 150–300 milligrams daily.

7. Exercise.

We will talk more about the effects of exercise in chapter thirteen. Exercise increases the release of endorphins, which have a calming effect and increase your feeling of well-being.

8. Pray.

There are many, many scriptures that advise us to lead nonstressful lives. Perhaps you would like to do your own study, but here are some of my favorites. My all-time favorite is, "Be anxious for nothing, but in everything by prayer and supplication, with thanksgiving, let your request be made known to God" (Phil. 4:6, NKJV). I also like Isaiah 43:1–3, Romans 5:1–11 and Romans 8:37.

9. Get more sleep.

When libido stalls, try getting just one extra hour of sleep per night for one week. The results may amaze you.

148

10. Let go of any stress or anxiety you have attached to sexual performance.

Enjoy your mate and yourself sexually to the best of your ability—at whatever level of function each of you is now at. This act of giving will not go unrewarded. In some way you will reap what you sow. I think you will also find a hidden lining of joy and peace, both of which are powerful anti-stressors.

HOW DOES STRESS AFFECT MY SLEEP?

The adrenal malfunction associated with prolonged stress can cause a disturbance of the body's circadian rhythm, the mechanism by which the body distinguishes between day and night. Also, a depressed immune system can cause sleep disturbances. Insomnia may be a very big problem for you. Follow some of the remedies below to find a way to overcome your insomnia and sleep loss.

For women: natural progesterone cream

Each hormone in the body is related to or made from another, or can be turned back into another, so any imbalance has a profound effect on the body. By restoring hormone balance through the use of natural progesterone, you can restore normal sleep patterns. I have many women patients who tell me they have had insomnia for years. They go to bed at a normal time, struggle to sleep for hours or sleep fitfully, finally getting to sleep at 2 or 3 A.M. Then they get up at 7 A.M. totally unrested. Some patients sleep through the night after only two to three days' usage of natural progesterone.

For premenopause, use ¼ teaspoon twice daily on days 12 through 26 of your cycle. For menopause, use ¼ teaspoon twice daily twenty-five days of the month.

Calcium

Calcium has a calming effect on the central nervous system and will aid sleep if taken before bed. Calcium has also been found to be more readily absorbed by the body at night when your body is not using it at the same pace. I recommend calcium citrate as the preferred form for best absorption. You can purchase a good brand of calcium citrate and use as directed.

149

Magnesium

Magnesium is a natural sedative. It is also essential for calcium utilization. Calcium and magnesium work together as a team and promote relaxation. If you are deficient in these minerals you may experience muscle cramps at night that can interrupt sleep. As with calcium, magnesium is very effective as a sleep aid when taken at bedtime. There are many fine calcium-magnesium supplements on the market today.

B vitamins

The B vitamins are extremely important. All of the B vitamins work to promote healthy nerves to help prevent insomnia, anxiety and depression. B_6 helps regulate the body's use of tryptophan, an amino acid that converts to serotonin, which is very calming. Low levels of B_6 increase the risk that you will develop insomnia. Vitamin B_3, also known as niacin, is said to prolong REM sleep. *Note:* Some forms of niacin can cause flushing of the skin, stomach irritation and itching. Two forms of niacin called *inositiol hexaniacinate* and *niacinamide* do not cause these side effects. If you are taking a separate supplement of niacin in addition to your B complex, avoid taking it on a empty stomach to avoid gastrointestinal distress. I recommend a good B-complex supplement daily.

HERBS

Herbs that have been found to have a positive effect on insomnia are valerian and chamomile (taken about forty-five minutes before bedtime), passion flower and kava kava.

Kava kava promotes a feeling of relaxation and relieves anxiety that can cause insomnia, but unlike alcohol or Valium, it does not decrease mental clarity. In fact, it induces a slight feeling of alertness when first taken. It will have a sedating effect a few hours later when it is time to sleep. Take it late in the afternoon or early evening. It is available in tea or in capsules. My friends have personally tried it in tea form and found it to be very effective, although I will warn you they report that it is slightly bitter. It has no reported side effects with recommended dosages. Kava has also been reported to increase libido, which may be due to its positive effect on mood and the way that it works to alleviate stress and promote relaxation. Kava should not be taken in conjunction with other antidepressants or with any other drugs that affect the central nervous system.

Valerian root has been used as an aid to sleep for many centuries. It is extremely effective if the insomnia is a result of anxiety and nervousness. Valerian has a mild tranquilizing effect on the central nervous system and muscles. It seems to work as well as prescription sleeping pills but without the side effects. Patients who use valerian for insomnia have told me that they experience no morning "hangover" or drowsy feeling.

5-HTP

The supplement 5-HTP (5-hydroxytryptophan), a precursor to serotonin, helps increase natural serotonin levels, giving the body a feeling of contentment and helping us sleep. When you boost your level of serotonin, you are also increasing your level of melatonin, the natural hormone that regulates sleep-wake cycles. Other benefits include the fact that it is a natural anti-depressant and stress reducer. It also is found to suppress appetite in some people.

MELATONIN

The natural hormone melatonin has been found to be extremely effective in treating insomnia. It is produced in the pineal gland and controls the body's circadian rhythm, which is the mechanism that tells us when to wake up and when to sleep. Melatonin levels decrease as we age, and therefore many older people have sleep disturbance problems.

Studies have shown that taking melatonin supplements can help bring melatonin levels back to normal levels and thus aid sleep. You should only take melatonin at night, one-half hour to two hours before bed. Most people report that they begin to feel drowsy within about thirty minutes, but for others it may take longer. You will need to experiment. Because melatonin is a hormone, I do not recommend regular usage or exceeding the recommended dosage. A range of .5 milligrams to 2 milligrams should be quite sufficient, although some people report needing higher doses. If you wake up groggy, reduce your dose. I do not advise taking melatonin every night. Taking it too often can cause your own body to decrease its production of your natural melatonin. Side effects are minimal. Some people report vivid dreams, occasional nightmares or mild headaches, but this usually occurs at higher doses. Also, some people have reported depressed feelings. However, people taking 1 milligram or less experience little or no side effects.

There is a way to increase melatonin levels naturally. Expose yourself to daylight for ten to twenty minutes within one hour of waking up. This can stimulate the pituitary gland and help "reset" your body clock. Often insomnia results when not enough sunlight enters the eyes when the person is awake. Try to take a short walk if you can. If not, let as much early morning light into your house and eyes as you can. At night, your body needs to be exposed to darkness to keep your circadian rhythm. Therefore do not sleep with the lights on, and try to keep street light from permeating your bedroom.

You might want to try including foods in your diet that are high in melatonin. The best sources are brown rice, rolled oats, bananas, tomatoes and corn.

Do some physical activity in the late afternoon or early evening. Your muscles need to be tired for a good night's sleep. The best sleep occurs when the body is cool, so take hot baths one to two hours before bedtime—not immediately before retiring.

HOW DOES STRESS AFFECT THE LIBIDO?

The effects of chronic stress on the libido are profound, because the balance of the sex hormones is so intricately involved with the balance of the adrenal hormones. Healthy adrenal glands are critical to a healthy libido. In addition to the ovaries and testes, testosterone is also produced by the adrenal gland. Therefore, the adrenal fatigue or adrenal burn-out that is caused by chronic stress has a direct, negative effect on the libido in both men and women.

In fact, a menstruating woman who is under enough stress will often have abnormal menstrual periods or even a total cessation of periods. Exhausted adrenal glands begin to shut down their progesterone production. In a man, the body will begin to "steal" testosterone in order to make cortisone out of it, which is the reason a man under stress loses his sex drive.

Adrenal exhaustion reduces the desire for sex. This served a distinct purpose in ancient times. Reduced sexual desire led to reduced intercourse, which led to fewer births and less mouths to feed. In this way, the lack of desire due to stress is programmed into your body!

INSOMNIA AND LIBIDO

Long hours, hard work and stress that lead to sleep disturbances have reached a record high in our society and play a large role in the libido loss picture. For many couples, doing without sleep too often means doing without sex, and that is not good.

You have probably had at least one bout with a serious case of insomnia. For highly stressed people and for menopausal women, insomnia sometimes seems just to be a fact of life. One very negative effect of insomnia is loss of libido. Even the loss of one hour of sleep per night can make your sex systems stall or crash.

The cumulative effect of not sleeping night after night will dampen even the strongest of sex drives—not to mention what it does to those of you who have already been suffering from no desire. Your libido will become almost nonexistent. Some patients have told me that they become almost hostile to their husbands or wives. There is no way they want to make love—they just want to get some sleep. When desire wanes and a nap continually sounds more blissful than the idea of making love to your spouse, it is time to change.

DOCTOR'S SUGGESTIONS FOR PROLONGED INSOMNIA

Alternate usage of the following to avoid developing a tolerance:

- One to two nights—Use melatonin (½ milligram to 1 milligram) before bedtime, or drink melatonin tea (1 cup equals ½ milligram).
- One to two nights—Use a herbal supplement like kava kava, chamomile or valerian (see above).
- One to two nights—Use nothing.
- Once a week—Use 5-HTP. Do not combine 5-HTP with MAO inhibitor-type medications.

CHAPTER 12

Sex Despite Medical Problems

Most of us eventually encounter some physical road-block, anything from sleep deprivation to a stroke, that causes our sex drive to plummet or even temporarily cease. Episodes of bad health happen, yet even such potentially serious challenges as heart disease, arthritis or prostate cancer need not always bring lovemaking to an end.

In fact, it is especially at times like these that both partners should seek to reestablish their sexual union as soon as possible for its many health-giving and spirit-lifting benefits.

ISSUES CONFRONTING MEN

Many illnesses formerly believed to cause permanent erection loss often do not. Even diabetes, multiple sclerosis and other neurological (nervous system) diseases need not necessarily bring one's sex life to a halt. Some men with these problems do indeed lose the ability to achieve erections, so physicians will often tell all other men with these conditions that they will experience the same fate.

My advice is to realize that the expectation of sexual problems can become a self-fulfilling prophecy. Whenever you are told for any reason that your libido or sexual abilities may be affected or lost, become proactive. Look further for answers.

A little effort toward sexual restoration can provide big personal and marital dividends. Your efforts and your positive personal attitude could make a big difference in your marriage and your life.

This chapter will cover a number of common maladies that can interrupt sexual function. I will make some recommendations for averting or curing problems that can rob you of you lovemaking—at least for a season. I will also offer some suggestions for working around pain, discomfort and other physical challenges.

The following paragraphs, in no particular order, highlight some of the questions I am asked most often about medical problems that interfere with sexual intercourse. Common sense tells us to go to our physician for answers about any health problem we're having—even sex. But too often we take it upon ourselves to shoulder the entire burden of a sexual problem, or we "just wait and see," tending to withdraw from sexual activity. Then, when there's a life-threatening event (that heart attack!), we tend to forget about future sex entirely.

Remind yourself always to place your sexual health as a high priority, and seek the appropriate answers. I find that patients usually feel quite encouraged about their health once they have adequate information to deal with their problem. But remember it is your responsibility to ask!

HEART DISEASE

Studies have shown that men suffer many more heart problems than women (though women are catching up with their male counterparts). Wives who have experienced their husband's heart crisis—a sudden attack or a coronary bypass operation—know how quickly their man can change from a hard-driving charger into someone cautious, even fearful of physical exertion.

Some men respond by giving up sexual activity completely, even after experiencing only minor heart problems. One of my patients told me, "We've made a lot of adjustments in our health routines—good diet, low-impact exercise and plenty of rest. My husband recovered quickly. He lost some weight, looks great and his cardiologist congratulates him on his progress. He told us we could resume sex, but Frank is totally disinterested." She asked me, "Where do we go from here?"

Her husband's behavior is not unusual. Most women are conditioned to think that men are such sexual creatures that almost nothing would deter them from sexual activity. However, 25 percent of all men who suffer heart attacks decide to give up sex completely.[1] Some 50 percent markedly decrease the frequency of their sexual encounters. Only the remaining 25 percent resume lovemaking as often as before.[2] Once some men are brought face to face with their mortality, they find that the trauma of even a slight heart attack can drastically affect their sex drive.

As most cardiologists believe, it is rarely necessary for a man to totally give up his sexual relations following a heart attack, nor is it desirable. Fully 80 percent of heart attack "graduates" can resume their sexual relations with no serious risks. The other 20 percent need not abstain, but should adjust their lovemaking to reflect their specific exercise toler- ance, according to their doctor's instructions.

But, you ask, after such a traumatic event, should sex really matter any longer? Absolutely! Resuming sex signals your return to "real life." It pumps up your confidence and sense of self. Now, perhaps more than at any other time, it becomes a renewing force, able to restore both partners' outlooks on life.

However, as a medical doctor, I know that some post- coronary or bypass individuals (or their spouses) still worry. What if chest pain recurs? Is sex too strenuous now? What if his pulse rate gets too high? Is sex really safe? Some men even fear they might die during intercourse. Others wonder, *Will I always feel this weak? Will sex ever be the way it used to be?*

Your cardiologist can reassure you. In a study of a large group of men with heart disease who died suddenly, fewer than ½ of 1 percent died while having sex. Moreover, most of those few were shown to have been having sexual intercourse with someone other than their wife—and having consumed exces- sive amounts of alcohol, a situation that dramatically increases heart rate and blood pressure levels and burdens the heart.

After a heart attack or coronary bypass surgery, be sure to counsel with your physician concerning what activities you can tolerate and what ones you can't. Get all your questions answered so that underlying worries will not create tension during lovemaking and lessen your enjoyment. It is a good idea for husband and wife to consult with the doctor together, so all questions get answered.

Let me give you a few sensible precautions as you resume your sex life following a heart episode. These should ease both your mind and your partner's mind.

- Make yourself comfortable and relaxed. Don't begin sex when you feel pressured or worried about your job, bills or personal issues. Chose a familiar place like your own bedroom and a time when you can relax fully and feel free to enjoy yourself with your spouse.

- Start slowly. The first several times, simply pet and caress one another, with no idea of having intercourse. Allow arousal to happen and, if desired, come to climax through manual stimulation. Experience pleasure and allow apprehensions to drain away.

157

- It is wise to postpone sexual relations if you have just consumed a large meal or had several alcoholic drinks. Digestion requires considerable amounts of energy and blood flow, which makes them less available for physical activity. You should probably wait until your body is less stressed.

- New positions may help. When the man is on top, supporting his weight on his arms, he expends more energy than might feel comfortable. You might try the spoon position, or one in which the wife is on top, or where the two of you are side by side. The important thing is that the recovering individual not feel unduly taxed.

- Give pleasure to one another without intercourse. If you simply lack the energy for lovemaking, you may enjoy bringing your partner to climax via manual petting, and allowing him or her to do the same for you.

ॐ Enjoy the moment and don't fret if you "aren't quite up to it."

Remember: If you experience angina pain during sexual relations (one of the most common reasons men give up sex or develop impotence after a heart attack), report the occurrence to your doctor. He may prescribe nitroglycerin or a similar drug that you can take before lovemaking.

Sex after a heart attack actually carries little risk of jeopardizing your health and can even promote recovery.

OTHER NOTES FOR HEART PATIENTS

ॐ Beta-blockers such as Inderol lower your maximum pulse rate during exertion and intercourse and thus decrease your chances of getting chest pain, but unfortunately they can result in a loss of sex drive or the ability to become erect. Should this happen, notify your doctor and ask if he can substitute another medication. Do not be hesitant about saying that your sex life is important to you.

ॐ Depression can be a natural occurrence following a heart attack. It is often related to the physical reaction of facing a life-threatening event, and it often passes with time. Anxiety over physical health can hover over you like a dark cloud, making it difficult to desire or enjoy sex. But sex in any form helps relieve tension and anxiety, and can restore feelings of well-being and fulfillment.

ॐ If depression and lack of sexual desire persist for several months, perhaps your doctor will want to refer you for some counseling or to a support group to help you.

Sexual relations should be embraced, not feared. Good health to you!

ARTHRITIS AND LOWER BACK PAIN

Undoubtedly, arthritis, with its pain, stiffness, fatigue and limited motion, can produce some daunting challenges to lovemaking, as can lower back pain. Both seem to choose people above age forty, and both maladies are common-place. Arthritis in some form, in fact, affects more people in this country than any other disease.

If you have arthritis, you may lose the easy, comfortable movements you once had. Finger dexterity and fine movements of hands may become undependable or even impossible, and mobility in some joints may be lost. Naturally, those limitations can discourage or even curb a person's sexual relations—if he or she allows it.

Arthritis pain can make it difficult to reach orgasm. Worse, chronic pain anywhere in the body can dampen sexual desire and "interrupt the moment" during lovemaking. In addition, if arthritis causes swelling and deformity in some joints, self-confidence concerning one's physical appearance can plummet.

Despite all that, there are powerful reasons to stay as sexually active as you can. Lovemaking works wonders in restoring self-confidence, self-image and self-esteem. It reinforces your femininity or masculinity. Equally important perhaps, sex often relieves pain. Some even experience pain relief for six to eight hours following sexual intercourse. This has been attributed to the body's release of endorphins (its internal painkillers) during sexual stimulation and orgasm.

159

It is healthy, therefore, to work with your partner to make love despite physical limitations. If he or she feels guilty about the possibility of causing pain or discomfort for you, explain that it is to your mutual advantage to work past the challenges and actively seek ways to have the sex life you want and deserve. "No pain, no gain" was never more true.

Teach your partner which tender areas of your body need to be avoided. Guide your partner's hand to those spots, pointing out the painful touches and explaining why other touches feel wonderful. Next, show your partner how he or she can stimulate you sexually without causing pain.

Knowing that your partner understands what hurts and what doesn't raises the trust level for each of you prior to attempting sexual relations. The next step is that of developing some sort of signal by which the arthritic partner can warn his or her mate of discomfort. Instead of exclaiming "Stop!" or "That hurts!", for example, you might agree on a nonverbal signal. A squeeze of the hand or tap on the shoulder, for example, will be much less intrusive during lovemaking.

Before making love, you might adopt a ritual of a few non-strenuous exercises or a hot bath or shower together to loosen stiff joints and diminish pain. This can become a sensuous experience, enjoyable for both of you.

It also helps to deliberately choose the time of day that best suits the partner with arthritis, a time when his or her body has loosened up, but before undue fatigue has set in. With a little experience, you will learn what is best. You also will want to plan around medication schedules, especially if you take pain mediations at specified hours. Give yourself time for the medication to take effect so as to begin love-making when you are most relaxed and comfortable.

Some forms of arthritis cause a decrease in bodily secretions, including vaginal lubrication. Should that occur, applying a water-based lubricant will make lovemaking much more comfortable. One especially important way to avoid the pain of arthritis or lower back pain during intercourse is to experiment with new positions, adapting according to your special needs. Pillows placed beneath knees or buttocks help in some positions, and kneepads purchased from a nearby medical supply house can cushion painful joints.

When arthritis flare-ups seem especially bad, you may find intercourse simply too painful, yet you still yearn for the intimacy it brings. At times like those, you and your spouse can use manual stimulation to bring pleasure to one another. Sex may be impossible for the moment, but lovemaking can still be achieved!

The secret, of course, lies in motivation and a strong, positive attitude toward your love life, your sex life, your spouse, your marriage and yourself.

URINARY STRESS INCONTINENCE

"Dr. Pensanti, I have a little problem..." I hear this quite often. My patient continued, "Sometimes I lose a little urine when I laugh, sneeze or pick up something heavy. Whenever we have sex I'm always afraid I'll lose control of my bladder."

This patient certainly is not suffering alone; more and more Americans in our steadily aging population are echoing her concerns. This involuntary loss of urine when coughing or sneezing is a condition called *urinary stress incontinence*. The good news for men and women is that Kegel exercises often can rectify the problem. These exercises were devised by Dr. Arnold Kegel, a gynecologist, for his patients with urinary stress incontinence. He taught them to strengthen their pubococcygeal muscles (pelvic muscles) for normal control of urination. Not only did the exercises work, but the women reported having more and better orgasms as well, with stronger uterine contractions.

Men who responded to a survey about Kegel exercises reported an enhanced ability to have more intense orgasms and fewer episodes of premature ejaculation.

KEGEL EXERCISES

The exercises are simple:

161

- ❧ Stop urine flow midstream.

- ❧ Do this five times during each bathroom visit.

- ❧ Once you learn how the muscle feels, contract it in sets of three seconds at other times during the day, then relax. Repeat ten times. Work your way from holding for three seconds to holding the contracted muscle for the count of ten.

- ❧ Do these exercises daily. Try to do five sets of ten seconds each.

This simple procedure can work wonders. If you decide to try it, give yourself at least a month to strengthen those important pelvic muscles. Enjoy your success!

THYROID DISORDERS

A thyroid disorder can make a person feel distinctly disinterested in sex. It has been estimated that at least 10 percent of our general population suffer from thyroid dysfunction, but I believe this figure is too low. I believe the figure is closer to 20 percent. These numbers may even be low in my opinion. The incidence is higher in women than men by about ten to one. Unfortunately, many people are not aware of their condition and needlessly suffer with the chronic symptoms of low (hypo) or high (hyper) thyroid until finally symptoms become impossible to ignore. The bad news is that one risks suffering even more than just libido loss—such serious health problems as clogged arteries, osteoporosis and even heart attack may ensue.

The thyroid gland is located at the base of the neck. The hormones it secretes regulate your metabolism. As we age, hormone production often dips (hypothyroidism) and can cause many of the problems just mentioned.

The thyroid hormone is influenced by shifts in the body's other hormones, and therefore hypothyroidism becomes more common in the perimenopausal and menopausal years. It may be yet another cause of low sexual desire. Treatment for hypothyroidism has been found to restore sex drive in many of my patients. You should seek treatment if you suspect that you may suffer from this condition.

Symptoms of low thyroid hormones or hypothyroidism are:

- Fatigue
- Depression
- Cold hands and feet
- Dry or coarse skin and hair
- Hair loss
- Weight gain
- Slow heart rate
- Constipation
- Low basal body temperature

The severity of symptoms is dependent on the degree of thyroid deficiency. Hypothyroidism often goes undiagnosed, either because physicians do not test for it, or they use a test that is not sensitive enough, especially if you have a borderline case. A test that measures the TSH (thyroid-stimulating hormone) in your blood is the most reliable. Some doctors test only for the two thyroid hormones T_4 and T_3 (thyroxine and triodothyronine), and these may be normal in cases of hypothyroidism.

Less frequently, the thyroid gland may overproduce (hyperthyroidism), speeding up metabolism and making one feel weak, jittery and spent.

Symptoms of excess thyroid hormones or hyperthyroidism are:

- Rapid heartbeat
- Intolerance to heat
- Nervousness and irritability
- Weight loss
- Excessive sweating
- Extremely high energy

Fortunately, such thyroid dysfunction is easily treated once the disorder is diagnosed. If you have symptoms that lead you to believe you may have a dysfunctional thyroid, see your physician about having a TSH test. You can also do a self-test at home, which I will teach you to do.

Once you are diagnosed, unless you are seeing a naturopathic physician or a doctor who is in tune with natural treatments, he or she will probably prescribe a drug called Synthroid. This is a synthetic form of T_4. It does nothing to support the T_3 hormone or the other elements that are found in a healthy thyroid.

Ask your doctor if he will prescribe natural desiccated thyroid for you. If you are currently on thyroid medication, I urge you to switch to natural. Natural thyroid is derived from porcine (pig) thyroid glands, and it contains all of the gland's hormones and factors. Because it is a more complete supplement, it has been shown to result in more effective treatment than T_4 alone. Many patients who have made the switch have reported rapid and even dramatic improvement. An excellent source of natural thyroid is Armour Desiccated Thyroid Hormone by Forest Pharmaceuticals. You will need a prescription for it. If your doctor is resistant, ask him if he will just agree to give you at least a three-month trial.

163

The good news is that once you have been diagnosed and begin treatment, men and women often improve rapidly. The effect of thyroid supplementation is often noticeable within the first two weeks. In fact, once treatment begins, many patients are so happy to have discovered what was causing their debilitating symptoms that they find their mood and outlook on life improve within days. Women especially have told me that their libido makes a remarkable comeback.

THYROID AND NATURAL PROGESTERONE

My esteemed colleague Dr. John R. Lee has been prescribing natural progesterone to his patients for over twenty years. He often noticed that after a few months of using progesterone cream, women who were taking thyroid medication found that they could reduce their dose of thyroid medication. In fact, many patients were eventually able to totally discontinue their thyroid supplement.

Dr. Lee concluded after many years of study that estrogen dominance appears to affect negatively thyroid hormone activity, while natural progesterone actually promotes healthy thyroid function. Synthetic progestins like Provera do not have the same balancing effect on the thyroid. Dr. Lee determined through his research, and taught me, that estrogen, progesterone and thyroid hormones are interrelated. When symptoms of hypothyroidism occur in women who are estrogen-dominant and progesterone-deficient, the use of natural progesterone can restore balance. The need for thyroid supplements often decreases. Now I advise my thyroid patients who are on natural progesterone to monitor their thyroid hormone levels carefully to check for improvement.

SELF-TEST FOR THYROID

Hypothyroidism is characterized by a low body temperature, which indicates that your metabolism is slow. Normal temperature taken by mouth is between 97.8 and 98.2 degrees.

Menstruating women must perform the following test on the second, third and fourth days of menstruation. Men and postmenopausal women may perform the test at any time of the month.

∽ Shake down an oral thermometer to below 90 degrees before you go to bed and place it within easy reach of your bed.

∽ Immediately upon awakening in the morning, before you move at all, place the thermometer in your armpit. Leave it in place for ten minutes. Lie very still.

∽ Record the temperature. Do this for four consecutive days to get an average temperature reading. If your temperature is less than 97.8 degrees, you probably have hypothyroidism, or inadequate thyroid production. NOTE: Women who are still menstruating should know that only temperatures taken on the first through fourth day of their cycle are accurate.

YEAST INFECTIONS

Yeast infections can seem equally bothersome and painful with accompanying irritation and burning. There is a risk of cross-infecting your partner—causing partners to infect each other numerous times (unless both receive simultaneous treatments). Such infections can become real sexual turnoffs (and sometimes should).

Symptoms include constant itching or burning and often a "crawling" feeling inside the vagina. The itching can be almost unbearable if not treated. There may also be a vaginal discharge accompanied by odor. Yeast infections need to be treated to stop the cycle of passing it back and forth between husband and wife.

There are several over-the-counter preparations that treat yeast infections in three to seven days. They include Monistat and Femstat. My colleague, Dr. Perry Ratcliff, and I have patented an over-the-counter vaginal gel that is inserted into the vagina. It kills yeast at a 99 percent rate in one hour. No more 3 A.M. itching nightmares, and a prescription is not necessary!

ANEMIA

Simple anemia, especially in premenopausal women or those with endometriosis, hemorrhoids or other conditions that cause steady blood loss, can make one's sex drive plummet. Anemia can sap one's energy to the point that life loses much of its color and interest—even in sex! If heavy menstrual periods or other abnormal blood loss lowers your blood count significantly, causing you to become one of the 3.3 million women with anemia, do not dose yourself with iron supplements.

Let your doctor treat you. Too much iron can cause liver disease and possibly even lead to heart disease. Blood count and iron supplementation need careful monitoring.

ALLERGIES/ASTHMA

Hay fever and allergy sufferers readily admit that their libido doesn't stand a chance when spring and autumn allergy seasons come into full bloom. Even otherwise healthy individuals can become flattened by such sneezing, coughing, weepy-eyed misery. Add drowsiness from strong antihistamines to the mix, plus fatigue from an oxygen-reducing stuffed-up nose, and few among us in that condition look or feel sexy. When allergies graduate into full-blown asthma, things get even worse.

Asthma is on the rise in America for reasons not yet fully clear. Two-thirds of the asthma patients in a recent survey said the illness put a damper on their sex life. While 47 percent reported some limitations in their sex life due to asthma, another 19 percent said they had not had sex at all during the past two weeks.[3]

Researchers speculate that just as some forms of exercise can induce asthma attacks, so can lovemaking.[4] Here are suggestions for heading off the limitations allergies and asthma place on your sex life.

- Change positions. Be careful not to place pressure on your chest, thus causing shortness of breath. If episodes are brought on by lying down, you may need to remain upright during sex.

- Take your medications beforehand. If you use a bronchodilator prior to engaging in sports or other physical activity, ask your doctor whether you should use such medications before you engage in sex.

∾ Tell your physician if wheezing, coughing or shortness of breath affect you during sexual intimacy. This is important to discuss with him, as he will base his advice on this.

YOU CAN FIND AN ANSWER

Clearly, any sort of medical imbalance, whether simple to treat, as mild anemia, or as complicated as one of the major diseases, also affects, immediately and directly, the state of your libido and lovemaking.

Health problems, mild or major, invariably affect your sex life. At times you can work around them, as with arthritis or a broken ankle. But many physical challenges, including those listed here or the many we did not mention, may require a certain amount of patience on your part. Don't give up. There is no medical problem, including E.D,. that you should allow to cause the extinction of your sexual life with your spouse. However, some ailments may take some dogged detective work.

Consider fifty-four-year-old Brad, for example, who developed a persistent pain in one leg. First a twinge, then a mild ache and gradually the pain progressed to the point that Brad and Evelyn agreed to postpone all sexual activity.

Brad was smart enough to seek medical help. He actually went to see three doctors, and then a fourth. He visited a rheumatologist, an orthopedist and a chiropractor before he dropped in for his scheduled dental check-up. Dental x-rays revealed an abscessed, but painless molar. When the tooth was treated and antibiotics administered, the mysterious leg pain vanished.

Who would imagine that a painless but deeply infected tooth would impinge on a couple's lovemaking? The moral is this: Whenever you discover a physical ill that needs attention, don't put it off, and don't give up hope for treatment. When you boost and protect your general health, at the same time you enhance and ensure the continued quality of your sex life and the pleasures of lovemaking.

CHAPTER 13

Is the Answer in Hormone Supplementation?

I n both men and women, sex hormone production decreases with age. This often leads to a decline in both sexual desire and performance. There is no need to be alarmed or discouraged, however. There are many natural ways to maintain hormone levels and prevent disappointing changes in your sexual activity. We will discuss them here in detail so that you can have better sex *naturally*.

TESTOSTERONE AND WOMEN

Testosterone is produced in a woman's ovaries and her adrenal glands. Testosterone serves several important functions in a woman: It contributes to the health of her bones and muscles, and it is the precursor to estriol and estradiol. There are testosterone receptors in the nipples as well as in the clitoris and the vagina, which make them sensitive to sexual stimulation. In addition, research has shown that testosterone receptors are concentrated in areas of the brain involved in sexual response and emotions. Thus testosterone contributes to the woman's libido by increasing her receptivity to the psychological aspects of sex and increasing the sensitivity of her genitalia.

Testosterone levels decrease gradually as a woman ages.

This is due to diminished production by the ovaries and/or adrenals, aging of the body and its testosterone receptors and reduction in enzyme function. Some women notice symptoms of decreased testosterone, and others go decades longer without being aware of any effect.

Many women actually report an increase in sexual desire after menopause. This may be due to the shift in hormone balance—the decrease in estrogen levels actually causes the testosterone in her body to have a stronger effect.

If a woman of any age has her ovaries removed surgically, this is called an *oophorectomy*. Oophorectomies are common with many hysterectomies; some physicians perform them routinely using the reasoning that the woman does not need her ovaries since her uterus is gone.

This is unfortunate because half of a woman's circulating testosterone comes from her ovaries. After the ovaries are gone, no matter what her age, she is likely to develop testosterone deficiency, because her adrenal glands will react to the loss of the ovaries and produce less of the androgens. Not only will she lose her ovarian estrogen, progesterone and testosterone, but also a portion of her adrenal testosterone and other androgens from the adrenals as well.

169

As a result of menopause, surgical removal of ovaries or their destruction by chemotherapy, many women fit this profile. Unfortunately, too many of them resort to synthetic estrogen replacement alone in an attempt to boost their flagging hormone level—exactly the wrong idea. Many doctors still mistakenly believe that libido comes from estrogen, but adding estrogen alone makes her become even more estrogen-dominant. The male hormone levels in her body become even less significant, and her hormonal balance tips even further from the norm, possibly crushing libido. In my clinical experience and from other hormone specialists, I have learned that taking synthetic hormone replacement therapy may reduce the amount of free testosterone in your bloodstream by up to 30 percent. Now you know what may have happened to one-third of your sex drive!

An excess of estrogen and lack of sufficient androgens produce these symptoms:

- Loss of sexual desire
- Loss of clitoral sensation
- No energy
- Anorgasmic condition (inability to achieve orgasm)
- Lost feelings of well-being
- Loss of pubic hair (a sign of lowered testosterone)

Remember, supplemental estrogen without accompanying progesterone only makes this condition worse. This is because supplemental estrogen makes any testosterone the woman has less available. The biological pathways of the body are such that the rate at which available testosterone is utilized in a woman's body is related to her hormone balance.

Some women, eager to boost flagging energy levels, try taking the male hormone testosterone. I do not advise this— at least not as a first step. As the ovarian function gradually decreases, women begin to show the signs of becoming more androgen-dominant (androgen is the male hormone), and testosterone will exacerbate this condition. Even at low dosages, testosterone can create in women some very unwanted masculine effects—facial hair, acne, male-pattern baldness and a deepening of the voice for example. Any excess dose can lead to much more serious side effects, including impaired liver function and heart disease.

A current treatment of choice in the mainstream medical community is to give a woman an androgen-estrogen combination. Estratest consists of methyltestosterone (a synthetic) combined with synthetic estrogen. It is a fixed dose, which is much too high for many women. It is taken orally and may cause serious side effects, including liver damage. It may also interfere with the body's production of HDL, which is known as the "good cholesterol," thereby exposing a woman to high amounts of "bad cholesterol" and to heart disease.

Other physicians like to use injections, or testosterone implants, which are inserted underneath the skin. These are not reversible. If you develop side effects, you will be forced to endure them for up to several months.

Using testosterone to increase sex drive is usually effective only when your levels are actually low. Research has also demonstrated that raising the level of testosterone above the normal range does not cause a further increase in libido.[1] In addition, if a woman is taking more testosterone than she needs, she will feel worse, not better. Women have told me that they feel agitated, angry and often depressed. If she continues to take a higher level than she needs, she will develop all the masculine symptoms of excessive testosterone.

I strongly believe that testosterone replacement therapy must always be administered by very responsible physicians who adhere to strict testing criteria. Testosterone should not be used as a "tonic" for women or men unless they have been diagnosed as suffering from legitimately low testosterone levels determined by reliable testing.

Doses must be tailored to the individual need of the patient. True, recent developments include patches, pellets, creams and gels. However, remember that any excess testosterone in the body can be converted to estrogen, which is not desirable; this alters the testosterone-estrogen balance and can lead to even worse symptoms.

As I talk to women all over the United States, I find that most women wish they could find an answer that did not involve taking any synthetic hormones, especially testosterone. However, at the same time, they are really mourning the loss of their sex drive and the loss of feelings of well-being and sexuality. I have seen this condition reversed over and over again with women regaining normal sexual desire by using natural progesterone. If you remember the hormonal pathways in the body, you know that natural progesterone is a precursor to the more potent testosterone your body needs. Because women differ in the amount and sensitivity of testosterone receptors and in the intricate balance of their other hormones, a "one-dose-fits-all" drug like Estratest is not the answer (not to mention its potential serious side effects). That is why progesterone is such a valid choice. In

171

addition to being a precursor to testosterone, progesterone has a balancing effect on the body.

Progesterone, in my opinion, offers a much more conservative and natural approach to restoring one's sex drive. Progesterone supplementation has the ability to enhance energy and sexual libido and also heighten feelings of well-being. Therefore, for a woman suffering from a reduced sex drive, I recommend progesterone as a first step.

While natural progesterone has been known to restore libido, the synthetic progestins can actually decrease it. Therefore, synthetic hormone combinations, even if they include testosterone, may cancel out any positive effect on the libido. You must learn the difference between *progestins (synthetic)* and *natural progesterone* just as surely as you learned your ABCs.

A small percentage of women may ultimately need testosterone replacement. If you have used natural progesterone for a minimum of six months and have not had any increase in your libido and are feeling miserable, you may be one of those women.

I confess to you that I actually used to administer testosterone shots to some of my patients before I discovered natural testosterone creams and testosterone boosters. My patients did notice an increase in sex drive, but they reported that it was a very strange, unnatural feeling, not the warm, loving desire they were hoping for. Some said that it was almost a nonhuman feeling, more "animal-like." I was so happy when I discovered there were other alternatives. Since that day I have "marched forward in the natural," and I intend to stay there.

Natural testosterone creams are available by prescription only, and you must bring the prescription to a compounding pharmacy. The advantage of using a compounding pharmacist is that the dose can be easily adjusted for the individual woman and kept at the lowest possible dose that will yield results.

The creams are the safest method because they bypass the liver—unlike oral pills. Formulas and percentages may vary depending on which compounding pharmacy your doctor uses, since the absorption of the testosterone will vary according to the composition of the cream base and absorption enhancers that are used. Some creams may be applied directly to the genital area. You must be very careful to avoid over-dosage, because even at low doses you may notice androgenic (maculinizing) symptoms. If so, discontinue for a while or reduce the dose. The most common dosage is 2 percent, but it can vary from 1–3 percent, depending upon the patient.

As with oral testosterone, testosterone that is absorbed into the body topically can metabolize into estradiol. Therefore women who have a history of or are at risk for breast cancer or uterine and ovarian cancer should not consider testosterone supplementation. In addition, hirsuit (hairy) women should beware of using testosterone. Pregnant women and women who are planning to conceive should never use testosterone in any form as it can lead to development problems in the repro-ductive and genital organs of the fetus.

TESTOSTERONE AND MEN AT MIDLIFE

"Is there some kind of hormone booster shot for men?" I have heard this question many times, and I usually do not treat male patients. My physician colleagues who are men and the doctors who are guests on my television show *Doctor to Doctor* tell me that it is a very common concern. When a man has an episode of "a problem in the bedroom," which is how it is usually described, he can become quite dis-concerted. He needs to be reassured that his sex life will not be going downhill from then on.

Between the ages of forty-five and fifty-five, men experience a gradual reduction in testosterone production. This hormonal decline can cause a man to lose some amount of strength and muscle mass and may cause a reduction in sexual interest.

A man may experience some feelings of general discon-tentment as well. This life stage in men has often been called *andropause.* Testosterone clearly plays a large role in men's sexuality and sex drive. It increases energy and libido and helps maintain muscle mass, skin elasticity and bone strength. It promotes a sense of vitality and well-being. When men begin to sense a physical decline, unlike women, they are usually very reluctant to talk about it, especially in terms of changing sexual function.

As men enter their forties, it has been estimated by many experts I have interviewed that about 20 percent have some testosterone deficiency. That percentage, of course, increases as men reach their fifties, sixties and beyond. Because this decline is very gradual, there is no specific way for a man to know his testosterone levels are low, as women know their hormones are low with menopause. Men do not have definitive symptoms like night sweats or hot flashes. However, testosterone decline can cause a decrease in sexual desire, and possibly a diminished ability to achieve orgasm. A man may also notice a loss of muscle mass, decreased energy and a decline in his overall sense of well-being. In the longer term, lowered testosterone can lead to decreased bone mass.

TESTOSTERONE SUPPLEMENTATION

At midlife, when testosterone levels may begin to dip and libido begins to dwindle, it's natural for a man to wonder about the possibility of testosterone supplementation. Again, I would like to stress the importance of obtaining a blood test to determine whether testosterone is really low. Replacing hormones in men is not as beneficial as it is in women. Men need a minimal amount of testosterone, and if they already have it, testosterone supplementation will usually not help. Men who respond well to testosterone supplementation are those whose hormone levels are in the low to low-normal normal range.

Decreased libido, impotence and ejaculation problems in men can be caused by a variety of factors besides low testosterone. They may benefit from other herbs and supplements or other physical help besides testosterone, as we will discuss later in this chapter.

Although I am not a big fan of testosterone supplementation, even in men, some of my most distinguished colleagues, including Dr. Julian Whitaker of the Whitaker Wellness Institute in Newport Beach, California, recommend testosterone supplements without reservation. I am much more hesitant to take this approach due to some cases I have observed with very negative side effects. However, these were cases using the patch, and there are other ways to supplement. I will present the information to you so that you can make an informed decision as to whether this is a route you would like to pursue. Of course, you must be under a doctor's care to receive testosterone. I urge you to seek out a doctor who is well versed in natural medicine, so you will avoid being given strong doses of harmful synthetic drugs. (Just take a look at muscle builders on steroids and their end result to see what I mean.)

Testosterone supplements stimulate cells of the prostate gland, so they are contraindicated for any man with prostate cancer, as it could stimulate growth of cancer cells. (It is a good idea, therefore, to have one's prostate examined before beginning testosterone supplementation. Let me emphasize, however, that it is not believed to cause prostate cancer.)

If you are taking supplemental testosterone, you should also have a PSA (prostate-specific antigen) test regularly to monitor for prostate cancer. You should also take 160 milligrams of saw palmetto a day. Saw palmetto blocks the conversion of testosterone to dihydrotestosterone, which is much stronger and is responsible for excess cell growth in the prostate.

Large doses of testosterone can signal the pituitary gland that the testicles are producing adequate hormones, thus causing the pituitary gland to produce even less of the hormones that usually stimulate the testicles. This vicious circle can result in a lowered sperm count, which becomes a problem for a couple trying to conceive. Large doses can also cause a reduction in the size of the testes as they have less work to do.

Testosterone's possible side effects may include retention of salt and water in the kidneys, which would not be advisable for anyone with kidney or liver problems or coronary heart disease. It also may stimulate the sebaceous glands, which can cause acne—not usually a problem, however, for older men.

Prescription testosterone is available as a patch, injection, lozenge or transdermal gel. There is also a procedure available where testosterone pellets are implanted under the skin, but this involves a minor surgical procedure. You must see a doctor to obtain any of these testosterone treatments.

One of my colleagues and mentors, Julian Whitaker, M.D., is founder of the Whitaker Wellness Clinic and is totally devoted to natural healing and optimal health. He feels that well-monitored testosterone supplementation in men is very safe when administered in physiological doses (small amounts aimed at restoring testosterone to young adult level, but no higher), and generally done by injection. According to Dr. Whitaker side effects are minor, one of them being weight gain associated with increased muscle mass. (Oral doses of testosterone, however, can negatively affect the liver, so these are not usually recommended.)

Benefits of supplemental testosterone, according to Dr. Whitaker, are restored libido, increased muscle mass and tone, increased sense of well-being and improved bone density.

Men, if you are considering supplemental testosterone, be sure that your doctor tests your levels first. This can be accomplished either by blood test or by saliva test. A man's testosterone is at its peak in the early morning, so that is the ideal time to test your existing level.

My suggestion is that a man aim only to increase his testosterone level to that of a twenty-five- to thirty-year-old male.

Dr. Whitaker has been prescribing supplemental testosterone for many years. His preferred method is an injection using either testosterone cyprionate (100 milligrams per week) or testosterone enanthate (200 milligrams every other week).

I feel somewhat comfortable with the injection method as long as the dose is kept at the lowest minimum required to obtain results.

Rx: Please proceed with care in the case of testosterone supplements.

My own best recommendation for low testosterone is a natural product. Now, for the first time, a man or woman can walk into a health food store and buy a product that can help boost their testosterone level. I like a product called Testron SX, which includes tribulus terrestris, an herb that Russian weightlifters have used for years prior to Olympic trials.

There are several other natural substances that can effectively boost libido, which we will address at the end of this chapter. I personally favor the use of natural testosterone boosters as a way to enhance sexual desire and function. I have seen good results and no adverse effects from this approach.

Now, please read on to learn how natural progesterone may help.

PROGESTERONE AND MEN

Will progesterone, which helps raise a woman's sex drive, also help men who suffer with lowered libido? Perhaps. Researcher John R. Lee, M.D., told me that "in animal studies large doses of progesterone inhibited sexual behavior, but a physiologic dose (equivalent to what the body would produce) stimulated male copulatory behavior."[2]

A study done some years ago addressed the issue of progesterone supplementation in men. The results showed that when progesterone is given to young men, their testosterone levels fell.[3] We know that progesterone is the precursor of testosterone in men. It is synthesized in their testes to produce testosterone. Dr. John Lee, who has done such extensive study and teaching on hormones, suggests that because many testosterone receptors accept progesterone, it is very probable that a biofeedback signal in the brain automatically reduces testosterone production when it senses a higher level of progesterone in the body in young men.[4]

However, other research seems to suggest that in men over age fifty-five, progesterone supplementation can increase libido.[5] From my own experience, a number of my male patients who are over fifty-five have reported that the use of ¼ teaspoon of natural progesterone rubbed on the perineum has helped boost sex drive and assisted in erections.

Progesterone can play a very important role in men with prostate cancer who have either had surgery or have been given medication that prevents them from making as little testosterone as possible. This can bring on osteoporosis very quickly, because testosterone is similar to progesterone in stimulating new bone growth and increasing bone density.

Dr. Lee suggests that progesterone may be a safe supplement for these men to prevent osteoporosis.

I had Dr. Lee as a guest on my television show *Doctor to Doctor* to do a series on natural hormones. During one of the shows he told our audience that men over fifty-five could use natural progesterone to keep their testosterone from splitting into metabolites. These metabolites can cause the prostate to enlarge, causing benign prostatic hypertrophy (BPH). He concluded that natural progesterone might be just as powerful as saw palmetto for keeping the prostate healthy.

Progesterone cream has also been found to provide relief from pain and swelling of rheumatoid arthritis in older men who rubbed it on their joints. I would suggest a dose of ¼ to ½ teaspoon twice daily.

So, you can see that natural progesterone does have some very positive benefits for men. I am sure further research will identify even more potential benefits from the use of this remarkable hormone.

SOME NATURAL SEX BOOSTERS

What can you do to retain your youthful vigor? There are several things I am going to recommend for you. Some are old, some are new (after all, we *have* entered the twenty-first century).

First of all, it has been proven that exercise is revitalizing to the body and releases those wonderful endorphins. Exercise should be your first step. However, assuming that you have already realized the benefits of exercise, I want to discuss some natural remedies. Please know that although I go along with medical prescription drugs for many health conditions, I like first to try *natural* products that do not have deleterious side effects.

> My philosophy is this: God and natural first. If that fails, then go to man-made.

TRIBULUS TERRESTRIS

Tribulus terrestris has been found to have a stimulating effect in both men and women on libido and sexual performance. Tribulus terrestris is a small vine belonging to the natural order *Zygophyllaceae*. Its common name is *puncture vine.* Tribulus was used by the ancient Greeks, and has been used in India and in China for many years. The most common cross-cultural use of tribulus has been in the treatment of infertility in women, impotence in men and for increasing the libido of both men and women.

Studies have been conducted at the Chemical Pharmaceutical Research Institute in Sofia, Bulgaria, which in 1981 showed that tribulus taken for just five days increased testosterone levels by a significant 30 percent or more.[6] It thus became very popular with world-class Russian athletes, especially prior to competition, due to its fitness-enhancing benefits. It is now used also by American athletes.

Since the early 1980s, tribulus terrestis has been used in Europe to treat impotence and infertility. The action of tribulus is based on an increase in testosterone levels. Tribulus appears to cause the release of a luteinizing hormone (LH), which is formed in the pituitary gland. The LH sends a message to cells to produce more testosterone. Thus, tribulus can help supplement natural testosterone production and help to naturally increase libido, energy and muscle mass formation.

In women, tribulus has been found to have a favorable effect on vasomotor manifestations during menopause and relieves subjective complaints such as general tenseness, irritability and apathy (loss of interest in sex). Results will not be immediate, as the testosterone levels will need to build. You should allow forty to fifty days for effects to be noticed.

Men who choose to take tribulus have been reported to experience increased libido, increased potency and increased frequency and strength of erections. Other positive changes observed were reduction of cholesterol and positive psychological effects such as increased self-confidence and improved mood. No serious side effects were noted in any of the clinical studies. It has a long and diverse history of safe use and apparent absence of toxicity.

For women, this is a unique sexual stimulator because there are no reported androgenic effects in women such as facial

179

hair, which sometimes occurs with DHEA supplementation.

I have seen many specific benefits of tribulus use. In males, tribulus appears to increase the testosterone level. It increases libido and improves strength of erection. It also improves formation and development of sperm. In females, tribulus usage increases libido, may decrease menopause symptoms and reduces apathy (loss of interest in sex.)

At this time, many products are beginning to emerge in the United States that contain a preparation of the tribulus plant. Try to purchase from a reputable dealer as you would any health food product. The product that I recommend is Testron SX, which is manufactured by Nutraceutics Corporation.

AVENA SATIVA

Whoever coined the phrase "Sow your wild oats" probably had avena sativa in mind. Avena sativa is believed by many researchers to be a true aphrodisiac. Studies have shown that it reliably increases libido in both men and women.[7] It is not a hormone, and studies have shown no reports of unwanted hair growth or acne.

Avena sativa is made from green oats extract, which comes from the flowering oat plant. First, let's look at the benefits of avena sativa usage for men.

Older men may produce as much testosterone as a younger man, but the body is not able to use it as effectively as it once did. Testosterone is found in the blood in two forms—free and bound. Free testosterone is biologically active. Bound testosterone is either bound to albumin or globulin. Albumin-bound testosterone is biologically active, while globulin-bound testosterone is not. As a man ages, his globulin-bound testosterone levels rise, so his testosterone is not as biologically available to his body. Avena sativa appears to contain substances that have a similar make-up to natural testosterone. These substances can bind with the globulin proteins and cause the albumin-bound testosterone to increase. This is the testosterone that is available for the body to use.

A 1990 Hungarian double-blind study showed that testosterone excreted in the urine increased dramatically in men who were taking avena sativa as compared to those using a placebo. From a medical standpoint, the good news is that this increase occurred in men whose baseline levels of testosterone were low normal or normal. Men with an initial high level of testosterone did not show an increase in testosterone excretion.

This means that avena sativa will raise a man's testosterone's levels without taking him to excessive levels. This makes it a very safe product to use.

Men using avena sativa report that:

- Erections become more frequent and firmer.
- They have heightened and "more youthful" sexual response.
- They experience stronger orgasms.
- They have increased sexual energy.
- They engage in more frequent sexual activity.

Men who had complained of impotence reported occurrence of erections due to increased sexual excitement.

Avena sativa also appears to improve immune function and to improve mood. One of my patients reported that her husband's sex drive increased so dramatically on avena sativa that she actually resorted to hiding the supplement bottle. He was chasing her around the kitchen in the middle of the day!

What does avena sativa do for women? Women who take avena sativa do not report as consistent an increase in libido as men do. In my experience, some women report quite dramatic increases, and some do not note an increase. However, in the women who get a positive reaction, the feelings of sexuality are reported to be quite intense.

Women who take supplemental avena sativa have told me that they have experienced an increase in the number of climaxes as well as an increase in overall sexual activity.

My patients on avena sativa have also reported that they have noticed an increase in vaginal secretions. This supplement may not work for all women, but there is enough evidence to make it worth trying. A second interesting benefit is that many of my patients have reported that avena sativa has reduced their cravings for sweets. It may be that this supplement affects the same area of the body that signals the brain to crave sugar. In any event, it is a wonderful side effect for many people.

Grab your sweetie instead of those sweets!

DHEA

DHEA is short for dehydroepiandrosterone. It is a hormone that is produced mainly by the adrenal glands in both men and women, but it is also made in the testicles, ovaries and brain. DHEA affects many hormone-related functions from the pituitary and thyroid to the adrenal glands and reproductive organs. DHEA is known as the body's "mother hormone." It is a precursor of both estrogen and testosterone. It is a very complex hormone, and researchers have found it difficult to separate the effects of DHEA from those of the primary sex steroids into which it is metabolized. DHEA may essentially serve a general purpose in the body and act as a buffer against age-related bodily changes.

DHEA declines significantly with age. By our late sixties we will have just about 10 percent of the DHEA we had in our youth. As I said, DHEA is the precursor to the steroid sex hormones, including estrogen and testosterone.

Can DHEA help increase libido? Because DHEA is the master hormone that controls the production of the sex hormones, when loss of libido is the result of DHEA or sex hormone deficiency, using it as a supplement can increase sex drive and enhance libido.

From the doctors I interviewed at the 7th Annual Conference on Anti-Aging Medicine in December 1999, I learned that DHEA is very effective in increasing testosterone levels in women. According to many anti-aging experts, taking between 10 to 25 milligrams per day can increase testosterone levels by one and one-half times to two times. I recommend the lower dose for women who want to take DHEA, as is wise when beginning any supplement.

In some women DHEA has also been found to reduce vaginal atrophy along with increasing libido.

In men, DHEA has been found to have a positive effect on erectile dysfunction. Men in a double-blind controlled study noticed moderate improvement in erections after eight weeks and significant improvement after sixteen weeks.[8]

Men and women who take DHEA have reported significant increases in energy and psychological well-being, and they report that they begin to feel more amorous. Some men have even said that they feel an increase in libido about thirty minutes after an evening dose.

DHEA has been reported to be safe in humans in low daily doses. However, it has been my experience that most people who take supplemental DHEA take too much. Most of the DHEA pills on the market come in 25- and 50-milligram dosages. I feel that 5 to 10 milligrams is a much more appropriate starting dose. You should still achieve some increase in your testosterone production at the lower levels.

Known side effects of too much DHEA supplementation are acne, heart palpitations, unwanted hair growth in women and irritability or mood changes—much the same side effects as too much testosterone. If doses are too high, estrogen levels are raised in men, and they can experience breast swelling. Optimally you should check your DHEA levels before beginning supplementation with pharmaceutical-grade DHEA. If you have regular medical checkups, have your DHEA level checked along with your other blood work. Otherwise, consider a saliva test prior to starting, and repeat the saliva test after three to four months. Ideal levels are those of a young adult—you do not want to exceed this. No one under the age of thirty-five should take DHEA unless specifically advised to do so by a physician.

DHEA affects a number of hormones in the body, and there are doctors who believe that comprehensive testing should be done before you can make an intelligent choice regarding a pharmaceutical-grade DHEA dose. That is why I like to recommend a product called DHEA PLUS, which contains special phytonutrients from the Dioscorea wild yam. This product offers a base of phytogenins and phytosterols, which the body seems to adapt to better than pharmaceutical DHEA. Also, the human body normally releases DHEA throughout the day while most capsules or tablets release all of the DHEA at once.

I like DHEA PLUS because it offers a delivery system that releases its phytonutrients over a twelve- to fifteen-hour time period. It is all natural and virtually free of side effects.

DHEA PLUS works in total harmony with the body to help supplement your own DHEA production. Note: No one who has a hormone-responsive cancer such as prostate, ovarian, cervical or breast should take DHEA. People with thyroid disorders should also not take it.

L-ARGININE

L-arginine has been called an herbal alternative to Viagra. It has been found to be equally effective in many men, although most reports are based on anecdotal evidence and scientific reasoning rather than exact science. There is also evidence that women who take it also note heightened sexual interest and response.

How does it work? L-arginine is an amino acid that is the precursor to nitric oxide (NO). The use of arginine increases NO levels in both men and women. It has very widespread influence on the body's blood vessels. In men, erections occur when the brain signals the body to produce NO. In turn, the NO triggers the release of a compound that causes relaxation of the smooth muscles inside the penis. This allows the tissues inside the penis to engorge with blood, and an erection occurs. If a man is deficient in NO, he will not have a firm—or perhaps any—erection at all.

Anecdotal reports of the success of L-arginine in treatment of depressed libido and erectile dysfunction have been documented quite frequently in medical literature. According to anti-aging experts I have interviewed, men who take L-arginine have reported improvement in erectile function, firmer erections and longer periods of remaining erect. Other extremely important benefits are protection against heart disease by preventing formation of plaque, assistance in lowering blood pressure because it is a powerful vaso-dilator and helping the body to shed fat and build and tone muscle. Naturopathic doctors have told me that arginine helps restore normal function in arteries damaged by high cholesterol. Because erectile dysfunction is often associated with hypertension and atherosclerosis due to decreased circulation, L-arginine has many positive benefits.

Women have reported increased sensitivity and lubrication in the genital area, which leads to enhancement of libido. Arginine is found in health food stores in both capsule and powder form. The usual dose is 1 gram three times per day, although some people require more initially to notice benefits.

If you have chronic herpes outbreaks, taking arginine may trigger this condition. To counteract the effects of arginine in this regard, take 500 milligrams of lysine daily.

Arginine is found in many foods, including chocolate, nuts, sunflower seeds and protein-rich foods. However, foods with high arginine levels were not found to produce the same effects as synthesized free arginine.

ANDROSTENEDIONE

Androstenedione is a steroid hormone that is a direct precursor to testosterone and is believed to raise testosterone levels quite rapidly after administration. It produces the same enhancing effects as testosterone, including increased energy, increased libido, increased tolerance for stress and a general sense of well-being. It may be used by both men and women. In men it is made mainly in the testes. In women it is produced in the adrenal glands and ovaries.

If a woman's ovaries have been removed surgically or have diminished function due to aging or menopause, her adrenal glands become the main source of her androgens by producing androstenedione. Her body then converts this into testosterone.

Androstenedione may also have an effect on maintaining bone strength since it is converted to estradiol in the bones. Estradiol is known to help slow bone loss. Some studies are being conducted to see if it actually can be found to help reverse osteoporosis, although I have not seen any completed studies to date. Androstenedione is currently available in oral form, transdermal form and as a nasal spray. Clinical studies filed with German patent authorities showed that peak plasma levels were obtained within thirty to ninety minutes and remained elevated for approximately three hours. The oral spray was said to work in minutes. One study showed that oral doses raised testosterone levels by 140 to 237 percent and were much more effective than DHEA.

The greatest significance was that the increase lasted only two to three hours and more closely mimicked the physiology of our bodies. Because androstenedione has a very short half-life, it may effectively and significantly raise testosterone levels for a short term, but it has little long-term effect.

That is why many men like to use it just prior to intercourse. This short half-life means that androstenedione does not have a detrimental effect on the body or what we call the *negative feedback factor*, which occurs when your body begins to decrease its own testosterone production because of the outside supplementation.

This short half-life does not make it valuable for increases in muscle mass, but it does have a performance-enhancing result that is embraced by athletes and bodybuilders who want to boost their performance.

If you are experiencing symptoms of diminished testosterone but do not wish to supplement with testosterone, this may be a good alternative. Use it with great caution. Start with the lowest possible dose. When you notice improvement in your libido and energy, do not exceed that dose. It should not be used by men who have a history of prostate disease, as it is a testosterone-boosting product.

Women who use androstenedione should take care to decrease the dose or discontinue its use if they begin to develop unwanted facial hair, a deepening of their voice or acne. Please be aware that it can also increase estrogen levels in women.

If you wish to try this supplement to enhance libido, I suggest you use the nasal spray, which seems to be more effective and does not tax the liver. It is recommended that you use androstenedione supplements in a cycle. Use the supplement for three to four weeks, then take one to three weeks off. I personally recommend a product called ANDROGENX Spray, which is manufactured by Phamacologic Laboratories.

Human growth hormone

If your libido is lagging, your energy low, your muscles soft and you are also worried about diseases of aging such as heart disease and atherosclerosis, I highly recommend an oral human growth hormone product. I am not referring to synthetic growth hormone injections, but rather a natural secretagog that will stimulate the body's own growth hormone to be released.

Human growth hormone, or HGH, is one of many endocrine hormones such as estrogen, progesterone, testosterone, melatonin and DHEA that decline with age. HGH, which is also known as somatotropin, is secreted by the pituitary gland. The decline of growth hormone (GH) with age has been directly associated with decreased energy and sexual function. Research has suggested that changes in hormones like somatostatin, which regulate growth hormones, are responsible for GH decline. However, evidence shows that the pituitary gland maintains the ability to release growth hormone if it is properly stimulated. Secretagogues are substances that stimulate the pituitary gland to secrete growth hormone. These cutting-edge substances may be able to re-create the body's youthful growth hormone secretion pattern according to the many experts I have spoken with at the anti-aging conferences I attend. Clinical studies and anecdotal evidence certainly seem to support this.

187

Studies published in the *New England Journal of Medicine* and other journals show that HGH may:

- ∾ Restore muscle mass
- ∾ Decrease body fat
- ∾ Reduce wrinkles
- ∾ Restore hair and/or hair color
- ∾ Increase energy
- ∾ Increase sexual function
- ∾ Improve cholesterol profile
- ∾ Improve vision

- ∾ Improve memory
- ∾ Elevate mood
- ∾ Improve sleep patterns
- ∾ Normalize blood pressure
- ∾ Improve immune function
- ∾ Increase cardiac output and stamina

Anti-aging experts whom I have interviewed on *Doctor to Doctor* say that the response to sex hormones like testosterone is enhanced with growth hormone therapy. This can explain the reported increase in sex drive in both men and women. In addition, GH helps increase circulation, which enhances sexual pleasure in women and helps a man maintain an erection.

The decline in a man's potency closely parallels the decline of the release of HGH in his body. Clinical studies have indicated that a significant number of men who were placed on HGH therapy reported improvement in their sexual function—in potency, frequency of intercourse and the time their erections lasted.[9]

HGH enhances natural hormone production in a woman, and it has a positive effect on diminished libido related to hormonal imbalance and decreased testosterone production.

A study done by the Palm Springs Life Extension Institute revealed the following positive effects on libido and sexual function:

- ∾ Sexual potency/frequency—75 percent
- ∾ Duration of erection—62 percent
- ∾ Decreased hot flashes—58 percent
- ∾ Energy level—84 percent
- ∾ Improved mood—78 percent[10]

These improvements occurred within one to three months of supplementation with maximum benefits being noticed after six months.

I have recommended HGH secretagogue to my patients for over five years and have found it to dramatically increase sex drive, energy and muscle strength in my patients. Almost everyone, both male and female, reported some degree of sexual rejuvenation. Other reported benefits from my patients are improved skin texture and elasticity, wrinkle disappearance, new hair growth, increased emotional stability, mood elevation and improved memory.

Due to the remarkable results reported with the use of human growth hormone, many new products have appeared on the market. Most use a combination of amino acids, which have been shown to increase production of HGH in the body. The most common ones contain some combination of arginine, ornithine, glutamine, lysine, and/or glycine.

Contrary to the cost of synthetic GH injections, which is between $800 to $1,200 per month and which I do not recommend as they utilize synthesized growth hormone, the natural substances can cost very little in relation to the benefits. They can be found at most health food stores. Some of them do not have any clinical studies attached to them, so please buy from a reputable vendor.

189

My personal recommendation is a product known as PRO-hGH, which was developed by third-generation pharmacologist James Jamieson. He has been working on his formula for the past two decades to be sure that he has achieved effective absorption and delivery to the proper receptor sites. It is an all-natural compound that releases growth hormone in the form of a pleasant-tasting tablet that dissolves into an effervescent drink. It is manufactured by Nutraceutics Corporation.

YOHIMBE

Yohimbe is a herb that is a much weaker version of yohimbine hydrochloride, which is available by prescription only. Yohimbine is the only FDA-approved drug for the treatment of erectile dysfunction and is often prescribed for impotence, but it has many serious side effects, including anxiety, hallucinations, elevated blood pressure or sudden drop in blood pressure, headache and dizziness. It has also been known to cause paralysis.

Please do not confuse these two products: Yohimbine requires a prescription; yohimbe can be found in health food stores.

Yohimbe is derived from the bark of a tree found in West Africa. It appears to act as a central nervous system stimulant and also dilates blood vessels. Reports indicate that it helps increase blood flow to the penis and therefore aids in erectile dysfunction.

I include mention of yohimbe here because some studies have concluded that yohimbe's benefits for men with E.D. may outweigh its risks. However, I do not recommend use of this supplement. I have never personally prescribed it, but I have heard of many powerful and undesirable side effects. There have been instances of severe adverse reactions due to some dangerous brands on the market. Yohimbe contains yohimbine bark extract, and some products have unsafe levels.

Certainly do not use this supplement if you have any history of kidney disease, low blood pressure, heart problems or take antidepressant medication. If you do take yohimbe, do so only under a physician's supervision. My recommendation is that you try tribulus terrestis, avena sativa, gingko biloba or L-arginine instead.

STINGING NETTLE (*URTICA DIOCA*)

Urtica has been found to be effective in the treatment of erectile dysfunction and cases of enlarged prostate. A rather large study done in 1995 showed that men with enlarged prostates improved after taking a mixture of urtica and saw palmetto. According to the study, urtica suppresses prostate cell metabolism and growth by allowing more male hormone to be distributed through the blood.[11] Urtica has been used for many years in Germany as a treatment for enlarged prostate. Urtica helps reduce the sexual dysfunction of an enlarged prostate and can also protect men from the side effects of taking powerful prescription drugs for prostate enlargement.

For men with E.D., urtica may be very helpful. The nettle root extract increases the level of free testosterone and has a positive effect on the libido. It does this by acting as a decoy for the sex hormone-binding globulin. When testosterone binds to this globulin, it loses its biological availability in the body. Nettle, in essence, fools the globulin and causes it to bind with the nettle. This leaves more testosterone to be free in the body. Thus, libido is increased.

The other positive benefits were related to the prostate and showed that stinging nettle increased urinary flow, decreased urinary frequency and assisted urination with men having less residual urine in the bladder after urination.

Ginkgo biloba

Ginkgo biloba is one of the most commonly prescribed supplements in Europe. Ginkgo biloba has been shown to help blood flow more freely, especially to the extremities. Its work seems to be done by preventing platelets from clumping together. Therefore your blood has a more free-flowing consistency. Gingko is also rich in flavonoids, which are powerful antioxidants. It helps to strengthen capillaries—the tiny vessels that carry blood to tissues.

Gingko has been found to be helpful to men with erectile dysfunction caused by decreased blood flow. In one promising study 50 percent of the men regained potency within six months of taking 60 milligrams of ginkgo extract per day.[12]

Ginkgo should be very helpful to people who have poor blood flow, specifically smokers, diabetics, people with narrowing of the arteries and high cholesterol. Remember, the three main causes of low testosterone levels and erectile difficulties in men are smoking, diabetes and heart disease.

Gingko also has been effective as a mood elevator. Many women who take it say that they have found themselves more interested in sex. This may be due to the fact that ginkgo appears to have an anti-aging effect on the body. It is well known for its restorative effects on the brain and appears to increase the brain's ability to utilize glucose and produce energy. This is what I like to call a "tonic effect," as it gives an overall boost to mood and feelings of well-being, which can translate into much more interest in the bedroom.

Remember to give ginkgo biloba time to work. Many

people start to notice its benefits in two to three weeks, but it may take up to three months to notice your improvement. When selecting your gingko, be sure the product is standardized to contain 24 percent gingko flavonglycosides. This should be clearly marked on the label of the product.

Because of its blood-thinning properties, people who take aspirin, Coumadin or other medications that thin the blood should consult their doctor before taking gingko, as should patients with any bleeding problems. You should stop using gingko for three to four weeks prior to surgery and advise your doctor that you have been taking it.

GINSENG

Panax ginseng has long been popular as a Chinese herbal aphrodisiac. Ginseng belongs to the group of herbs known as *adaptogens*. Adaptogens work to help the body return to a balanced state. Ginseng contains substances that help increase the production of sex hormones.

In the 1990s, researchers in the United States found that the ginsenosides in ginseng help release nitric oxide, which is an important factor in erections. It triggers a response in the body that allows the smooth muscle of the spongy tissue of the penis to relax and fill with blood during the period of sexual arousal. A 1995 study published in the *International Journal of Impotency Research* showed that about 60 percent of men who took Panax ginseng had higher libido and higher incidences of penile rigidity.[13]

Benefits for both men and women include improved mental stamina, higher energy levels and improved mood. It is recommended as an anti-aging "tonic" by many naturopathic physicians. Ginseng also reduces the negative effects of chronic stress on the body, which we know is responsible for diminished sexual drive. Studies have shown Panax ginseng to boost libido in both men and women.

High doses of Panax ginseng may cause insomnia, headache, heart palpitations and may elevate blood pressure. You should not take ginseng if you have high blood pressure or if you take heart medication. It has occasionally been found to cause vaginal bleeding in postmenopausal women. Siberian ginseng is usually less potent than Panax ginseng and does not have a history of side effects.

My patients report that ginseng appears to enhance the effects of avena sativa, so you may want to try adding this if your avena sativa trial does not reap benefits. Or you may wish to start by taking both together to obtain optimum libido enhancement.

Choose your ginseng wisely. Quality control of this supplement has been known to fluctuate dependent on the manufacturer.

L-TYROSINE

L-tyrosine is an amino acid and a precurser to neurotransmitters that determine mood, energy level and sex drive. Studies have shown that tyrosine increase the rate at which the brain produces dopamine and norepinephrine. Increased dopamine levels have been associated with an improvement in libido. It is also a natural antidepressant and helps to counteract the effects of stress on the body. The usual dose is 1,000 milligrams twice daily, thirty minutes before meals.

MUIRA PAUMA EXTRACT

Muira pauma means "potent wood" and is extracted from a shrub that grows in Brazil. It has long been used as an aphrodisiac in South America. It has recently gained a reputation as a sexual enhancer for men.

Several studies done in the 1990s have indicated that muira pauma is safe and effective in improving libido. Both studies were conducted in Paris. In the first study 356 men participated, and over 60 percent reported improvement in libido and sexual function.[14] In the second study involving men who were complaining of lack of desire and the inability to achieve or maintain an erection, 66 percent reported a significant increase in frequency of intercourse, and 55 percent reported firmer and more reliable erections.[15] Of the men who had complained of failing to be able to achieve erections, 51 percent reported satisfactory results. Some of these results were reported within two weeks, but the full effects were not noticed until sometime thereafter, indicating that muira pauma has a cumulative effect. The daily dose used in the studies was 1 to 1½ grams of standardized extract.

All of the studies were performed on men, and researchers are not sure exactly how muira puama works to improve sexual performance and libido. Patients stated that they felt both physical and psychological benefits.

SAW PALMETTO

Saw palmetto *(serenoa repens)* is a species of dwarf palm trees that grow in the Southeastern United States. The crushed berries from the saw palmetto plant contain compounds that help inhibit the production of dihydrotestosterone, which contributes to enlargement of the prostate.

Saw palmetto is used extensively in Europe and now in the United States to treat benign prostate hypertrophy. It helps reduce prostate size, pain and blockage, increases urine flow and decreases nighttime urination in men with BPH. It improves general prostate health. It may help stimulate the libido, but this is probably due to a man feeling more motivated to engage in sex after improvement of prostate and urinary conditions.

Studies have shown saw palmetto to work just as well as the prescription drug Proscar. Proscar has caused some men to experience decreased libido, ejaculation problems and even impotence. Switching to saw palmetto may definitely enhance libido in these patients.

ZINC

Zinc is essential for testosterone production. Although the exact role zinc plays is not fully understood, it may influence the action of enzymes that cause testosterone to be synthesized from other hormones.

Zinc is essential for hormone activity, and it is the most important nutrient of the prostate gland. It is also a major component of seminal fluid. Low levels of zinc have been associated with low testosterone levels, decreased sperm count and benign prostatic hyperplasia (enlarged prostate).

194

Impotent men are more likely to have low levels of zinc.

Studies show that getting sufficient zinc relieves BPH. Some believe, in fact, that supplementary doses of zinc, about 50 milligrams per day, may help prevent or reverse prostate enlargement. One very significant study showed that when young men (age twenty-seven to twenty-eight) were put on a zinc-restricted diet, their testosterone levels decreased by over 70 percent within five months. Conversely, when older men (age fifty-five to seventy-three) who had slight zinc deficiency were given zinc as a supplement, their testosterone levels increased by an average of 92.8 percent![16]

Oysters are high in zinc, and this is probably the reason that they have earned their reputation as an aphrodisiac. Other foods high in zinc include lean meat, poultry, pumpkin seeds, lima beans and organ meats.

Studies have indicated that if you are not deficient in zinc, taking extra zinc will not increase your testosterone production.

VIP Gel for men

195

Jim Jamieson, a third-generation pharmacologist from one of America's leading families in pharmaceutical research and one of the most extraordinary researchers I have ever encountered, has provided us with a "natural" alternative to Viagra. It is not taken orally or injected, but rather it is applied topically.

The product is a vaso-active peptide called VIP Gel. It is a powerful vasodilator. Like Viagra, it causes the release of nitrous oxide (NO), which in turn activates an enzyme cascade that results in the metabolite cyclic GMP, otherwise known as cGMP. The cGMP relaxes muscles in the corpora cavernosa, which is the spongy tissue in the penis. The relaxation allows the tissue to engorge with blood, resulting in an erection.

Unlike Viagra, VIP Gel does not have potentially fatal side effects. It is applied directly to the penis fifteen to thirty minutes prior to intercourse. The goal is to produce an erection capable of sustaining intercourse. As with any treatment, there will be a variance in the time for optimum results. Some men may notice immediate results, while others may need a longer course of therapy.

According to Jim Jamieson, Viagra is known to be about 50 percent effective while his anecdotal evidence shows VIP Gel to be effective in 75 percent of the men who used it.

Women may also use VIP Gel to enhance or restore sexual pleasure. It stimulates the woman's clitoris by dilating the capillaries.

Please see the Product Source Guide in the back of the book for information on how to obtain VIP Gel, which is available only through physicians.

APHRODISIACS

"Are there foods that really do act as aphrodisiacs?" Many foods have been touted as aphrodisiacs throughout the ages. Many people proclaim the aphrodisiac qualities of certain foods. It would be presumptuous to say that they do not work for some people. However, any libido-enhancing results may be due to the strong placebo effect. With the exception of oysters, which are high in zinc, research is purely anecdotal to date. However, if you are interested in experimenting, here are some other foods reputed to be aphrodisiacs:

- Tomatoes ("love apples")
- Garlic (believe it or not!)
- Figs
- Artichokes
- Chilis
- Balsamic vinegar
- Okra
- Cloves
- Nutmeg
- Saffron
- Vanilla

I personally believe that it may not be these foods that are the enhancer, but the anticipation and the fact that you eat them with your beloved with the idea that a romantic interlude may occur. However, with all the busy researchers in the world today, I do not rule out the possibility that some of these "sexy" foods will some day be scientifically proven to enhance libido. In the meantime, if you are looking for something that has been documented to have libido-enhancing effects, don't forget your wild green oats (avena sativa)!

SOME TIPS FOR SEXUAL NUTRITION

1. Limit animal fat. Choose fish, soy and legumes for protein.

2. Increase foods that are high in vitamin B, especially B_3 and B_6, which assist in the production of sex hormones. These include wheat germ, eggs, avocados, dates, figs and fish (vitamin B_3), and soybeans, black strap molasses, spinach and cantaloupe (vitamin B_6).

3. Imbibe small amounts of alcohol only.

4. Increase amounts of fruits and vegetables, as these provide the broadest range of nutrients of any of the food groups and are very high in crucial antioxidants.

5. Snack on pumpkin seeds, which are high in zinc.

197

EXERCISE

I know you have all been informed over and over again about the benefits of exercise. You may be groaning to see this section included. However, I want to briefly address the effects of exercise on the libido.

Researchers and scientists are in agreement that women who exercise regularly have a tendency to enjoy sex more and to have more of it. First of all, fitness improves health, and a healthy body should lead to a healthier libido due to increased stamina and improved mood.

After moderate exercise a woman's autonomic nervous system moves into an excited state and her heart rate increases. This increases blood flow to the genital area. I find that even women with dramatically reduced libidos are more susceptible to arousal due to increased blood flow to the vagina after pedaling an exercise bike for twenty minutes. If your sex drive is suffering (and this applies to men also), exercising just three times per week can jump-start sexual interest through a boost in energy.

Another way exercise improves libido is by increasing positive body image, especially for women. Men seem to have a more well-rounded approach to seeing themselves as a total human being, incorporating all of their attributes—good father, good provider, good golfer, good husband. That is why men seldom seem to be alarmed if they put on a few pounds. Women are much more focused on their bodies as the major part of their image. If a woman does not feel good about her body, she is likely to inhibit her libido and sexual nature. She will spend more time during sex trying to hide her body than she will in concentrating on her sexual feelings.

Exercising stimulates the adrenal glands, which we know convert androstenedione into estrogen and testosterone. Regular exercise sessions can help keep your estrogen levels up during menopause.

Exercise is known to improve mood through the release of endorphins. I can personally vouch for this. When I am faithful enough to get on my treadmill, I notice a very significant difference in my thinking patterns. I usually pray for the hour I am on the treadmill.

We all have heard that long-term exercise means stronger bones and a lowered risk of osteoporosis. Another benefit is increased flexibility in your joints, which will come in very handy when you are still making love with your spouse into your eighties! No pulled muscles!

So, exercise should be on our list of "things to do," as it helps us control our bodies and our emotions. I hate to add anything to anyone's list—most people have lists that are long enough—but since exercise is also a stress reducer, I will not feel guilty!

CHAPTER 14

Tips for a Better Love Life

D ear Readers: These are some of the tips that I have either gleaned from my patients over the many years I have spent discussing sexual issues with them, or from my friends or people I know with happy, loving marriages. I hope some of them will be of help to you!

GENERAL TIPS

∾ Look positively at the mystery of figuring out how men and women differ! Do not look at it in a disgruntled manner or as inconvenient or too much trouble. Enjoy the differences; they are a gift from God!

∾ Men like to make love with a *spotlight* (focus on genitals); women like to make love with a *floodlight* (focus on whole body).

∾ Sweet breath is very important for lovemaking. There is a product called CloSYS, which is remarkable for clearing up even the worse cases of halitosis. I have a folder of letters testifying to its value in keeping some love lives alive! It is a patented, extremely effective mouthwash made with chlorine dioxide, which, when used, keeps breath fresh for up to eight hours. You can use it at night and wake up with good breath.

If you can't get close, use CloSYS to help you in the first step toward intimacy—loving kisses.

ॐ Don't play try to "catch-up" sexually when it's time for bed. If you allow yourself sexual thoughts throughout the day, arousal will be much easier. If sex is always the last thing on your mind, eventually it will become the last thing in your life.

A NOTE FROM DR. PENSANTI

Dear Readers: I think it is important that you forgive him or her all his or her trespasses, though they be many!

Worship God, forgive others and intercede for others. These three things will bring you to a wonderful state of mind and refresh you body, mind and spirit.

TIPS FOR MEN

ॐ Women's loss of desire has much to do with a lack of foreplay. This does not need to be sexual. Some well-placed tenderness, flowers, compliments, a backrub or a take-out meal can go a long way to creating a spark. One woman noted that whenever her husband leans over to kiss her and then takes out the garbage, she feels a surge of sexual interest.

ॐ The more a man does nonsexual things, the more receptive a woman is sexually.

ॐ Open the car door for her; she will love it!

ॐ Stand when she enters or leaves the room.

ॐ Pull out her chair for her.

ॐ Have good table manners.

ॐ Pay attention when she is talking to you.

ॐ Make positive comments about her body. Most women question their looks in some way. Ask her what she likes best about yours. Her answer may surprise you!

ॐ Fifty percent of women have difficulty achieving orgasm through intercourse alone, no matter how long it lasts. She may require manual or oral stimulation to increase her arousal level before you begin intercourse, or you can add manual stimulation of the clitoris during intercourse. Countless studies show that women whose husbands give them a little extra clitoral stimulation during lovemaking are more apt to climax on a consistent basis.

∾ The female actually has a greater capacity for sexual response than a male. She has an organ (the clitoris) with no other known purpose than sexual pleasure.

∾ Try not to immediately place your hands on your wife's breasts or genitals. Give her a little time to "warm up."

TIPS FOR WOMEN

∾ Men like stronger, deeper caresses and pressure. Testosterone makes their skin thicker.

∾ Men have revealed to me that they are really looking for the same things from sex that women are—love, acceptance and intimacy. They are not just "sexual animals" as they are often portrayed.

201

∾ Most men are not as enthralled with oral sex as we are led to believe. They prefer more standard forms of intercourse. So do not be intimidated or feel guilty if this is not something you like or desire.

∾ Studies show that testosterone surges around 7 or 8 A.M. This is the ideal time to approach your man for a positive response. However, anytime up to 10 A.M. may be just as strong. By the way, did you know that 10 A.M. is your peak time?

∾ Be careful of criticism and nagging. This is men's number one complaint about their wives. Men say they want to feel appreciated. When was the last time you paid your husband a compliment? Remember to "brag, don't nag."

∾ A very sensitive area on men is on the neck and throat (where their whiskers end), also where the neck joins the shoulder.

❧ Spray your sheets lightly with your cologne. This will impart a subtle message to him. He may not even realize what you have done.

❧ A man's nipples are often as sensitive as a woman's. As a matter of fact, if a man has trouble climaxing, it is often helpful to stimulate his nipples during intercourse.

❧ Realize that men think about sex more than women do. A study showed that 58 percent of men say they have sexual thoughts at least two to three times per week (less than 20 percent of women do).[1]

❧ Many men are too shy to speak up about where they like to be touched. Experiment!

❧ As I did my own survey for this book, an overwhelming majority of men (about 90 percent) said they liked to have their ears touched or caressed; they especially mentioned a light, sexy whisper.

❧ Give a man time for arousal. A woman's response is internal, not easily apparent. For the man, his lack of response is obvious. Imagine trying to make yourself get lubricated. That is the kind of pressure men face—if he becomes anxious or stressed, he will not be able to get an erection.

❧ Many men like talking during sexual intercourse. It enables them to totally focus on the sexual experience and relieves them of other anxieties and distractions. Try it and see!

❧ Men have reported that they like the feeling of their wives lovingly stroking their faces during lovemaking. This makes them feel that their wife really wants them and cherishes them.

❧ The majority of men like to feel their wife's hands gripping their derrières during intercourse. They like the feeling that you are pulling them tighter toward you, as if you just want to get lost in him. This works to your advantage because you can also use this to guide his rhythm.

~ The patch of skin between the testicles and anus is called the perineum. This has been called a man's "G-spot." Pressure on this spot with one or two fingers can send waves of pleasure through his body.

~ Increasing your husband's libido can be done by influencing his emotions. Use smell (your shampoo, perfume, scented candles) or music. A very soft voice stimulates his parasympathetic system. Remember Marilyn Monroe's soft sexy voice? She knew what she was doing!

~ Not really in the mood? Suggest a "quickie." This gives a man permission not to worry about foreplay. It will be fast. Men love it. And it is conspiratorial and humorous. The two of you can chuckle about it throughout the rest of the day.

~ Want to really excite and please him? Try a written invitation for a "romantic interlude." The anticipation for him will be delicious!

~ Want to have some more fun "teasing" your husband? You can create some wonderful sexual anticipation by planting a little seed during the daily routine. Try making a sexy phone call to him at work (without disturbing any big projects or meetings, of course) or flash a little breast with the morning coffee. I know it may sound contrived, but men are very much aroused by thinking of their wives in a sexual manner. This is something that is often drowned out by the stress and business of our daily agendas.

203

~ If you're feeling really brave, try revealing something new about yourself to your husband before sex. The mental connection is very powerful and leads to greater intimacy and greater pleasure.

CHAPTER 15

Common Questions About Natural Hormones

W omen, as you can now see, I firmly believe that you can jump-start your sex drive using natural hormones. Here is a quick review of the material I have presented in question-and-answer form. These are the questions I am most frequently asked in my lectures on natural hormones.

1. WHAT IS USP PROGESTERONE?

USP stands for *United States Pharmacopoeia*. The diosgenin used, which is the source of the progesterone, is extracted from a very specific type of wild yam that grows in Mexico or from soybeans. The USP means that it was taken into a laboratory and synthesized or converted into standardized form.

You will see products on the market that simply say "wild yam extract," not USP Progesterone. This means that it has not been converted or standardized. Many naturopathic doctors believe that this same conversion can take place in the human body, but others disagree. I have much anecdotal evidence that shows that some patients do get as much relief from their symptoms on wild yam extract as on USP Progesterone. However, it always depends on the patient and on the integrity of the product, so I prefer a standardized product. That way we know what we have.

2. How do I know if I should use natural progesterone?

❧ *If you have PMS or estrogen dominance symptoms.* PMS symptoms occur regularly seven to ten days before your period and stop after the period. Symptoms for both PMS and estrogen dominance include water retention, mood swings, loss of libido, swollen or tender breasts, irritability, anxiety, headaches and food cravings.

❧ *If you have menopausal symptoms.* These symptoms include hot flashes, night sweats, insomnia, vaginal dryness, loss of libido, emotional instability, lack of energy, rapid skin aging, loss of tone in breasts and forgetfulness or "fuzzy" thinking.

❧ *If you have osteoporosis.* Dr. Lee has studied the effect of natural progesterone on osteoporosis and found that it can help prevent and even build new bones.

3. Does natural progesterone help vaginal dryness?

Yes. Vaginal dryness can occur in women of all ages for various reasons. It is primarily present in postmenopausal women as hormone levels drop. A good non-irritating progesterone cream can be inserted intravaginally to attempt to restore moisture to the vaginal tissue.

However, if there is atrophy of the tissue and the progesterone cream does not help after a three-month trial, I would suggest switching to a phytoestrogen/phytoprogesterone blend (provided you have no history of breast or reproductive cancer). See chapter seven for a more in-depth discussion of vaginal dryness and painful intercourse. I also suggest vitamin E (inserted into vagina) and essential fatty acids taken orally to help lubricate vaginal tissues.

4. I am postmenopausal. Will I start menstruating again or have breakthrough bleeding if I use natural hormones?

The postmenopausal age group should not have any side effects at all. Occasionally upon beginning use of natural hormone supplements, postmenopausal women could experience some breakthrough bleeding or a "period." This rarely happens, but if it should, it is a perfectly normal response and is

205

nothing to be alarmed about. The progesterone is simply causing the body to rid itself of excess estrogen stored in the
endometrium and can sometimes stimulate a uterine shedding.
There have been reports of temporary incidental spotting, but
this stops after three months. Any persistent problems lasting
beyond that time period should be checked by a physician.

**5. How do I know whether I need natural progesterone
alone or natural progesterone with natural estrogen?**

If you are postmenopausal and have a history of reproductive organ or breast cancer, I recommend only natural progesterone. If you have breast pain or tenderness, you should
stick with natural progesterone, too. All others can use a
combination of natural progesterone and natural estrogen.

PMS sufferers usually exhibit the same symptoms as estrogen dominance. Therefore I recommend only natural progesterone. Usually PMS sufferers are too young to add natural
estrogen to their hormone mix anyway.

**6. I think I have estrogen dominance, but I felt worse after
I started natural progesterone. Why?**

During my many conversations with Dr. John R. Lee, I
learned that estrogen dominance prompts your body to "tune
down" estrogen receptors. The body is trying to protect itself
from too much estrogen, so it decreases the sensitivity of the
estrogen receptors. When progesterone is started, it
temporarily increases the sensitivity of these estrogen receptors. Your body is actually restoring estrogen dominance for a
while as the receptors resume normal sensitivity. At this time
there may be a period of adjustment when some women experience various uncomfortable symptoms that flare up, such as
swollen breasts, weight gain, water retention and headaches.
These estrogen side effects last only for the first month or
two. By the third month the body's progesterone level will rise
sufficiently to oppose this action. Therefore, if you will just
persevere for two to three months, these symptoms will subside, and you will begin to feel great and should obtain a
noticeable increase in your libido.

7. CAN I MIX SYNTHETIC ESTROGEN WITH NATURAL PROGESTERONE?

If you are unwilling or unable to discontinue your synthetic estrogen, please try adding natural progesterone to your daily regime. It will decrease your cancer risk at the same time it enhances your libido.

8. WHY IS TRANSDERMAL APPLICATION SO GOOD?

Natural hormones are small, fat-soluble molecules that are readily absorbed through the skin. They pass directly into the skin to the subcutaneous fat layers, then to blood circulation. So first the progesterone or progesterone/estrogen blend goes into body fats, and then into the blood.

9. HOW LONG BEFORE I NOTICE CHANGES IN MY LIBIDO?

Some women report immediate improvement. However, it may require up to three months use before maximum benefits are experienced. Do not give up too quickly. Use the adequacy of vaginal secretions as your guide. If you notice your vagina is moist and your mood is great, you are on the right track! Persevere, and you will be rewarded!

207

10. HOW SAFE IS NATURAL PROGESTERONE?

The safety of natural progesterone is well established. There have been no reports to the FDA of problems with it, hence the FDA permits the sale of progesterone and phytoprogesterone-estrogen creams at the levels we offer without a prescription.

However, please be careful about choosing over-the-counter natural progesterone products. You should buy only from reputable companies that are concerned with purity and high-quality ingredients. I had one patient who purchased a very cheap yam cream for $7.00 at a local health food store, and ended up in the hospital with cardiac arrhythmia. Her physician attributed it to an ingredient in the cream that triggered an allergic episode leading to an irregular heartbeat. Buyer, beware!

11. WHAT HAPPENS IF I USE TOO MUCH NATURAL PROGESTERONE?

If you are using too much, you may begin to feel drowsy.

Some women will also notice abdominal bloating. Simply cut back on your dose. You should be feeling energetic, not lethargic, on natural progesterone.

12. I HAVE HAD A HYSTERECTOMY, BUT STILL HAVE MY OVARIES. DO I NEED NATURAL HORMONES?

Yes. The blood supply to the ovaries is from a branch of the uterine artery that is cut and tied off (ligated) during a hysterectomy. This results in a loss of the ovarian function. Even though it appears that your ovaries have been saved, they usually stop functioning within two to three years. They atrophy and stop producing hormones. This contributes to a dramatic loss of libido in many women.

13. WHAT IF I DON'T HAVE A UTERUS AND AM TAKING ESTROGEN? MY DOCTOR SAYS I DO NOT NEED PROGESTERONE.

Although this is a twenty-year-old approach to treating women, it is very misguided according to experts in the field of hormones. You should always take progesterone along with estrogen, with or without a uterus, due to the increased risk of breast cancer associated with estrogen dominance. I believe that this applies to some of the soy products on the market today. Estrogen use without progesterone can lead to the highly undesirable state of estrogen dominance, which, as I have discussed, can lead to a diminished libido.

14. I HAVE BEEN TOLD THAT I HAVE VERY LOW ESTROGEN LEVELS, YET I FIT INTO THE SYMPTOMS OF ESTROGEN DOMINANCE. HOW CAN THIS BE?

Estrogen dominance, the phrase coined by Dr. John Lee after his extensive research in women's hormones, describes a condition in a woman's body where she has deficient, normal or excessive estrogen, but has little or no progesterone to balance its effects in the body.

Therefore, even a woman with low estrogen levels can be estrogen dominant. We add natural progesterone cream to restore hormonal balance and help bring back the woman's libido.

15. WHAT IF I HAVE HOT FLASHES AND VAGINAL DRYNESS THAT ARE AFFECTING MY LIBIDO, BUT I HAVE HAD BREAST CANCER—WHAT CAN I DO TO GET RELIEF?

In addition to using natural progesterone (stay away from estrogen since you have had breast cancer), there are several other things you can do to help with hot flashes: First, use your natural progesterone cream, using ¼ teaspoon twice daily. This is safe to use even if you have had breast cancer. Actually, this may alleviate up to 85 percent of your hot flashes, according to a recent study.[1] I also advise you to take vitamin E, up to 1000 international units per day. Take a good essential fatty acid supplement daily. More importantly, take a good B-complex containing vitamin B_6. Decrease your consumption of caffeine, spicy foods and large meals during periods of increased hot flashes. Because hot flashes are a temperature-control problem (changes in the hypothalmus associated with lower hormone levels trigger a cooling response at inappropriate times), keep a thermos of ice water on your nightstand or in your refrigerator and sip it during hot flashes.

Keep your room temperature at home at 65 degrees. Use deep breathing techniques. Do some slight exercises as exercise has been shown to increase the amount of estrogen circulating in the blood. Important tip: During severe episodes of hot flashes, apply ¼ teaspoon of progesterone cream every fifteen minutes for one hour following the episode.

For vaginal dryness: Use ¼ to ½ teaspoon of progesterone cream once a day intravaginally. This may be used in addition to, or instead of, your daily applications, dependent on severity of your symptoms. Many women also report success with the insertion of a vitamin E capsule into the vagina once daily until symptoms are relieved.

See chapter seven for more discussion on vaginal dryness and hot flashes.

16. HOW DO I USE NATURAL PROGESTERONE FOR TREATMENT OF PMS?

Excess estrogen and/or progesterone deficiency can cause some of the symptoms commonly referred to as PMS.

209

A woman's monthly cycle is regulated by the rise and fall of estrogen and progesterone. From day 1 through 12 of the menstrual cycle, estrogen is the dominating hormone causing the uterine lining to build up in preparation for a fertilized egg. The estrogen levels off just prior to ovulation when the egg is mature enough to produce progesterone. The progesterone causes the body temperature to rise and cervical secretions to thin. This is the time of month when libido is most likely to be high in a woman with normal hormone balance. If no pregnancy occurs within ten to twelve days following ovulation, both the estrogen and progesterone levels fall, and the uterine lining sheds in what is called menstruation. This is the natural ebb and flow of hormones. If progesterone levels are low and there is a hormonal imbalance, the negative effects of the excess estrogen can cause some of the symptoms of PMS, as well as loss of libido. Therefore, natural progesterone is one of the most effective remedies available to treat PMS. I recommend you take plenty of B vitamins, especially 250 milligrams of B_6 daily, or a good quality PMS vitamin formula.

17. I HAVE FACIAL HAIR, ESPECIALLY ABOVE MY UPPER LIP, WHICH MAKES ME FEEL VERY UNFEMININE. SOMETIMES I EVEN HAVE TO SHAVE. CAN YOU HELP ME?

Any excessive growth of facial and body hair is called *hirsutism*. It can be indicative of a hormonal imbalance between your estrogen, testosterone and progesterone. Because progesterone helps to regulate the entire hormone system, natural progesterone is the right choice for this condition. I have been treating women with unwanted facial hair with natural progesterone for almost ten years. My patients report that the facial hair and/or body hair either decreases or completely disappears after four to six months. The process is gradual, but effective. You should apply the cream twice daily. Use the instructions that apply to you if you are still menstruating or menopausal. You can actually rub a little of the cream directly on the face.

18. CAN NATURAL PROGESTERONE HELP WITH HOT FLASHES?

Postmenopausal women are still making estrogen. Estrogen continues to be made after menopause by the conversion of androstenediol, an adrenal steroid that is found in body fat cells. In fact, estrogen levels decrease only about 40 to 60 percent as compared to progesterone, which drops to very low levels. For this reason, and because progesterone is a precursor to estrogen, hot flashes often respond well to progesterone supplementation. Many women respond to a three-month trial of progesterone along with vitamin B_6 and vitamin C. (See more about hot flash therapies in chapter seven.)

If you are still experiencing too many flashes after three months, switch to a natural phytoestrogen/phytoprogesterone blend. Remember that estrogen is not recommended for women with a history of breast or uterine cancer.

I recommend that many of my patients begin right away with the phytoestrogen/phytoprogesterone blend, especially if their hot flashes are accompanied with night sweats and vaginal dryness.

Whichever cream you choose, my patients have reported dramatic relief and often cessation of hot flashes in as little as three weeks. In other women it may take a more gradual course, but usually they receive optimum benefits after eight to twelve weeks.

19. I HAVE HAD BREAST CANCER. WHY IS NATURAL PROGESTERONE SAFE FOR ME? I LIVE IN FEAR THAT MY CANCER WILL COME BACK. IT IS AFFECTING EVERYTHING I DO, INCLUDING MY SEX LIFE WITH MY HUSBAND.

Not only is natural progesterone safe for you, but it is actually protective against a recurrence of your cancer! First of all, excess estrogen is thought to be a major contributing cause to the increasing number of breast cancers in the United States. Progesterone balances the estrogen level in the body, so it lowers a woman's risk of getting breast cancer in the first place.

Many studies offer solid evidence that natural progesterone has an important role in preventing and treating breast cancer. Several distinct studies have revealed some very important mechanisms by which natural progesterone does this. The research showed that:

꙰ Excessive cell proliferation (hyperplasia) is a recognized signpost of potential cancer development. A 1995 study by Dr. K. J. Chang indicated that unopposed estrogen increased cell proliferation by 230 percent, whereas natural progesterone decreased it by more than 400 percent.[2]

꙰ A second study by Dr. William Hrushesky in Albany, New York, revealed that estrogen promotes delayed apoptosis. Apoptosis is the system our body uses to destroy old cells. Normal cells are programmed to live for only a specified time and then die as new cells replace them. If old cells are not destroyed, it increases their risk of becoming cancerous. Natural progesterone was found to decrease delayed apoptosis.[3]

꙰ The metastasis or spread of cancer cells depends on the permeability of blood vessels that allow the cancer cells to pass through their walls. Natural progesterone is found to reduce blood vessel permeability and thus helps protect against cancer cell metastasis.[4]

꙰ A link has been established between cancer and progesterone on the genetic level. Researchers grew cultures of cancer cells and then treated them with estrogen and progesterone. They found that estrogen alone promoted cancer growth, but when progesterone was added, tumor suppressor genes were stimulated and the cancer growth was stopped.[5]

꙰ A study at John Hopkins showed that the incidence of breast cancer was 5.4 times greater in women with low progesterone than in women who had good progesterone levels (regardless of age or history). The incidence of all kinds of neoplasms was ten times higher in women with low progesterone levels as compared to women with good progesterone levels.[6]

This is all very good news for women who worry about getting breast cancer and for those who have already been diagnosed. Please remember that we are talking about natural progesterone—not synthetic progestins. So please start using a good natural progesterone cream right away and protect against breast cancer. Remember: The bonus is that it will also increase your libido!

NOTE: Unopposed estrogen is a known cause of endometrial cancer, so natural progesterone is safe for women who have had uterine cancer, too.

20. CAN NATURAL PROGESTERONE HELP ME WITH MY "FUZZY THINKING"? SOMETIMES I FEEL AS IF I AM LOSING MY MIND OR MY MEMORY.

Yes, yes, yes. Hormonal imbalance is a prime cause of short-term memory loss and what you called "fuzzy thinking" in women. One of my patients told me that she had become a "walking Post-it note" because she had to write everything down and then stick the notes all over her body, purse, house and car! Progesterone has been found to be highly concentrated in brain cells, and although we do not know the exact mechanism, this strongly suggests that it serves an important purpose. I can tell you that one of the major improvements my patients relate to me is clearer thinking, usually within three weeks.

For those with more clogged memory channels, I recommend a product called GEROVITAL GH3; also, gingko biloba and pregnenolone.

21. WILL NATURAL HORMONES AFFECT MY THYROID MEDICATION?

It seems to be true that estrogen dominance interferes with or inhibits thyroid hormone activity, and progesterone facilitates it. Therefore, you may need a reduced dose of your thyroid medication after a few months of progesterone therapy. Some women eventually are able to discontinue thyroid supplementation entirely. When I first used natural progesterone, I lost four pounds. Amazed, I asked Dr. Lee what had happened. He reminded me of the fact that natural progesterone will often help stimulate a sluggish thyroid without the use of thyroid medication.

22. HOW OLD IS TOO OLD FOR NATURAL HORMONES?

Natural hormone supplementation is beneficial to women

213

of all ages who want to maintain optimal health and sexual vitality. In addition, it is particularly beneficial in the area of osteoporosis prevention. A study was conducted with one hundred patients who ranged in age for thirty-eight to eighty-three years. They were all menopausal. Each patient was followed for a minimum of three years. Of the sixty-three women who were given natural progesterone, the benefit proved to be extraordinary, showing that in three years, instead of losing 4.5 percent of bone as expected, the women actually increased their bone density by an a average of 15.4 percent, regardless of their age.[7]

Further, the study refuted the myth that osteoporosis is irreversible for older women, or even that it is more difficult to correct. Indeed, the women over the age of seventy showed even better results than the younger women!

23. WHY DOESN'T MY DOCTOR KNOW MORE ABOUT NATURAL HORMONE THERAPY?

Many doctors have little enough time to keep up with the world of rapidly changing and evolving prescription drugs. They focus their reading on the *Journal of the American Medical Association* and the *New England Journal of Medicine,* among others, and tend to be completely in the dark regarding what is going on in the field of naturopathic medicine—specifically natural hormones. Until recently, their use has not been taught in medical schools or promoted by any pharmaceutical companies (the other major source of information for nearly all "conventional" physicians). With no multinational drug industry to pay the enormous costs, the large definitive reports that might demonstrate the efficacy and safety of natural hormones are not being done. Doctors tend to see only reports of the benefits and risks of Premarin, Provera and other patentable hormone studies, which the pharmaceutical industry has either conducted itself or underwritten. The good news is that it has been announced that Harvard Medical School is adding classes in naturopathic medicine to its curriculum. Hopefully the rest of the medical community will follow suit!

Also, you will be heartened to know that I get calls almost daily from physicians wanting more information about natural hormones.

24. WHY IS IT IMPORTANT TO STAY ON NATURAL HORMONES EVEN AFTER MY LIBIDO IS RESTORED?

Estrogen and progesterone are two of the steroid hormones. The others include pregnenolone, androstenedione, testosterone, DHEA and cortisol. These hormones affect the brain, bones, circulation muscles, kidneys, liver, reproductive organs, nerves, immune system and even digestion. They have a powerful effect on the body's ability to resist disease, especially cancer, heart disease, respiratory disease, circulatory disease (stroke), brain disease, osteoporosis and arthritis. Each of these hormones is related to or made from another or can be turned back into another. Therefore, any imbalance has a profound effect! As we age, our progesterone levels fall to zero, and we lose the intrinsic effects of progesterone. Therefore I believe that women should be supplementing with natural hormones for about three weeks out of the month even if they are asymptomatic. Once you discontinue the use of the natural hormones you will lose the positive effects on your libido.

215

25. WHAT DO I SAY TO MY PHYSICIAN WHO THINKS THIS IS SILLY?

The base used for natural progesterone is the same base as that of four hundred FDA drugs on the market today. We just don't add synthetic chemicals to our natural hormones as pharmaceutical companies do when making their drugs. More and more physicians are finding out that synthetic hormones have many undesirable side effects. And remember, I receive inquiries almost every day from doctors who want to switch their patients to natural hormones, so times are changing.

26. ARE THERE ANY OTHER BENEFITS OF NATURAL PROGESTERONE USE?

Additional benefits of using natural progesterone are:

ᘐ Improvement and/or resolution of fibrocystic breasts

ᘐ Improvement in migraine headaches. Natural progesterone

helps restore normal vascular conditions and works against the blood vessel dilation that can cause the headache. Estrogen causes dilation of blood vessels, and therefore estrogen dominant women often have migraines.

෴ Improved sleep patterns

෴ Clearer skin and resolution of many skin problems, especially acne and rosacea

෴ Increased energy

෴ Decrease in nonspecific joint and muscle pain

෴ Enhances fertility in women attempting to get pregnant

෴ Resolution of ovarian cysts

෴ May help reduce uterine fibroids. Fibroid tumors are stimulated to grow by estrogen. Lack of estrogen causes them to atrophy and shrink. When a sufficient amount of natural progesterone is used, the fibroids may stop growing or decrease in size. After menopause they will naturally atrophy. Many women tell me they have avoided surgery for fibroids with the use of natural progesterone.

෴ Has helped successfully treat endometriosis, which may be one of the biggest enemies of a woman's sex drive because she spends so much of the month in pain. The treatment requires patience, but has been very successful with quite a few women. The progesterone halts the proliferation of the endometrial cells, which grow outside of the uterus. You must use natural progesterone cream from day 6 of your cycle to day 26 each month, using 1 ounce of cream per week for three weeks. You stop the cream just before your period. It may take four to six months and may not totally stop all of the discomfort, but for some women the avoidance of surgery was the end result.

27. HOW LONG SHOULD I STAY ON NATURAL HORMONES?

Estrogen and progesterone are two of the steroid hormones. The others include pregnenolone, androstenedione, testosterone, DHEA and cortisol. These hormones affect:

- ∾ Reproductive organs
- ∾ Brain
- ∾ Bones
- ∾ Circulation
- ∾ Muscles
- ∾ Kidneys
- ∾ Nerves
- ∾ Immune system
- ∾ Digestion

Each of these hormones are related to or made from one another or can be turned back into one another. Therefore, any imbalance has a profound effect. As I have explained, as we age our progesterone levels fall to zero, and we lose the intrinsic effects of progesterone. Progesterone is an excellent protector against osteoporosis (as demonstrated by bone density testing). It is also a great help for sexually active females with vaginal dryness causing painful intercourse. It is recommended that women should use natural hormones a minimum of five years, but each individual woman should use them as long as she feels the hormones are of benefit to her bone density and libido.

I find that women feel younger, more mentally alert and have a stronger libido if they use natural hormones indefinitely three weeks out of the month.

After menopause women should have natural hormones on their "shopping list" for the rest of their lives in order to have optimal health. This includes a healthy sex life!

Anti-aging experts agree that women should be supplementing with natural hormones for about three weeks out of the month, even if they are asymptomatic. My research and patient testimonials show me that these women have much more active and satisfying sex lives.

CONCLUSION

Sexual changes are one of the most challenging aspects in the life of a married couple. I want you to know that this is nothing new. Throughout history man has searched for the "fountain of youth"—a tonic, an elixir, a vitamin or some special combination of things that will allow him or her to stay forever young, especially sexually. You can look in any bookstore and see by the titles in the health section how diligently man is pursuing his lost or waning youth.

This book is not about "recapturing" your youth. This book is about enjoying whatever wonderful season of life you are now in sexually—your forties, fifties, sixties, seventies and beyond. Scripture tells us that "to everything there is a season" (Eccles. 3:1, NKJV). If you and your spouse are committed and caring, together you can discover ways and means to use this current season—and those ahead—to deepen your relationship and increase your intimacy instead of becoming estranged. As a couple you can focus on maintaining a healthy body and healthy sex life by using many of the nutritional, hormonal and general tips in this book. I sincerely want to help you to enjoy every season of your life.

So, whether you are . . .

- ✎ a premenopausal or postmenopausal woman suffering from lack of libido
- ✎ a man with some degree of erectile dysfunction
- ✎ a woman with PMS who is cranky and irritable or depressed two weeks out of every month
- ✎ an exhausted, stressed individual who cannot find the time to even think about sex
- ✎ interested in sex, but unable to become aroused
- ✎ a man who contends with premature ejaculation
- ✎ feeling emotionally distant from your mate

- feeling hormonally "out of sync" or depleted
- a woman suffering from headaches, hot flashes or vaginal dryness
- a man who suffers with a painful prostate
- a woman who has had a hysterectomy and is feeling very disinterested in sex
- coping with the symptoms of a dysfunctional thyroid
- wishing you had a prescription for Viagra
- feeling like the sexual desire of your youth has left home forever

...you can sustain your sexual longevity.

Of course, even as this book goes to press, new and exciting breakthroughs are being made in the field of medicine, both naturopathic and what we call conventional or mainstream medicine. Every interview I conduct for *Doctor to Doctor* holds the potential for more current valuable information that I can pass on to you. There is much to be learned, and my experience has taught me to be open-minded and always on the lookout for new naturopathic and, yes, even conventional medical therapies, or a combination of both.

219

I would like to pass all of this new information on to you. Right now there are on-going studies about transdermal testosterone patches. Are they effective and safe for women who have had their ovaries removed at a very young age and have lost their sex drive? We will see. The medical literature reflects a great surge of research in the area of sexual function, and I see that new studies are begun on what seems to be a monthly basis, if not weekly. With the aging of the baby-boomer generation, researchers are working overtime to find new treatments for sexual dysfunction, especially for E.D. Over the next year or so I expect we will see even more media coverage of potential new therapies, drugs and natural herbal treatments.

I will be closely following all of these test groups and analyzing the completed data. I attend many anti-aging conferences both as a participant and also to interview the physicians and researchers who attend and present their findings. As you can see, I am constantly updating my medical information.

I want your testimonies, too. If ever you see me in person, or if you want to write to me, I would LOVE to hear from you. I am collecting material all the time to add to my research, and I want to hear your success story!

If you would like to be on my mailing list, please write to me at:

Helen Pensanti, M.D.
P.O. Box 7530
Newport Beach, CA 92658

Phone: (714) 542-8333
Fax: (949) 509-1500
E-mail: info@askdrhelen.com
Websites: www.askdrhelen.com and
www.doctortodoctor.com

PRODUCT SOURCE GUIDE

Many of the specific name-brand products recommended by Dr. Pensanti can be obtained from physicians who practice naturopathic medicine or a combination of naturopathic and conventional medicine. They are also available through many chiropractors. All of them can be ordered directly from BETTER HEALTH NATURALLY:

BETTER HEALTH NATURALLY
P.O. Box 5033
Irvine, CA 92616
Phone: (877) 880-0170
Fax: (949) 509-1500

BETTER HEALTH NATURALLY's
NUTRITIONAL LINE INCLUDES:

ANDROGENX™ Spray

DHEA PLUS™

Helen Pensanti, M.D.'s Vaginal Gel™

Menopause Relief Cream

Ostaderm V™

PMS Vitamin Formula

PRO-hGH™

VIP Gel

CloSYS II Oral Rinse

GEROVITAL GH3

Isocort™ Adrenal Formula

Ostaderm™

Osteo Support Formula

Pro HELP

Testron SX™

Vital Vulva

After years of research, these are products that Dr. Pensanti has found to produce reliable, consistent and often dramatic results. They are of the highest quality, and their efficacy has been clinically proven.

Although the specific products listed above are usually obtained only through physicians, you may find a close equivalent at health food stores. Please feel free to give us a call if you have any questions.

All of the other vitamins, herbs, and supplements listed in this book such as avena sativa, ginseng, L-arginine, etc. can be found at most health food stores across the nation.

NOTES

CHAPTER 1
THE NUMBER ONE QUESTION

1. Edward O. Laumann, Ph.D., Anthony Paik, M.A. and Raymond C. Rosen, Ph.D., "Sexual Dysfunction in the United States: Prevalence and Predictors," *Journal of the American Medical Association* 281 (February 10, 1999).

CHAPTER 2
IN THE MOOD

1. Source obtained from the Internet: "AARP/*Modern Maturity* Sexuality Survey," *Modern Maturity* (September/October 1999): research.aarp.org/health/mmsexsurvey_1.

CHAPTER 6
FROM SEXUAL AROUSAL TO ORGASM

1. B. D. Starr and M. B. Weiner, *The Starr-Weiner Report on Sex and Sexuality in the Mature Years* (New York: McGraw-Hill, 1981).

CHAPTER 7
WOMEN AT MIDLIFE

1. John R. Lee, M.D., with Virginia Hopkins, *What Your Doctor May Not Tell You About Menopause* (Warner Books, 1996); John R. Lee, M.D., Jesse Hanley, M.D. and Virginia Hopkins, *What Your Doctor May Not Tell You About Premenopause* (Warner Books, 1999).
2. *Physicians' Desk Reference*, 54th ed. (Montvale, NJ: Medical Economics Company, 2000), s.v. "Premarin."
3. Graham A. Colditz et al., "Hormone Replacement Therapy and Risk of Breast Cancer: Results of Epidemiologic Studies," *American Journal of Obstetrics and Gynecology* 168, no. 5 (May 1993): 1473 (8).
4. M. J. Stampfer, G. A. Colditz, W. C. Willet et al., "The Use of Estrogens and Progestins and the Risk of Breast Cancer in Postmenopausal Women," *New England Journal of Medicine* 332 (1995): 1589–1993.
5. Ibid.
6. Ibid.
7. Gina Kolata, "Estrogen Tied to Slight Increase in Risks to Heart," *New York Times* (April 5, 2000): A1.
8. You need a prescription to obtain anything from a compounding pharmacy. If your doctor does not know of one, you can contact the Professional Compounding Centers of America, Inc., at (800) 331-2498 or the International Academy of Compounding Pharmacies at (800) 927-4227.
9. Lee, *What Your Doctor May Not Tell You About Menopause*, 123.
10. Ibid., 41.
11. Ibid.
12. J. F. DeBold and C. A. Frye, "Progesterone and the Neural Mechanisms of Hamster Sexual Behavior," *Psychoneuroendocrinology* 19 (1994): 563–566.

13. H. Leonetti, M.D., "Report on the First FDA-Approved Study of Natural Progesterone Cream," *The John R. Lee Medical Newsletter* (November 1998): 6.

CHAPTER 9
MEN AT MIDLIFE

1. Robert W. Stock, "Lost and Found," *Modern Maturity* (September/October 1999): 51.
2. William H. Masters and Virginia E. Johnson, *Human Sexual Inadequacy* (Boston, MA: Little, Brown & Co., 1970).
3. Shari Roan, "Herbal Remedy Offers Hope for Cancer Patients," *Los Angeles Times* (October 21, 2000): A-1.

CHAPTER 10
ENJOY SEX FOREVER

1. Source obtained from the Internet: "AARP/*Modern Maturity* Sexuality Survey," *Modern Maturity* (September/October 1999): research.aarp.org/health/mmsexsurvey_1.

CHAPTER 11
DON'T LET STRESS DESTROY YOUR SEX LIFE!

1. Susan Jacoby, "Great Sex: What's Age Got to Do With It?", *Modern Maturity* (September/October 1999): 43.

CHAPTER 12
SEX DESPITE MEDICAL PROBLEMS

1. Alan Francis, *Sex After 40* (n.p.: Andrews McMeel Publishing, 1996), 152.
2. Ibid.
3. Survey findings presented at the 96th International Conference of the American Thoracic Society, May 2000.
4. Ibid.

CHAPTER 13
IS THE ANSWER IN HORMONE SUPPLEMENTATION?

1. Susan Rako, M.D., *The Hormone of Desire* (New York: Three Rivers Press, 1996), 46.
2. Lee, *What Your Doctor May Not Tell You About Menopause*, 102.
3. Ibid., 79.
4. Ibid.
5. Ibid.
6. Maleeva Milanov and Sopharma Taskov, Chemical Pharmaceutical Research Institute, 1981.
7. Stuart W. Fine, M.D. and Brenda D. Adderly, M.H.A., *The Libido Breakthrough* (Los Angeles: Newstar Publishing, 1999), 64.
8. Source obtained from the Internet: "Restoring Your Sex Drive With Natural Hormones, Supplements and Herbs," *Health Concerns* (September 13, 2000), www.vitamin-resource.com/ health/detail.cfm?id=131.
9. James Jamieson and Dr. L. E. Dorman, *Growth Hormone: Reversing Human Aging Naturally* (n.p.: Safegoods and LNN Publishing, 1997), 31.
10. Ibid.
11. T. Hirano, M. Homma and K. Oka, "Effect of Stinging Nettle Root Extracts and Their Steroidal Components on Benign Prostatic Hyperplasia," *Planta Medica* 60 (1) (1994): 30–33.

12. R. Sikora et al., "Gingko Biloba Extract in the Therapy of Erectile Dysfunction," *Journal of Urology* 141 (1989): 188A.
13. H. K. Choi, D. H. Seong and K. H. Rha, "Clinical Efficacy of Korean Red Ginseng for Erectile Dysfunction," *International Journal of Impotency Research* 7 (3) (1995): 181–186.
14. Jacques Waynberg, M.D., Institute of Sexology, Paris, France, n.d.
15. Ibid.
16. William Faloon, *Nutrition News* XXIII, No. 6 (1999).

CHAPTER 14
TIPS FOR A BETTER LOVE LIFE

1. Jacoby, "Great Sex," 43.

CHAPTER 15
COMMON QUESTIONS ABOUT NATURAL HORMONES

1. H. Leonetti, M.D., "Report on the First FDA-Approved Study of Natural Progesterone Cream," *The John R. Lee Medical Newsletter* (November 1998): 6.
2. K. J. Chang et al., "Influences of Percutaneous Administration of Estradiol and Progesterone on Human Breast Epithelial Cell Cycle in Vivo," *Fertility and Sterility* 63 (1995): 785–791.
3. William J. Hrushesky, "Breast Cancer, Timing of Surgery, and the Menstrual Cycle," *Journal of Women's Health* 5 (1996): 555–556.
4. Ibid.
5. Chang, "Influences of Percutaneous Administration of Estradiol and Progesterone on Human Breast Epithelial Cell Cycle in Vivo."
6. L. D. Cowan, L. Gordis, J.A. Tonascia and G. S. Jones, "Breast Cancer Incidence in Women With a History of Progesterone Deficiency," *American Journal of Epidemiology* 114: 209–217.
7. J. Lee, "Is Natural Progesterone the Missing Link in Osteoporosis Prevention and Treatment?", *Medical Hypothesis* 35 (1991): 316–318.

Receive 3 Issues of
Charisma
& CHRISTIAN LIFE
FREE

Compliments of

STRANG COMMUNICATIONS :
the publisher of
CHARISMA
magazine,
Creation House
and Siloam Press
Books.

3 FREE!

CHARISMA magazine
* the Country's Leading Christian Publication!

FREE Offer Certificate

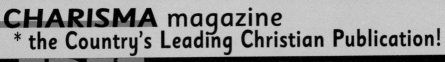

☑ **YES**, I'd like to receive a FREE 3 MONTH (3 issues)
subscription to **CHARISMA** magazine. I understand that I am
not obligated to make any additional purchases and that this is
a FREE offer.

Name _____

Address _____

City_____ State_____ Zip _____

Telephone_____

E-mail _____

Valid in the USA only.

91ADEF

0823A